LOOKING FOR A STORY

Looking for a Story

A COMPLETE GUIDE
TO THE WRITINGS OF JOHN MCPHEE

NOEL RUBINTON

WITH A FOREWORD BY
PETER HESSLER

PRINCETON UNIVERSITY PRESS
PRINCETON & OXFORD

Copyright © 2025 by Princeton University Press
Foreword copyright © 2025 by Peter Hessler

Princeton University Press is committed to the protection of copyright and the intellectual property our authors entrust to us. Copyright promotes the progress and integrity of knowledge created by humans. Thank you for supporting free speech and the global exchange of ideas by purchasing an authorized edition of this book. If you wish to reproduce or distribute any part of it in any form, please obtain permission.

Requests for permission to reproduce material from this work should be sent to permissions@press.princeton.edu

Published by Princeton University Press
41 William Street, Princeton, New Jersey 08540
99 Banbury Road, Oxford OX2 6JX

press.princeton.edu

All Rights Reserved

Library of Congress Cataloging-in-Publication Data

Names: Rubinton, Noel, author. | Hessler, Peter, 1969– writer of foreword.
Title: Looking for a story : a complete guide to the writings of John McPhee / Noel Rubinton ; with a foreword by Peter Hessler.
Description: Princeton : Princeton University Press, [2025] | Includes bibliographical references and index.
Identifiers: LCCN 2024052186 (print) | LCCN 2024052187 (ebook) | ISBN 9780691244921 (hardback) | ISBN 9780691244938 (ebook)
Subjects: LCSH: McPhee, John, 1931—Bibliography. | BISAC: LITERARY CRITICISM / American / General | LITERARY CRITICISM / Modern / 21st Century | LCGFT: Bibliographies.
Classification: LCC Z8561.19 .R83 2025 (print) | LCC Z8561.19 (ebook) | DDC 016.8080092—dc23/eng/20241210
LC record available at https://lccn.loc.gov/2024052186
LC ebook record available at https://lccn.loc.gov/2024052187

British Library Cataloging-in-Publication Data is available

Editorial: Anne Savarese and James Collier
Production Editorial: Karen Carter
Jacket/Cover Design: Haley Jin Mee Chung
Production: Erin Suydam
Publicity: Alyssa Sanford
Copyeditor: Anne Sanow

Jacket/Cover Credit: Art by Kirsten Sparenborg / TurnoftheCenturies.com

This book has been composed in Arno

Printed in the United States of America

10 9 8 7 6 5 4 3 2 1

To Amy, for so much

CONTENTS

Foreword by Peter Hessler   ix
Preface   xv
Chronology and Selected Honors   xxiii

PART I: WORKS BY JOHN MCPHEE   1

1 Books   3
   Introductions, Forewords, and Prefaces   26
   Digital and Audio Editions   32
   Anthologies   35
   Limited Editions   45

2 Periodicals   48
   Time *Magazine*   48
   The New Yorker   70

3 Other Publications   95
   Newspapers and Other Periodicals   95
   Time *Magazine Book Reviews*   104
   Juvenilia   106
   Television Screenplays   117
   Fiction   120

PART II: WORKS ABOUT JOHN MCPHEE — 123

4 Articles — 125

5 Interviews — 139

6 Book Reviews — 149

7 Books — 183

8 Theses — 186

PART III: MISCELLANY — 189

9 Readings and Speeches — 191

10 Book Dedications — 195

11 John McPhee's Editors at *The New Yorker* and Farrar, Straus and Giroux — 200

12 Film Adaptation — 202

13 Books by Former Students — 204

14 Books by John McPhee's Children — 217

Acknowledgments 221

Index 227

FOREWORD

IN THE spring of 1991, when I was a junior at Princeton, I took John McPhee's seminar on nonfiction writing. Back then, I was an English major who hoped to become a novelist, and I focused primarily on writing short stories. I had no real interest in nonfiction. I hadn't published a single word in any campus publication, and I had never considered a career in journalism. But John McPhee's course was famous for having produced authors, and writing—in the undisciplined, impractical, and insecure dreamworld of a 21-year-old mind—was what I hoped to do someday. So I signed up for the class.

By the time I arrived for the first session, in a beautiful, wood-paneled room on the ground floor of a gothic building called East Pyne Hall, the only piece of John McPhee's writing that I had ever read was the course description. In retrospect, I find this mortifying. But it was also characteristic of the 21-year-old dreamworld: everything was of the moment; nothing was carefully considered. One might assume that, before taking a course taught by John McPhee, who had been described by *The Washington Post* as "the best journalist in America," a student would feel inspired to read a couple of books or maybe even one magazine article by John McPhee. But this idea apparently never occurred to me.

As a result, I first became a McPhee reader in the margins of the essays that I submitted for class. He marked every paper in pencil, in a tight left-handed script. He crossed out words, and he drew boxes around phrases, and he inscribed long comments that sometimes ran perpendicular to the text. "You can't make a silk purse out of this," he wrote, in response to one of my poorly executed descriptions. Next to a sentence with oddly formal phrasing, he remarked, "This could be said with several pebbles removed from the mouth." Once, when I used a subject's name four times in the span of two sentences, McPhee wrote, "Listen to the character's name thudding like horseshoes. Vary it. Use pronouns here and there."

Other comments thudded in a way that made horseshoes seem soft:

"This sort of thing is irritatingly repetitive."
"The incongruity in this line isn't artful, it's just awkward."
"I wish you would listen more critically to the rhythms and sound of the prose."
"You are extraordinarily repetitive for someone who writes on your level."
"This is lame cleverness."

But there were also many instances of praise, when John McPhee wrote in the margins "yes," or "ah," or "a fine moment." At the end of my first paper, the neatly penciled script sent up sparks of encouragement:

"This piece is a pleasure—insightfully imagined and ably wrought.... It took care—please keep caring on the pieces to come."

I realized that it's possible to write both very well and very badly at the same time. My project was to learn how to do the one without the other, and every two weeks, as part of the course, I had an hour-long one-on-one tutorial with John McPhee in his office, on the top floor of East Pyne. That semester, I finally became a proper McPhee reader: for class, he photocopied sections of his books and talked in detail about various problems he had encountered and decisions he had made. While studying his prose we learned about structure, set pieces, and transitions that felt effortless but, when pulled apart, revealed something else. *It took care.* By the end of the semester my writing world had been transformed, and that summer I researched what became my first published article, about going door-to-door in East Moline, Illinois, with a group of missionaries from the Church of Jesus Christ of Latter-day Saints. And then I was off—after that, no matter where I lived, in England or China or Egypt, I was always researching, writing, and publishing. Everywhere

I went, I heard echoes of East Pyne. *Please keep caring on the pieces to come.*

———

John McPhee has compared the sensation of being a young writer to that of a canoeist floating downstream on a river. There are islands everywhere—to the left, to the right, to the front—and you decide where to stop and how long to stay. Time is moving, like the current, and it flows in only one direction. Poor decisions become costlier as the writer grows older. Lingering on the banks of one island might mean that you skip another, and from a distance it's hard to tell which of the two is barren.

McPhee has also said, "Don't look at my career through the wrong end of a telescope." One of the many pleasures of *Looking for a Story* is that it helps us orient the scope in the proper direction. We see the full body of McPhee's work, and we see it in order, thanks to the tireless research of Noel Rubinton. Rubinton seems to have uncovered everything—not just the books and the *New Yorker* articles, but also the old screenplays and the short fiction and the book reviews. There's even a chapter titled "Juvenilia," in which we observe the young writer effectively stepping out of the canoe and setting foot on different islands. At one point, McPhee seems determined to become a novelist; later he writes five prospective episodes for a television series called *Robert Montgomery Presents* (two of the scripts were made). Even the byline changes. For a brief spell, in the *Nassau Sovereign*, it's Johnny McPhee, and then it becomes John Angus McPhee in *The Nassau Literary Magazine*.

Rubinton illustrates how, at every stage of McPhee's long career, certain lodestars shine through. One is a pure love of language. It's fundamental to the geological writing, where McPhee takes a palpable pleasure in terminology: gabbros, plagiogranites, pillow basalts. The love is also clear in his use of a word like Haligonian, which sounds like a long-lost era when dinosaurs walked the earth and the big trees were kings; but in fact a Haligonian is simply a person from Halifax. Puns are another not-guilty pleasure. When the Princeton Board of Health shut down local hot dog vendors, the undergraduate McPhee's report was titled

"Imminent Ptomaine." "Zealous Island" is an account of a political activist detained on Ellis Island. "Phi Beta Football"—those words, which cleverly repeat and refigure three distinct consonant sounds, like a little snatch of jazz, were so pleasing to McPhee's ear that he used them as a title for four different pieces: first, in 1952, in *The Princeton Tiger*, and last, in 2014, in *The New Yorker*. Who says that a writer can't paddle back to an old island?

―――

Looking for a Story can be read in different ways. The book traces John McPhee's lifelong search for material, and often it's possible to see how one subject or character led to another. But this book will also help McPhee readers find stories that they didn't know existed, and subjects that might surprise them. For a former student of McPhee's, one of the many fascinating discoveries is a YouTube link to a video of a February 8, 1952, episode of *Twenty Questions*, on which McPhee appeared as a contestant. Today, very little of this world of black-and-white television is recognizable. For one thing, the game-show buzzer had apparently yet to be invented, and thus we are treated to the spectacle of five adults eagerly raising their hands in competition, like a pack of fourth graders. McPhee himself, in a light jacket, striped tie, and a full head of hair, is younger than I was when I entered his class. His face is unfamiliar—but every time he answers a question, the voice sounds almost exactly the same as the one I remember from East Pyne Hall.

After I graduated, in 1992, there was a stretch of many years when we communicated primarily through writing, and often on paper. On October 22, 1997, while living in a remote city on the southern bank of the Yangtze River, I mailed a long letter that began "Dear Mr. McPhee." To me, he was still the professor in the wood-paneled room, and I was often asking for advice. I didn't know anybody who was more sympathetic and more insightful about what it feels like to be a young writer steering through the rapids. In July of 2000, when I was living in Beijing and trying to juggle the edit of my first book with researching articles for *The New Yorker*, John sent a note of encouragement. "You are fully able to work on all those levels and should feel confidence about it," he wrote, and then continued: "Confidence never wrote a book, though, and in excess has killed unborn libraries." Later that year, he wrote again:

> I also remember your saying that you may be in eastern America in a month or so and would like to visit Princeton. I very much hope you do. If you would like to talk about books versus-and-plus *New Yorker* versus-and-plus whatever else comes to mind, now is a good time to do it, and I'd be pleased to be the sounding board.

Over time, "Mr. McPhee" became John. I lived abroad for more than 20 years, but Princeton was a regular stop on my annual visits back to the United States. As I settled into my writing life, the river became easier to navigate, and I no longer needed to ask John for advice. But every time I returned to campus, I gained a better understanding of what it means to sustain a career in writing nonfiction. For John, that's another lodestar: his drive and his dedication to the craft have never wavered. He has taught me many lessons, but the first remains the most powerful. *Please keep caring on the pieces to come.*

When John was my teacher, he called his course "The Literature of Fact." At other times, he used the title "Creative Nonfiction." He's often remarked on the problems of the various labels for the genre that he prefers to call "factual writing." Once, in the 1980s, he was asked to give a reading at the University of Utah, but the invitation was subsequently revoked because, as John remembers, "They didn't approve of the genre I write in."

Of the 121 authors who have been awarded a Nobel Prize in Literature, only one has specialized in nonfiction: Svetlana Alexievich, a journalist who depicted life during and after the Soviet Union. Even then, the description that was posted on the Nobel website emphasized that Alexievich's work "moves in the boundary between reporting and fiction." Once, while visiting John at his home, I remarked that I dislike it when people praise a nonfiction book by saying, "It reads like a novel!" John quickly agreed, which didn't surprise me: none of his books reads like a novel. All of them are beautifully written, but they also refer to source materials, and interviews, and the author's reporting in ways that a novel never would. Everything has to be true; there is no blurring of the boundary between fiction and nonfiction. From my perspective, one of John McPhee's greatest achievements is the way in which he has brought greater respect to his genre. There is no higher praise for a work of factual writing than to say that it reads like a John McPhee book.

In April of 2023, I made another journey back to Princeton. These days, John spends little time on campus; in 2020, he decided to retire from teaching, after a career that began in 1975. Over the course of those 45 years, he taught a total of 544 students, of whom 125—nearly a quarter—have published at least one book. In John's latter years, on several occasions, he taught the child of a former student.

He continues to write, and he's physically active; every other day, he bicycles hard for exercise. (The year after my visit, in a rare concession to age, he transitioned to using a stationary bicycle.) He describes himself as naturally shy, but his circle of friends, colleagues, and contacts must be among the widest of any nonagenarian on earth. In person he is engaging, good-humored, and quick-witted. He doesn't look much different from the teacher I remember from 1991. When I visited, we had lunch with his wife, Yolanda, in the home that they have shared since the 1970s. In a typical McPhee detail, he had earlier observed that he was 92 years old, from the Princeton class of '53, while I was 53 years old, from the class of '92.

Over lunch, we reminisced about the old days in East Pyne Hall. As always, we also talked about current work: John was editing *Tabula Rasa*, the most recent of his more than three dozen books, and I mentioned a project that I planned to start soon. Before I left, we took a photograph together in front of his house. The following day, John sent an email. He had already reached out to a couple of friends who might be helpful for my new project, and he included their contact information. They were ready to talk whenever I was ready to call.

Peter Hessler

PREFACE

IN A writing career of more than 70 years, John McPhee, best known for his graceful and compelling *New Yorker* articles that became books, has profoundly influenced readers and writers.

McPhee's subjects are idiosyncratic. To name but a few: nuclear energy, college basketball, Alaska, a silk parachute, oranges, and, of course, geology. Stylistically he has broken ground applying many devices and skills long associated with fiction to the literature of fact: the collection and presentation of details; structure; turns of phrase and movement through time; unusual choice of words and wordplay; and vivid physical descriptions, whether of the actress Sophia Loren or a guide in the Maine woods.

He has also been so prolific—more than 35 books, 160 articles in *The New Yorker*, and hundreds of varied pieces published elsewhere, including rarely read fiction—that it can be hard to track down and absorb all his writing, not to mention the huge numbers of interviews, reviews of his books, and articles about him. Naming McPhee's major works is a task akin to naming all the countries of the world, or all of Shakespeare's plays and poems. Searches on the internet cannot come close to locating all his work, with some of it only existing in hard-to-find, nondigitized places.

Thus comes the central aim of this book: to provide a complete guide to McPhee's writings, to help his current readers navigate their way to finding and appreciating more of his work and learning more about him, and also to offer guidance to generations of new readers curious about McPhee's work.

The first part catalogs McPhee's published work, organized by category and including dates and summaries of his books; his articles in

FIGURE 1. In the late 1960s McPhee wrote in a shed in his Princeton backyard, surrounded by notes. (From the estate of David Gahr/Getty Images)

Time, The New Yorker, and other magazines and newspapers; his appearances in literary anthologies; and the availability of digital and audio editions. Some aspects of his writing, such as his books and *The New Yorker* articles that sparked them, are well known. But others, such as his varied writing while a Princeton University undergraduate and the many articles in *Time* magazine that have never been identified as his with a byline, have been largely unnoticed and unappreciated.

The second part of this book presents a selection of material about McPhee and his writing, including articles, interviews, and book reviews, many by other prominent writers in influential publications. This selection is not all-inclusive, as the many hundreds of items involved would be overwhelming. The choices here represent the full group.

Listings throughout the book include commentary to illuminate McPhee's biography and the many interwoven threads of his literary life. Cumulatively they tell the remarkable story of a writer who has lived almost all his life in Princeton, New Jersey, where his high school

English teacher, Olive McKee, taught him lasting lessons about structure and the sound of words. He has used that small town as a base from which to travel far with great imagination in a wider world.

Why has McPhee lived in Princeton for so long? The reason he often gives—he credits the quality of Princeton University's Firestone Library and says it was essential for his writing—might seem surprising at first, but in the context of his life and career, it makes sense. He says that Princeton has been "a kind of fixed foot" for him ("John McPhee Trolls the World, Lands a Shad," by Mark Feeney, *The Boston Globe*, December 11, 2002). He has written rhapsodically about the research resources at Princeton and particularly the rewards of the Firestone Library's open stacks, which provided him access to many adjacent books and unexpected discoveries. Driven to build his books in a highly layered way, he knew he needed the best and broadest possible platform for research.

To fully inventory McPhee's writing and select from all that has been written about him has been like constructing a similar library, the Library of McPhee. As with open stacks, his work leads you from one discovery to another, bumping into people and subjects in the many engrossing and surprising worlds about which he writes, as well as frequently introducing you to those who helped steer him to his stories and books (such as how a tennis game in Rhode Island with a high school friend led, in quintessential McPhee-like fashion, to him meeting the nuclear scientist he profiled in *The Curve of Binding Energy*).

To plumb his work has required exploration in many large research collections—primarily the Library of Congress, the Farrar, Straus and Giroux archive at the New York Public Library, the *Time* magazine archive at the The New York Historical, the Seeley G. Mudd Manuscript Library at Princeton University, and, yes, the Firestone Library. The unearthing of long unseen writing by McPhee has been aided most of all by the generous assistance of John McPhee himself and his prodigious memory.

Researching this book has been the source of much discovery and joy. McPhee's work at *Time* magazine is a prime example. From 1957 to 1965, he spent eight energy-filled years on the magazine's staff, a formative period in his late twenties and early thirties. Yet because *Time* carried no bylines then, McPhee's contributions have long been hidden from view. During this time he wrote, almost completely anonymously, nine cover stories (including on show business luminaries like Jackie Gleason, Barbra Streisand, Joan Baez, and Richard Burton). Few McPhee readers have ever known of his authorship of these profiles, which still sparkle. And until now, the other writing of his *Time* years has been even harder to discover.

After combing through every issue of *Time* during McPhee's tenure, using special copies in the magazine's archives in which copyeditors marked the initials of the writers of each story in red grease pencil or pen, I was able to identify for the first time more than 500 stories written by McPhee at *Time*. This book lists details and excerpts from dozens of the most interesting and inventive of the *Time* stories, including all the cover stories; his article on entertainer Carol Burnett; his analysis of a new hit television show, *The Flintstones*; his recounting of Beatlemania in America; and an account of Sidney Poitier becoming the first Black actor to win the Academy Award for Best Actor.

As a young, ambitious "back of the book" writer at *Time* whose reputation rose quickly, McPhee had creative freedom to write stories in his own style, and he experimented with many approaches. He gained considerable writing and organizational skills in his years at *Time*.

By early 1965, McPhee finally landed at *The New Yorker*, the place where he had wanted to work since he was a teenager. Starting from his first profile of Princeton basketball star Bill Bradley, he became one of the greatest and most identifiable writers for a magazine that was arguably America's most revered. His books that followed, almost all developed from *New Yorker* assignments, would be reviewed as widely as almost any other books published in his time. Over the years, beginning with *Coming into the Country* in 1977, they became best sellers.

McPhee also wrote for smaller publications, often out of his devotion to friends, like an English teacher, or causes, such as the environment. This book brings to light this writing, which is lesser known and frequently difficult to find. He also was openhanded in contributing to other people's books, where his many introductions, forewords, prefaces, and an afterword all reward readers with insight and wit.

Another highlight in the research of this book was uncovering a virtually unknown television screenplay that McPhee wrote for one of the leading television series of the 1950s, *Robert Montgomery Presents*. After completing his studies at Princeton and at Cambridge in England, McPhee decided he wanted to write television screenplays, and he devoted much time to studying the craft of screenwriting. His episode, "The Man Who Vanished," aired nationally in the United States in 1956. It was exhilarating to visit the UCLA Film and Television Archive and watch what appears to be the world's last remaining video copy of the program. The sophistication and skill of McPhee, then a 25-year-old who had written only a handful of screenplays, is astonishing.

Yet a further aspect of McPhee's writing that has mostly gone unnoticed is his large body of creative work while he was an undergraduate at Princeton. Reading this work, detailed in the "Juvenilia" section, imparts intriguing glimpses of the writer he would become. His 1953 profile, for example, of the musicologist Sigmund Spaeth in *The Princeton Tiger* student magazine is a preview of his later *New Yorker* profiles. In a still closer connection, McPhee covered the 1953 "Spring Riot" at Princeton, once an annual campus rite, as a correspondent for *Princeton Alumni Weekly*. Two weeks later, the same events were covered in a "Talk of the Town" piece in *The New Yorker* by two staff writers who would later become McPhee's colleagues at the magazine. McPhee's undergraduate years also marked the only time in his life that he worked as an editor. He remade *The Princeton Tiger*, a struggling humor magazine, into something that resembled the weekly he already admired over all others: *The New Yorker*. His makeover included getting a *New Yorker* contributor who lived in Princeton, John O'Hara, to contribute a short story.

The third and final section of this book is titled "Miscellany" as an homage to the classic weekly feature in *Time* that covered the world in short, clever bits. It is one of the places where new-to-the-staff McPhee distinguished himself when he started writing regularly for the magazine in 1958.

One part of this book's "Miscellany" section takes up a particularly important and compelling aspect of McPhee's legacy that has been largely unknown or overlooked: his record as an educator and mentor to generations of writers. On a few weeks' notice when a previous teacher quit, McPhee took over a writing seminar at Princeton University in 1975. He wasn't sure how it would work out; he ended up spending nearly 50 years in that role.

A striking measure of McPhee's impact as an educator is the accomplishments of his students in writing and other fields. Many of those who have become writers have expressed their enormous appreciation to him, regularly sending him copies of their own books with warm inscriptions and staying in touch for decades. Hundreds of their books filled McPhee's academic office. The "Books by Former Students" section here identifies 125 of McPhee's more than 500 students who have published books, including details of their first book (some have written up to 30). Their books show the range of writing that McPhee has encouraged and influenced. His Princeton students have won many top book and journalism awards, and many have ascended to high positions at newspapers and magazines. *New Yorker* editor David Remnick, *Time* managing editors Jim Kelly and Richard Stengel, and bestselling novelist Jennifer Weiner are only a few examples.

Beyond those fortunate enough to have had McPhee as a teacher at Princeton, a legion of writers around the world (McPhee's books have been translated into at least 11 languages other than English) claim him as a major inspiration, including those who use his advice in *Draft No. 4* as an essential resource. In this book, sections on interviews, readings, and speeches, which list the many recordings and transcripts of interviews and book events McPhee has conducted through the years, make clear the size of the appetite for McPhee's advice and the breadth of his wisdom.

McPhee has been called a leader of the "literary nonfiction" and "creative nonfiction" movements, but he truly defies classification. Modest as usual, he says his writing is about "real people in real places" (Lily Rothman, "John McPhee on Writing, Reading and How Working in Magazines Has Changed," *Time* magazine, October 18, 2017 [https://time.com/4983145/john-mcphee-draft-no-4-time-interview/]).

McPhee's ability to translate complicated subjects is extraordinary, with the most celebrated example his series of geology books. One of

FIGURE 2. McPhee posed for a portrait to go with a *Time* magazine story in 2018, sitting in his Princeton University office in a turret of the Department of Geosciences building. On the shelves are some of the hundreds of books written by former students of his, often inscribed to him. (Bryan Anselm/Redux)

them, *Annals of the Former World*, received a Pulitzer Prize. The many intricate yet nearly invisible structures he has designed to tell stories in his articles and books are widely studied.

McPhee has often talked about how much of what he wrote about grew from his interests when he was young. It is easy to see this in his books about the environment and sports, yet the range of subjects he has delved into during his whole career is vast. It seems he has engaged almost any subject conceivable, and plenty beyond that (think of the bright orange Aereon 26, an experimental aircraft he explored in *The Deltoid Pumpkin Seed*), shedding light on so many previously darkened corners of the world and knowledge.

Well into his nineties, McPhee hasn't lost his literary ambition, continuing to write and publish at a pace that would be enviable for someone half his age.

I read my first John McPhee when I was fourteen. I was bored at school and thinking about trying somewhere different. Somehow, I came across a copy of McPhee's *The Headmaster*. It was a book by a writer I'd never heard of, about a school, Deerfield Academy, I knew nothing about. By the time I finished the book, I knew where I would go to school next, and I had deep loyalty to a writer I would follow and read for decades to come.

One of McPhee's memorable books is *Looking for a Ship*, springing from the story of how second mate Andy Chase looked for work and navigated the choppy waters of a declining U.S. merchant marine industry. It can be said that McPhee has been on his own lifelong search for a story, or actually thousands of stories.

This guide aims to help readers discover or rediscover McPhee's writings, and there is tremendous pleasure ahead. Altogether, the range, extent, and style of his work is also a window into McPhee himself, revealing his ambition, curiosity, creativity, and determination. We are fortunate for it all.

CHRONOLOGY AND SELECTED HONORS

1931 Born in Princeton, New Jersey.
1937 Attends Keewaydin summer camp in Vermont, where he would return each summer through 1950, when he was a counselor as a college student.
1948 Graduates from Princeton High School.
1949 Graduates from a postgraduate high school year at Deerfield Academy, and enrolls at Princeton University.
1952 Named managing editor of *The Princeton Tiger* humor magazine, which he revamps as a general interest publication. Writes *New York Times Magazine* story on the death of college humor magazines. Chosen as campus columnist for *Princeton Alumni Weekly*.
1953 Graduates from Princeton University with a bachelor's degree in English Literature.
1954 Studies for a year at Magdalene College, University of Cambridge, England.
1955 Writes screenplays for *Robert Montgomery Presents* on NBC. Two of his dramas are produced and shown on national television.
1957 Hired as a writer for *Time* magazine. Becomes part of new Show Business department and writes more than 500 stories over the next eight years.
1960 Publishes his first *Time* cover story (August 15), on the comedian Mort Sahl, his first of nine cover stories for the magazine.
1963 Publishes his first *New Yorker* story (March 16), a freelance article about his playing for the Cambridge University basketball team.

FIGURE 3. McPhee at age nine in 1940 at the Keewaydin summer camp in Salisbury, Vermont, a place where he developed many of his lifelong interests. (Courtesy of John McPhee)

FIGURE 4. Olive McKee was McPhee's English teacher for three years at Princeton High School. He cites her as one of the greatest influences on his writing, particularly in terms of structure. (Princeton High School)

FIGURE 5. McPhee's senior portrait at Deerfield Academy in 1949. He attended the Massachusetts prep school for a year after graduating from Princeton High School. Deerfield's headmaster at the time, Frank Boyden, later became the subject of McPhee's second book. (Deerfield Academy Archives)

1965 Publishes a profile of Bill Bradley in *The New Yorker* (January 23). Leaves *Time* and becomes a staff writer for *The New Yorker*. His first book, *A Sense of Where You Are*, based on the Bradley article, is published in the fall by Farrar, Straus and Giroux.

1967 Travels in Europe throughout the spring and summer with his first wife, Pryde Brown, and their four children. While living on Colonsay in the Scottish Hebrides, researches what becomes *The Crofter and the Laird*, about the history and culture on the island, then goes elsewhere to report five other magazine articles, all written during the next two years.

1968 Publishes his last piece of fiction, a form that he had written occasionally since college, with the short story "Ruth, the Sun Is Shining," in *Playboy* in April.

1969 *A Roomful of Hovings and Other Profiles*, his fifth book and first collection of assorted *New Yorker* articles, is published.

1975 Becomes Ferris Professor of Journalism at Princeton University and begins teaching a seminar on the "Literature of Fact" (later renamed "Creative Nonfiction"). In the fall, he goes on the first of a series of long reporting trips to Alaska.

1976 The *John McPhee Reader* is published, including excerpts from his first 12 books and an introduction by Princeton English professor William Howarth.

1977 *Coming into the Country* is published and receives an enthusiastic front-page review in *The New York Times Book Review*. It becomes a national bestseller, McPhee's first, and goes on to sell a million copies.

1978 *Casey's Shadow*, a film starring Walter Matthau as a horse trainer and based on McPhee's *New Yorker* story "Ruidoso," opens and receives mostly positive reviews.

1979 McPhee's article "Brigade de Cuisine," published in *The New Yorker* (February 19), causes controversy when McPhee and the magazine grant anonymity to the chef featured. Within several days, the *New York Times* restaurant critic identifies the chef and criticizes his food and restaurant.

1981 *Basin and Range*, McPhee's first book in a series about geology that will span 20 years, is published.

1987 At the home of Princeton University president William Bowen, McPhee and his second wife, Yolanda Whitman, begin what becomes a 25-city tour of readings during the next decade from *Rising from the Plains*, his third book about geology.

1996 *The Second John McPhee Reader*, including excerpts from 11 more books since the 1975 *Reader*, is published with an

FIGURE 6. *Coming into the Country*, McPhee's 13th book, was his first bestseller, bringing him wide acclaim.

introduction by David Remnick, a former McPhee student who became editor of *The New Yorker* in 1998.
1998 *Annals of the Former World*, his fifth and last volume in his geology series, is published, including the four previous books and a new long essay.
1999 Receives the Pulitzer Prize for general nonfiction for *Annals of the Former World*, the final book in his geology series.
2010 *Silk Parachute*, a book of essays about his childhood and family, is published.
2017 *Draft No. 4* is published, including eight essays on the writing process drawn from McPhee's lifetime of experiences.

FIGURE 7. In 1999, McPhee received the Pulitzer Prize for his book *Annals of the Former World* from Columbia University, presented by provost Jonathan R. Cole. (University Archives, Rare Book & Manuscript Library, Columbia University Libraries, photograph by Eileen Barroso)

2018 *The Patch* is published. It includes essays and "An Album Quilt," consisting of dozens of story excerpts from McPhee's career.
2022 "The Ignocene," a poem by McPhee, appears in *Orion* magazine, his first published poetry in 70 years, since the *Nassau Literary Review* during college.
2023 *Tabula Rasa: Volume 1* is published. McPhee's self-described "old-man project" includes a montage of material drawn from articles he planned but never completed.

Selected Honors

1971 *Encounters with the Archdruid* is a finalist for a National Book Award.

1974 *The Curve of Binding Energy* is a finalist for a National Book Award.

1981 *Basin and Range* is a finalist for the Pulitzer Prize in general nonfiction.

1982 Receives the American Association of Petroleum Geologists Journalism Award (which he would win again in 1987). Princeton University presents McPhee with the Woodrow Wilson Award, given to an alumnus whose work exemplifies Wilson's vision of "Princeton in the nation's service."

1986 *Rising from the Plains* is a Pulitzer Prize finalist in general nonfiction. McPhee is elected a fellow of the Geological Society of America.

1988 Elected to the American Academy of Arts and Letters. Receives the John Wesley Powell award for "noteworthy contributions to the objectives and mission" from the United States Geological Survey.

1990 *Looking for a Ship* is a Pulitzer Prize finalist for general nonfiction.

1999 Receives the Pulitzer Prize for general nonfiction for *Annals of the Former World*, the final book in his geology series. He also receives the Princeton University President's Award for Distinguished Teaching.

2002 Accepts Public Service Award from the Geological Society of America.

2008 Awarded a George Polk Career Award for lifetime achievement for his "indelible mark on American journalism during his nearly half-century career."

2011 Receives the Wallace Stegner Award from the Center of the American West, for "an individual who has made a sustained contribution to the cultural identity of the West."

2018 Accepts the Ivan Sandrof Award for Lifetime Achievement from the National Book Critics Circle, the Medal of Honor for Literature from the National Arts Club, and the Audubon New York Award for Environmental Writing.

Honorary Degrees

Bates College (1978)
Colby College (1978)
Williams College (1979)
University of Alaska (1980)
College of William and Mary (1988)
Rutgers University (1988)
Maine Maritime Academy (1992)
Yale University (2009)
Lehigh University (2010)
Amherst College (2012)
University of Wyoming (2016)

PART I

Works by John McPhee

"Write what you're interested in, and hope that the world is interested too."

—FROM "THE REPORTER AS TEACHER:
A TALK WITH JOHN MCPHEE" BY HELLER MCALPIN,
BARNES & NOBLE READS, SEPTEMBER 13, 2017

1

Books

JOHN MCPHEE's books are almost all based on writing previously published in *The New Yorker*, often virtually verbatim and other times with some editing for continuity. Nearly all have been published by Farrar, Straus and Giroux, making it an unusually long publishing partnership. There have been more than 90 foreign editions of 30 of his books. His writing has been translated into at least 11 languages other than English.

McPhee's early books received strong reviews, but he did not have a national bestseller until his 13th book, *Coming into the Country*. After that success, his book sales increased dramatically and he had several more bestsellers, including some of his geology books and *The Control of Nature* and *Looking for a Ship*.

McPhee spent months and sometimes years on articles that later became books. His energy and goals did not end with the writing. He was also tenacious about getting the books into the right hands, regularly sending Farrar, Straus and Giroux lengthy lists of people to receive review copies, including people who had helped him in research and influential people he knew, such as Georgia governor and then President Jimmy Carter, New Jersey governors Brendan Byrne and Thomas Kean, and when it fit, a host of college basketball coaches. He often paid for these extra copies himself.

One of McPhee's strengths as an author, as his publisher saw early on, was the strong loyalty he generated in his readers and the relative timelessness of his work. McPhee has been cited as an example of an author whose backlist is exceptionally valuable to a publisher and

FIGURE 8. McPhee's first book, *A Sense of Where You Are*, chronicles the days of Princeton basketball star Bill Bradley.

McPhee has been vocal about keeping his previous books in print. As that backlist grew, McPhee made it a condition in his contracts with Farrar, Straus that the publisher would keep his books in print. He was also a fierce advocate for his precise writing style, down to punctuation and other elements, and McPhee was able to get his publisher to agree to preserve it for years to come as books were reprinted.

A Sense of Where You Are: A Profile of William Warren Bradley. New York: Farrar, Straus and Giroux, 1965.
John McPhee's first book is a profile of Bill Bradley, the cerebral Princeton basketball star and Rhodes Scholar. It was later republished as a paperback in 1978 and again in 1999, coinciding with Bradley's campaigns for United States Senate from New Jersey and then president.

~~Detail~~	A	Amherst 1879-1902
~~Showmanship~~	B	Personal Nature (incl. relations w/ Faculty)
	C	Paradoxes and Inconsistencies
	D	~~Detail~~ & Showmanship
	E	Charity & Good Works
Possible sections involving one or more of these	F	Admissions and Placement — scholarships
	G	Discipline — relations w/ the boys
	H	Mrs. Boyden
Interview w/ Callahan	I	Politics — town, state, nation
Vic Butterfield	J	1902-1924
Tour of School	K	Alumni
Day w/ Head	L	Statistics
Trip to N.Y.	M	Coach — and Athletics generally
week - Nov 4-10 p. 98	N	1924-29
Delap 110	O	One Full Day with FLB
	P	Fund Raising
	Q	Miscellany
should come before G	R	Principles — Basic — on which school built & runs
	S	Academic side
R - B - G - M	T	Public Funds Crisis — 1924
(in that order)	U	Campus & town now
	V	Cliché Schoolmaster
	W	~~Great Headmasters~~ — Deerfield headmasters
	Y	Traditions & Their history
	X	Future of Deerfield
	Z	Changed composition of student body

FIGURES 9, 10, AND 11. In his second book, *The Headmaster*, McPhee used a method for organizing his research that became a model for decades of future projects: he would type up his interviews and other notes, categorize and gather them by theme, and refer to them as he wrote from a carefully designed outline. (Deerfield Academy Archives/Courtesy of John McPhee)

BB/ G
B

November 5, 1965 -- all day with FLB

I thought I would just stick with him for a day. All day. Try to avoid his giving me the slip. Not interviewing him. Just seeing what he does.

7.00 a.m. Dictates. Works in a stand-up breakfast, a look at the newspaper. Boston paper. Fire going in fireplace. Letters to parents and alumni and about matters having to do with the 20 boards he serves on. 7.45. Goes to dining hall to talk to 40 boys who are going home for the weekend. Tells them not to bother the "older traveling public" -- to be sure to answer

G (parents' questions etc. Boys sitting on floor of dining hall lobby. Only about two or three look impatient or trapped.

Hirth asks him about Carlton Ray lecture tonight, explaining first who Ray is.

Goes back and continues dictating. Dictates rapidly. One letter after another. Writes 20. Can do 75 on a trip to NY. Severaldozen in a pre-school morning.

8.45   fifteen minute nap

As he dictates, there are papers all over the floor. He is pitching things into the fireplace; loves mail -- can't wait to get it. New mail more interesting than yesterday's. Answers today's mail. To heck with whathas been pending.

→ Letters take precedence over the whole routine.

→ Not interested in letters that require study.

His batting average has to be maintained.

For allthis he has the talent of giving everyone his undivided attention/. Only for a short time. But undivided.

B/P ("From years of looking at envelopes," says Louise, "he has x-ray eyes. He can tell by a sixth sense which letters have money in them and he will unfailingly pluck them from the pile."

E) No one knows the number of people the headmaster supports. Old Ed Bundy, who picked up papers, lost his birth certificate. Couldn't prove he was an American citizen. Head supported him for the rest of his life. "No one knows the number of people the headmaster supports."

gets in car -- drives to Wallingford -- attends funeral of Choate chef for 5 minutes, shakes with all relatives -- gets in car and goes back to Deerfield

FIGURES 9, 10, AND 11. (*continued*)

BOOKS   7

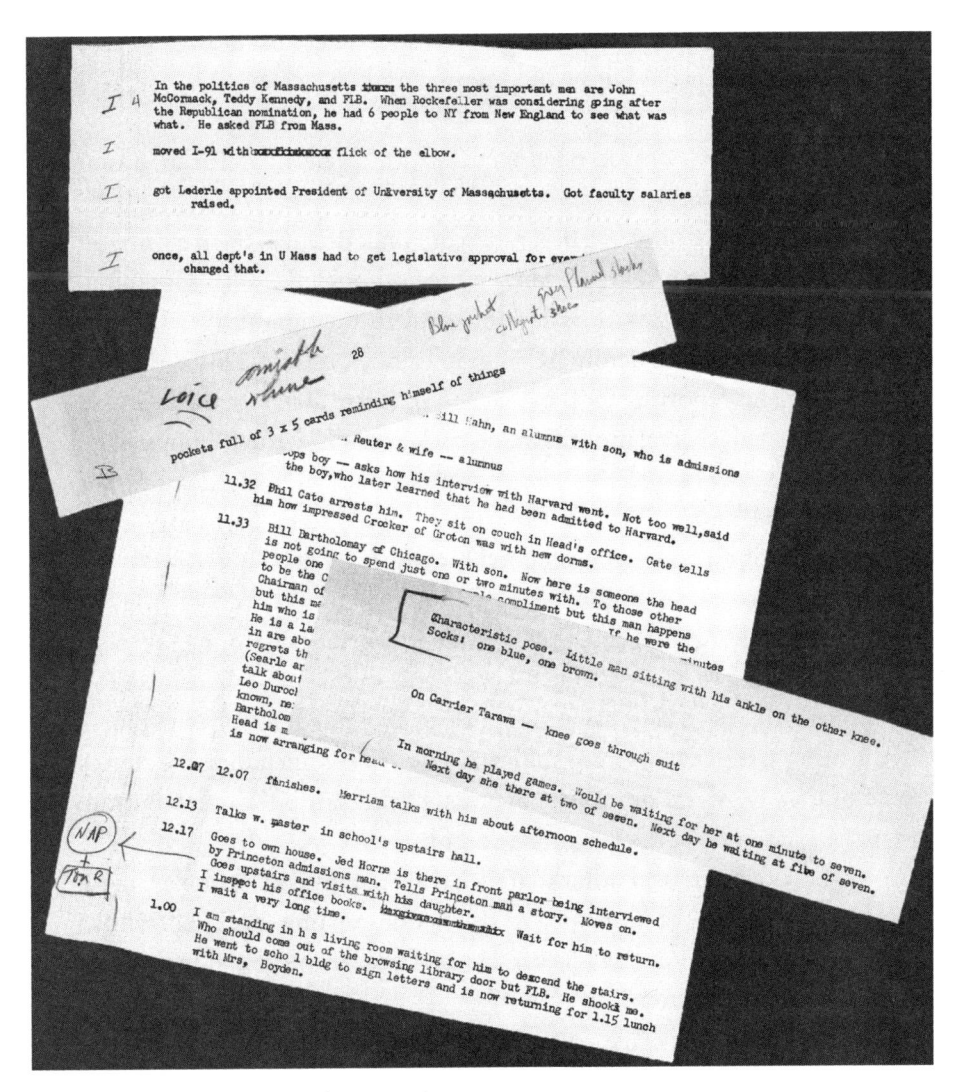

FIGURES 9, 10, AND 11. (*continued*)

In his introduction to *The Second John McPhee Reader*, writer David Remnick, a former student of McPhee's at Princeton and soon to become the editor of *The New Yorker*, writes: "By staying close to Bradley, day after day, McPhee accumulated the details necessary to describe Bradley's quest for perfection. With McPhee's gift for the telling anecdote, Bradley's game and his acute awareness of its angles came alive even to a reader who would never think, otherwise, to care."

The Headmaster: Frank L. Boyden of Deerfield. New York: Farrar, Straus and Giroux, 1966.
McPhee's second book is a biography of Frank Boyden, the headmaster for 66 years of Deerfield Academy, a prep school in western Massachusetts. McPhee had met Boyden in 1948 as a postgraduate student at Deerfield in the year before he entered Princeton University.

During his reporting for the *New Yorker* article that became the book, McPhee spent several months living back on the Deerfield campus. Besides appearing in *The New Yorker* and as a book, *The Headmaster* was chosen by *Reader's Digest* in the winter of 1967 to be part of its "condensed books" series, which gained him more readers.

Oranges. New York: Farrar, Straus and Giroux, 1967.
What began as a short article—an agricultural sketch—became a full book as McPhee's interest and reporting expanded. McPhee explores the history, significance, and cultivation of oranges, including the stories of orange growers, botanists, pickers, packers, modern concentrate makers, and one of the last orange barons.

Book reviewers and other writers have cited this as a prime example of how McPhee could make any subject interesting. McPhee, whose curiosity took him many places, says he became interested in oranges when, as a commuter into New York's Penn Station, he saw the wide range of colors in oranges used to make juice.

The Pine Barrens. New York: Farrar, Straus and Giroux, 1968.
This is the history of the rural, undeveloped land that makes up nearly 25 percent of New Jersey in the shadow of the megalopolis around it. It includes legends about the Pine Barrens, like the Jersey Devil; its agriculture, highlighting blueberries and cranberries; and the stories of some of the Pineys, the previously little-known people who live in the region.

McPhee's book was widely credited for contributing to the passage of the New Jersey Pineland Protection Act in 1979. "If there's one person without whom there wouldn't be a Pinelands Act it would have to be John McPhee," former New Jersey Governor Brendan Byrne told the *Philadelphia Inquirer*. "Until I read John's book, I didn't know a lot about the Pinelands." After reading the book, Byrne went on to seek advice from McPhee, and the two also became regular tennis partners.

McPhee says he particularly struggled with structure on this project. In *Draft No. 4*, McPhee writes, "I had assembled enough material to fill a silo, and now I had no idea what to do with it. The [magazine] piece would ultimately consist of some five thousand sentences, but for those two weeks I couldn't write even one." McPhee spent many days lying on the picnic table outside his house, until finally the lessons about structure that he had learned from his high school English teacher, Olive McKee, kicked in. He realized that Fred Brown, a 79-year-old Pine Barrens native with whom he had spent much time and who was connected to most of the subjects in the book, should be central to the story. "Obvious as it had not seemed," McPhee writes, "this organizing principle gave me a sense of a nearly complete structure, and I got off the table."

In May 1968, Farrar, Straus and Giroux placed a full-page ad in *The New York Times Book Review* for three of its strongest new books—*Slouching Towards Bethlehem* by Joan Didion, *Unspeakable Practices, Unnatural Acts* by Donald Barthelme, and McPhee's *The Pine Barrens*.

A Roomful of Hovings and Other Profiles. New York: Farrar, Straus and Giroux, 1968.
McPhee's first collection contains profiles of Thomas Hoving, director of the Metropolitan Museum of Art; Euell Gibbons, a leading advocate of gathering and eating wild foods; members of a program developed at the Massachusetts Institute of Technology to place highly qualified young men in civil-service jobs in emerging African nations; Robert Twynam, head groundskeeper of the All England Club, the site of Wimbledon; and travel-guide writer Temple Fielding.

Levels of the Game. New York: Farrar, Straus and Giroux, 1969.
A dual biography of two top American tennis players, Arthur Ashe and Clark Graebner, is told through the lens of their U.S. Open semifinal

FIGURE 12. *A Roomful of Hovings and Other Profiles* was McPhee's first collection of articles from *The New Yorker*. (Jacket design by Janet Halverson)

match at Forest Hills in 1968. Ashe and Graebner, both 25, had known each other for half their lives but came from widely different backgrounds—Ashe from the African American section of segregated Richmond, Virginia, and Graebner from an affluent and almost all-white suburb of Cleveland. Getting a tape of the match from CBS, which televised it, was crucial to McPhee in his reconstructing the contest. But archiving TV shows was not done systematically or anywhere near automatically at the time. When McPhee called to get the tape, he learned it had been scheduled to be taped over later that day, and he had almost missed out.

The Crofter and the Laird. New York: Farrar, Straus and Giroux, 1970. McPhee returned to the home of his ancestors—Colonsay, a small island in the Scottish Hebrides—and surveyed the island's history and the lives of its residents from early times to the present. For a time, every McPhee in the world lived on Colonsay at some point, before they were banished. McPhee examined the relationship of the crofters, or farmers, with the English laird who owned Colonsay and the land. Accompanied by his wife and their four young daughters, McPhee lived for a number of weeks in a crofthouse on the island, and his daughters went to the island school.

Encounters with the Archdruid. New York: Farrar, Straus and Giroux, 1971.
McPhee writes of environmental dilemmas in the United States through his profiles of David Brower, founder of Friends of the Earth and first executive director of the Sierra Club, and three natural enemies of his conservation efforts. It is told in three parts through a trio of wilderness trips McPhee took with Brower along with, one by one, his ideological opponents—a mining engineer, a real estate developer, and a federal dam builder. McPhee dubbed Brower the "Archdruid" of the environment movement, a moniker that would stick with him for the rest of his life. The book was a finalist for the National Book Award in the category of science.

Ever since his high school English teacher Olive McKee insisted that students read their writing aloud as a way to be more conscious of it, McPhee had embraced the practice. That reading took an unusual, extended form for this book. McPhee and his first wife, Pryde Brown, had divorced in 1969, and he says this led to a difficult period in his life that sapped his self-confidence. He got into a pattern of reading and discussing the draft of this book with his *New Yorker* editor Robert Bingham over the phone. He eventually read about 60,000 words to Bingham, and built his confidence back.

In 2001, 30 years after *Encounters* was first published, the University of Texas at Austin made it the common text to be read and discussed by more than 10,000 first-year students, and McPhee spoke on campus.

Wimbledon: A Celebration. New York: Viking, 1972.
This book is a pairing of two articles by McPhee and photographs by Alfred Eisenstaedt, one of the founding photographers of *Life* magazine.

McPhee visited Wimbledon for its tennis championships in 1970 and wrote "Hoad on Court 5," about the tournament scene and Australian champion Lew Hoad and other players. The article first appeared in *Playboy* and is paired in this book with McPhee's 1968 *New Yorker* article about the All England Club's head groundskeeper Robert Twynam. Eisenstaedt was commissioned to go to Wimbledon to take the photographs for this book.

The Deltoid Pumpkin Seed. New York: Farrar, Straus and Giroux, 1973. McPhee tells the story of the bright orange Aereon 26, an experimental aircraft that was a hybrid of an airplane and a rigid airship. The efforts to develop the wingless flying machine were led by William Miller, who was in McPhee's class at Princeton University. Miller became president of Aereon Corporation after a decade of pursuing theology studies and other religious work. The book includes a history of "lighter than air" flying machines and focuses on efforts to make the Aereon airborne. The cover was created by the noted graphic designer Milton Glaser.

As an odd sort of tribute to McPhee's novelistic-like writing and storytelling powers, the Library of Congress briefly catalogued the book as fiction, and then corrected the error.

The Curve of Binding Energy: A Journey into the Awesome and Alarming World of Theodore B. Taylor. New York: Farrar, Straus and Giroux, 1974. This book is a profile of Theodore B. Taylor, a theoretical physicist who designed the largest-yield fission bomb ever exploded. Taylor later spent years working to strengthen security practices to prevent the theft of nuclear materials, and McPhee visited American nuclear institutions with him. It was a finalist for the National Book Award in the category of science.

In 1976, when a novel, *The Seventh Power* by James Mills, took up many of the same themes of McPhee's book, Pete Hamill wrote in his *New York Times* review: "I think it's fair to say that 'The Seventh Power' would not exist if 'The Curve of Binding Energy' had not existed first."

Pieces of the Frame. New York: Farrar, Straus and Giroux, 1975.
McPhee's second collection contains eleven articles about travels through Georgia with two ecologists for the state; whitewater canoeing; the decline of Atlantic City, NJ, told through his search for Marvin Gardens, made famous by the Monopoly game; the Loch Ness Monster; a distillery in Scotland with its special Josie's Well; a walk in Macbeth country in Scotland; a season McPhee spent playing on a Cambridge University basketball team in England; a visit to the Wimbledon tennis championships; the physics of firewood; a profile of the director of the National Park Service; and the All-American Futurity quarter horse race in New Mexico.

McPhee's first editor at Farrar, Straus and Giroux, Harold Vursell, wrote to McPhee about the Marvin Gardens piece, which would go on to be studied by many academics for its inventive structure: "Wow! A real surprise. It pushes the borderline between fiction and nonfiction further than I've ever seen it in your work. It is technically brilliant and was great fun for me to read" (Farrar, Straus and Giroux archive at New York Public Library, September 14, 1972).

The Survival of the Bark Canoe. New York: Farrar, Straus and Giroux, 1975.
This book tells the story of the age-old craft of making birch-bark canoes. McPhee takes a 150-mile trip in the north Maine woods with Henri Vaillancourt, a New Hampshire man who makes canoes with the methods and tools that native Americans have used for countless generations. McPhee also writes of the history of canoes, the long canoe journeys of Henry David Thoreau in Maine, and the development of canoes by fur traders in Canada.

The John McPhee Reader. New York: Farrar, Straus and Giroux, 1976.
A collection of excerpts from McPhee's first twelve books, edited by William L. Howarth, a professor of English at Princeton.

This was the first study of McPhee and his literary nonfiction. In his 17-page introduction, Howarth assesses McPhee's development as a

FIGURE 13. The Japanese edition of *The Survival of the Bark Canoe* is one of more than 90 foreign editions of McPhee's books in at least 11 languages besides English.

writer and gives a long description of McPhee's reporting and writing process. "The resulting prose style," Howarth says, "is fresh, strong, unaffected, and yet entirely idiosyncratic."

Coming into the Country. New York: Farrar, Straus and Giroux, 1977. McPhee's book on Alaska and the people who live there came at a time of rapid change in the state. The Alaska Native Claims Settlement Act of 1971 led to greater economic ownership by Alaska natives and increased oil and gas exploration in the state. McPhee tells the story in three segments: wilderness, urban Alaska, and remote life in the bush. McPhee made four long reporting trips to Alaska, spanning nearly three years.

One of McPhee's inspirations for the book was a friend, John Kauffmann, whom he'd first met when they both taught at Princeton's Hun School in the mid-1950s. Kauffmann had gone on to plan national parks and monuments in Alaska for the National Park Service, and he accompanied McPhee on a trip there.

The book quickly became a bestseller and remains McPhee's greatest commercial success. The book ultimately sold more than a million copies and elevated McPhee's profile dramatically. "We have hit the jackpot," Farrar, Straus and Giroux chairman Roger Straus wrote at the time (Farrar, Straus and Giroux archive at New York Public Library, December 19, 1977).

Giving Good Weight. New York: Farrar, Straus and Giroux, 1979.
This collection of five articles contains the title story about New York City's Greenmarkets, and others about a company's plan to float nuclear power plants off the coast of New Jersey; a field trip with a grandmaster of pinball (and journalism), J. Anthony Lukas; a whitewater canoe trip in Maine; and one about the artistry of a chef and his wife.

"Brigade de Cuisine," the last and longest story in the collection, caused controversy when it was first published in *The New Yorker* because McPhee and the magazine had agreed not to disclose the chef's identity—he is called "Otto" in the article—or to reveal the name of the restaurant. The chef also says he guessed—later found to be wrong—that the ultra-luxe restaurant Lutèce in New York City served frozen fish. It was corrected in the book version.

The Pine Barrens, Special Edition with Photographs by Bill Curtsinger. New York: Farrar, Straus and Giroux, 1981.
This book contains the original text of McPhee's 1968 book about the rural, largely undeveloped area of New Jersey, plus a 14-page addendum by McPhee about his work with longtime National Geographic photographer Bill Curtsinger. McPhee provides updates on several people mentioned in the 1968 book, as well as on state and federal actions to protect land use. Curtsinger contributed more than 60 black-and-white photographs chronicling the Pine Barrens, often closely connected to McPhee's reporting.

Alaska: Images of the Country. San Francisco: Sierra Club Books, 1981.
In 1979, Galen Rowell, regarded as one of the most talented landscape photographers in the world, proposed a book that would combine text from McPhee's *Coming into the Country* and Rowell's photographs of Alaska. McPhee agreed, and Rowell made nine separate trips to Alaska, where he took more than 10,000 images that he culled down to 112 color photos for the book.

Rowell also selected the segments of McPhee text for the book and wrote in the preface: "Few if any writers have been as successful as John McPhee in giving solid journalism the taste of fine literature. The elegance and complexity of his style never obscure the substance of what he has to say."

Basin and Range. New York: Farrar, Straus and Giroux, 1981.
The first of what became a series of five books spanning 20 years, McPhee undertook to write about North American and, to some extent, global geology. He began by traveling west from Salt Lake City with the Princeton University geology professor Kenneth Deffeyes as his guide. In this volume McPhee coins the term "deep time," now widely used around the world, in a set piece on the timescale of geological events. Like McPhee's other geology books, it was later republished as part of *Annals of the Former World* in 1998.

The book includes an introduction to plate tectonics and the "New Geology" movement. Deffeyes later wrote in a letter to Roger Straus, chairman of Farrar, Straus and Giroux, "Working with John has been a continuing pleasure, he has been patient with the hundreds of changes that have been required to preserve factual precision. That he was able to hammer out a book of literary merit out of such stubborn material is a small miracle" (Farrar, Straus and Giroux archive at New York Public Library, December 8, 1980).

In Suspect Terrain. New York: Farrar, Straus and Giroux, 1983.
In the second book in his series on geology and geologists, McPhee traverses Interstate 80 between New York and Indiana with Anita Harris, a paleontologist with the U.S. Geological Survey. She discusses her

roots in Brooklyn, her decision to become a geologist, and her skepticism about the revolutionary theory of plate tectonics that was emerging at the time. Glaciation is another major topic, as the area that McPhee is exploring—New York, Pennsylvania, Ohio, and Indiana—was largely shaped by continental ice sheets. This book was later republished as part of *Annals of the Former World*, in 1998.

La Place de la Concorde Suisse. New York: Farrar, Straus and Giroux, 1984. In this book on the Swiss Army and its role in Swiss society, McPhee writes about some of the country's citizen-soldiers on their patrols and other military maneuvers, including tactical practice. The book also highlights the spectacular scenery surrounding the soldiers when they hike the meadows of the Alps, drink Valais wine, and eat fine food as picnic meals. He discusses how closely Switzerland is intertwined with its army although it has not fought a war in hundreds of years, and how the country holds on to the Porcupine Principle, in which "you roll up into a ball and brandish your quills."

Table of Contents. New York: Farrar, Straus and Giroux, 1985.
A collection of eight McPhee pieces: "Under the Snow," on a visit with bear cubs in Pennsylvania; "A Textbook Place for Bears," on travels with a state biologist who tracks New Jersey's wild bears; "Riding the Boom Extension," on the impact of telephone service coming to a small village near the Arctic Circle; "Heirs of General Practice," a book-length piece (later published as a separate book) about family practice doctors in Maine; "Open Man," on a day spent on a coastal boardwalk with Bill Bradley, the subject of his first book, now a Senator of New Jersey; "Ice Pond," on a return visit with Theodore B. Taylor, the subject of the *Curve of Binding Energy*, this time looking at Taylor's efforts to develop a cooling system using ice rather than fission or fossil fuel; "Minihydro," on how entrepreneurs in New York State were setting up mini hydroelectric facilities at former mill sites and selling the energy to power companies; and "North of the C.P. Line," on flights with a bush pilot and game warden in Maine who is also named John McPhee.

Heirs of General Practice. New York: Farrar, Straus and Giroux, 1986.
This book is the story of doctors in Maine who belong to a medical specialty that was new at the time, called family practice. McPhee shows how the doctors, with patients of every age, have embraced generalism at a time of great specialization in the medical world. The text is also included in the collection *Table of Contents* in 1985 and a special edition of *Heirs* was published by a medical society for delivery to doctors and medical students.

In the Highlands and Islands. London: Faber & Faber, 1986.
Published in London for distribution mainly in the United Kingdom and Europe, this is a collection of McPhee's work set in Scotland, including "The Crofter and the Laird" and three essays from *Pieces of the Frame* all originally published in 1969 and 1970: "Josie's Well," about whisky making; "Pieces of the Frame" on the Loch Ness Monster; and "From Birnam Wood to Dunsinane," on a journey walking through Macbeth country.

Rising from the Plains. New York: Farrar, Straus and Giroux, 1986.
This third book in McPhee's series on geology focuses on Wyoming and the Rocky Mountains. He tells much of the story through David Love, a field geologist for the U.S. Geological Survey who grew up on a ranch at the geographical center of Wyoming. McPhee spent many months with Love, and one day Love gave him something totally unexpected: the unpublished journals kept by Ethel Waxham, the geologist's mother. Waxham's journals covered the early years of the twentieth century, when she came to teach in rugged Wyoming after growing up in Denver and graduating Phi Beta Kappa from Wellesley College.

McPhee made Waxham's keen observations on ranch life, her wit, and the story of her romance with sheep rancher John Love a large part of the book. McPhee also says that working with her journal inspired him to buy his first computer in 1984. As he incorporated excerpts from her journal, he could not bear to keep retyping them in drafts on his typewriter, so he went out and bought his first computer and started using it the same afternoon. The book, which was a finalist for the Pulitzer Prize in General Nonfiction, was republished as part of *Annals of the Former World* in 1998.

Ten years after the book was published, the documentary filmmaker Ken Burns included the story of John Love and Ethel Waxham in episode 8, "One Sky Above Us," in his nine-part television series *The West*. In addition, two granddaughters of Waxham, Barbara Love and Frances Love Froidevaux, later published two volumes adapted from Waxham's journals and letters, *Lady's Choice* (with a foreword by McPhee) and *Life on Muskrat Creek*.

Outcroppings. Text and introduction by John McPhee, edited by Christopher Merrill, photographs by Tom Till. Layton, UT: Gibbs Smith, 1988.
This book pairs text from several John McPhee books, *Rising from the Plains*, *Basin and Range*, and *Encounters with the Archdruid*, with photographs by Tom Till, a prominent American landscape photographer.

In his preface, the book's editor, Christopher Merrill, says choosing the McPhee excerpts was "at once exhilarating and impossible." He expressed hope that the text and photographs "work in counterpoint, creating sparks across the page—poetry, if you will—to replace the poetry sacrificed in the initial editing."

The Control of Nature. New York: Farrar, Straus and Giroux, 1989.
McPhee's account is of four places around the world where people have been locked in battle to control nature: the U.S. Army Corps of Engineers' efforts to restrain the Atchafalaya and Mississippi rivers near Baton Rouge and New Orleans; people in Iceland working to cool and stop a lava flow; Hawaiians coping with an active volcano; and Los Angeles residents attempting to catch and control debris flows that travel down mountain canyons with disastrous force. In subsequent years, after Hurricane Katrina's destruction in the Louisiana area and crippling landslides in Los Angeles, McPhee's writing from this book has been widely cited and reprinted.

Looking for a Ship. New York: Farrar, Straus and Giroux, 1990.
The story of the fading U.S. Merchant Marine starts with McPhee accompanying Andy Chase, a veteran mariner, as Chase goes through the difficult process of waiting in union halls to try to get a job in a dwindling industry. Chase gets a spot as a second mate on the *S.S. Stella Lykes,* one of the last ships in the fleet, and McPhee rides along on the ship as it goes on a run through the Panama Canal and down the Pacific Coast of South America. Through stories from Chase, Captain Paul Washburn, and others in the crew, McPhee covers many aspects of maritime life—disaster, greed, courage, and more. The book was a finalist for the Pulitzer Prize in General Nonfiction.

Assembling California. New York: Farrar, Straus and Giroux, 1993.
In the fourth book in his series on geology, McPhee travels through California with the geologist Eldridge Moores, professor at University of California, Davis, and a leading expert on global plate tectonics. With Moores, McPhee explores how the state of California has been assembled over the last hundred million years as the result of a series of eruptions called "island arcs." The book ends with a vivid 17-page section about the 1989 Loma Prieta earthquake, providing a slice of what the human experience looked and felt like from Santa Cruz to San Francisco during the deadly quake. This book was republished as part of *Annals of the Former World* in 1998.

The Ransom of Russian Art. New York: Farrar, Straus and Giroux, 1994.
Sparked by a chance meeting on an Amtrak train, McPhee constructs a profile of Norton Dodge, an American professor of Soviet economics who bought thousands of paintings, prints, and other works by Soviet dissident artists and then smuggled the art from the USSR into the United States in the 1960s and 1970s. McPhee describes how Dodge saved the work of a generation of artists, often at great risk to him and the artists.

In striking contract to McPhee's other books, almost all of which had no photographs or illustrations and relied solely on his words for descriptions, the book includes 53 color illustrations of work that Dodge brought to the United States.

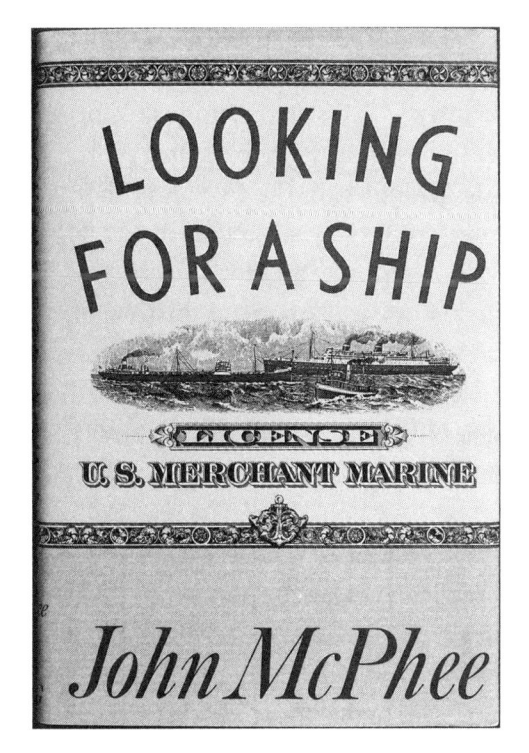

FIGURE 14. *Looking for a Ship* is McPhee's account of the dwindling U.S. merchant marine fleet. (Jacket design by Cynthia Krupat).

The Second John McPhee Reader. New York: Farrar, Straus and Giroux, 1996.
The second broad collection of McPhee work draws from 11 of his books published since 1975. The book is edited by Patricia Strachan, a former editor of McPhee's at Farrar, Straus and Giroux, and includes an introduction by David Remnick, who was a student of McPhee's at Princeton and became editor of *The New Yorker* in 1998.

"McPhee's reputation is substantial, far from a secret," Remnick writes. "He is a favorite of other writers, the sort of figure who is so good that he is beyond envying ... All the same, McPhee's reputation should be greater still. While much of the New Journalism of the sixties and seventies has long felt mannered or hysterical in the rereading, McPhee's work has the quality of permanence."

Irons in the Fire. New York: Farrar, Straus and Giroux, 1997.
This is a collection of seven essays, including one on travels in Nevada cattle-rustling country with a state Brand Inspector; a blind professor using a computer; 65 acres of virgin forest in a central New Jersey suburb; how forensic geologists in the FBI and other law-enforcement organizations solve crimes; a visit to the world's largest pile of scrap tires, about 34 million of them; an exotic car auction in Pennsylvania; and the geologic history and American history of Plymouth Rock, which McPhee describes while a mason repairs cracks in it.

Annals of the Former World. New York: Farrar, Straus and Giroux, 1998.
This book, a compilation with some adjustments of McPhee's four previously published geology books, won the 1999 Pulitzer Prize for General Nonfiction. It includes a new final section, "Crossing the Craton," a previously unpublished essay that describes the deep Precambrian basement that lies below the midwestern United States. The book is McPhee's only one with an index, running 31 pages.

The Pulitzer jury said of the book, "As clearly and succinctly written as it is profoundly informed, this is our finest popular survey of geology, and a masterpiece of modern nonfiction writing."

The Founding Fish. New York: Farrar, Straus and Giroux, 2002.
McPhee chronicles his decades in pursuit of shad, along with the history of the fish going back to the days of George Washington, who was a commercial shad fisherman, and Henry David Thoreau. Quirkily encyclopedic about shad, it includes subjects such as how the fish was critical to early American settlers, McPhee's personal history in fishing for shad, and recipes.

Uncommon Carriers. New York: Farrar, Straus and Giroux, 2006.
Transportation in various forms is the common thread in this collection of seven essays. It includes a coast-to-coast trip in an 18-wheel tanker truck; a school on a pond in France that trains the skippers of large oceangoing ships; riding on the Illinois River on barge rigs that are longer than any existing aircraft carrier; a New England canoe trip

FIGURE 15. *Annals of the Former World*, a compilation of four previously published books about geology and one new essay, won the Pulitzer Prize for general nonfiction in 1999. (Jacket design by Cynthia Krupat)

retracing the route of an 1839 journey by Henry David Thoreau; a visit to a UPS facility that sorts a million packages a day through loops and belts and machines at a Louisville air distribution hub; rides in the cabs of coal trains in the United States; and a follow-up with the 18-wheel truck driver.

Silk Parachute. New York: Farrar, Straus and Giroux, 2010.
For decades, critics and readers wondered why McPhee didn't reveal more of himself and his personal history. This collection of 10 essays is widely seen as breaking that pattern. The title essay, describing his boyhood adventures with his mother (Mary Ziegler McPhee, 99 years old

as he wrote about the memories) and the captivating toy, a silk parachute, that she gave him, received the most attention.

Other essays involve a trip with family on the massive chalk that is a prominent geological feature of Great Britain and Western Europe; canoeing at his childhood summer camp; his relationship with the headmaster of Deerfield Academy as they rode on fold-out jump seats in a car en route to basketball games; the history and growth of lacrosse and his experience as faculty fellow for the Princeton team; the technique of two collaborating photographers (one is his daughter Laura) who use a large view camera together; his lifetime list of exotic foods eaten; his decades of working with fact-checkers at *The New Yorker*; a report from attending the 2007 U.S. Open golf championship; and an answer to a question from a travel writer based in Tennessee about why he chose to keep living in New Jersey.

Draft No. 4: On the Writing Process. New York: Farrar, Straus and Giroux, 2017.
Though he has mentioned the writing process in many other books and articles, this is the closest to an instructional book about writing that McPhee has done. In eight essays, McPhee imparts his ideas on structure (including his picnic table crisis of 1966), elicitation (or how to conduct interviews and accumulate information in additional ways), and the title piece, *Draft No. 4*, about the keys to revising and improving your own writing.

The Patch. New York: Farrar, Straus and Giroux, 2018.
A book in two parts, this collection includes many McPhee articles previously unavailable in book form, mostly from *The New Yorker* and his work at *Time* magazine from 1957 to 1965. The first section is a collection of six essays with a connection to sports, although the title essay is more about McPhee's father than about the favorite fishing spot with that name. The others are on his memories of football coaches and a Princeton roommate, Dick Kazmaier, who won the Heisman Trophy; McPhee's compulsion to collect golf balls; the 2010 Open Championship at St. Andrews and the evolution of golf; lacrosse coach Bill Tierney's move from

FIGURE 16. *The Silk Parachute*, a collection of McPhee's articles, includes some of his most personal published writing, including the title essay about him and his mother. (Jacket design by Susan Mitchell)

Princeton to the University of Denver; and McPhee's longing to see a wild bear from the windows of his house.

The second section, "An Album Quilt," is a patchwork of more than 50 items, ranging in length from a few hundred to several thousand words, on widely disparate subjects. Fragments of his *Time* cover stories of show business celebrities, such as Richard Burton and Sophia Loren, are included, as are items on places like Radio City Music Hall, and more personal ones such as a eulogy for his longtime *New Yorker* editor Robert Bingham, and a high-school composition his youngest daughter wrote about him.

Some have called the book a covert memoir, although a review by Craig Taylor in *The New York Times* called it "just another chapter in an ongoing memoir of generous curiosity" (*The New York Times*, December 23, 2018).

Tabula Rasa: Volume 1. New York: Farrar, Straus and Giroux, 2023.
McPhee says this is his "old-man project." Since his late eighties, McPhee has been searching his memory and computer files for "saved-up, bypassed, intended pieces of writing" that were never written. In a format that resembles his 2018 "Album Quilt," McPhee includes items of widely different subjects and length, such as his early efforts to publish work in *The New Yorker*, a fateful conversation with writer and friend Peter Benchley, and being a teenaged night watchman at the Institute for Advanced Study in Princeton, where Albert Einstein and other luminaries had offices.

Introductions, Forewords, and Prefaces

"Writing is a matter strictly of developing oneself. You compete only with yourself."

—JOHN MCPHEE, DRAFT NO. 4 (2017): 82

John McPhee has contributed many introductions, forewords, and prefaces to books that were written by others, representing projects of special meaning to him and often on topics he has written about previously.

John McPhee, foreword to *10 Trial Street*, by Robert McGlynn. Deerfield, MA: The Deerfield Press, 1979.
As a student at Deerfield Academy in 1948–1949, McPhee met Robert McGlynn, an English teacher whom McPhee never had for a class but who became an important inspiration, mentor, and friend. Thirty years later, the Deerfield Press published a short story by McGlynn as a small book and McPhee writes in his foreword, "He led us up the hill to Joyce and Conrad, and down the other side to meet ourselves."

INTRODUCTIONS, FOREWORDS, AND PREFACES   27

John McPhee, remembrance of the author, in *Stalking the Wild Asparagus*, by Euell Gibbons. Putney, VT: Alan C. Hood & Co., 1987, xii.
McPhee's writing here, as part of a republication of Gibbons's classic text, is drawn from his April 6, 1968, profile of Gibbons in *The New Yorker*, which was later included in the collection *A Roomful of Hovings and Other Profiles*.

John McPhee, introduction to *Outcroppings*, photographs by Tom Till, edited by Christopher Merrill. Salt Lake City: Peregrine Smith Books, 1988, 1.
In this book, which pairs some of McPhee's writings about the West with photographs by Tom Till, McPhee responds to the book editor's question about what prompted him to write about the West. He starts out by saying "a tennis match at Forest Hills," explaining how his dual profile of Arthur Ashe and Clark Graebner in *Levels of the Game* led him to design a still more complicated structure in "Encounters with the Archdruid," much of which was set in the West.

McPhee then tells the story of his work with the geologist David Love during research for *Rising from the Plains* when Love gave McPhee the unpublished journals of his mother, Ethel Waxham Love, a schoolteacher on the Western frontier. McPhee writes, "When her son gave me her journal, she would have been over a hundred years old, and needless to say I never met her, but the admiration and affection I came to feel toward her is probably matched by no one I've encountered in my professional life. To the editor's question—why would this writer be drawn to the West?—she and her son are enough of an answer."

John McPhee, foreword to *Lady's Choice: Ethel Waxham's Journals and Letters, 1905–1910*, edited by Barbara Love and Frances Love Froidevaux. Albuquerque: University of New Mexico Press, 1993, ix.
McPhee addresses the early twentieth-century writings of Ethel Waxham Love. She was the mother of David Love of the U.S. Geological Survey, who was crucial to McPhee's understanding geology in Wyoming and elsewhere for his book *Rising from the Plains*, published in 1986. After Love and McPhee had worked together for months, Love gave McPhee

FIGURE 17. McPhee wrote the foreword to *10 Trial Street*, a book by Deerfield Academy English teacher Robert McGlynn, published in 1979. McPhee (left) and McGlynn (second from left) discuss the project with two other Deerfield teachers involved, Tim Engelland and John O'Brien. (Deerfield Academy Archives)

access to his mother's unpublished journals, and McPhee incorporated many excerpts of her portrait of the American West in his book.

"She recorded these things," McPhee says of Waxham's journals and later writings, "with such wit, insight, grace, irony, compassion, sarcasm, stylistic elegance, and embracing humor that I could not resist her."

Later, Waxham's granddaughters, Barbara Love and Frances Love Froidevaux, also turned Ethel Waxham's writing into a second volume (*Life on Muskrat Creek*, published by Lehigh University Press in 2018).

John McPhee, afterword to *No Ordinary Land: Encounters in a Changing Environment*, by Virginia Beahan and Laura McPhee. New York: Aperture, 1998, 99.
A "how they do it" piece describes two well-known fine art photographers who jointly operate a large-format Deardoff view camera. One

of the photographers is McPhee's daughter Laura, who, like her camera partner Virginia Beahan, grew up around Princeton—they met in a Princeton University course. John McPhee traces their partnership "under the dark cloth" that they use to block out light while focusing the camera. "Their own appearance, under the cloth, with the snout of the big camera protruding," writes McPhee, "is so incongruous and vaudevillian that snapshooters the world over have crowded in to take pictures of Laura and Virginia making pictures." Besides describing the work of Laura McPhee and Beahan, McPhee explores their artistic process and how the camera works. The piece was later republished in his collection *Silk Parachute*.

John McPhee, preface to *The Princeton Anthology of Writing: Favorite Pieces by the Ferris/McGraw Writers at Princeton University*, edited by John McPhee and Carol Rigolot. Princeton, NJ: Princeton University Press, 2001, v.
McPhee traces the history of the Ferris/McGraw writing programs at Princeton and nonfiction writing in general, saying that when he was a student at Princeton in the 1950s "we did not study contemporary journalistic prose . . . nonfiction was not yet a term, let alone a literary term." He adds, "Even as late as 1973, a Harvard anthology purporting to represent all the important writing in the United States since the Second World War did not include a single nonfiction example. As this book splendidly attests, factual writing has found its place in the regard of the academy, to the great pleasure of all of us represented here."

John McPhee, introduction to *Fishing in New Hampshire: A History (New Hampshire Fishing Series)*, by Jack Noon. Warner, NH: Moose Country Press, 2003, v.
While he lives in New Jersey, McPhee gives an account of his lifetime of experience fishing in New Hampshire. He describes fishing there every July for many years, staying with his family in a house loaned to him by John Kauffmann, who spent his summers working for the National Park Service in Alaska and was a key inspiration for McPhee's *Coming into the Country*. McPhee also writes with affection about the tastiness of an undervalued fish he grew accustomed to in New

Hampshire—the chain pickerel, a long torpedo-shaped fish with sharp teeth and many bones.

At the end, McPhee writes about how *An Annotated Bibliography of the Chain Pickerel* has a prominent spot on his bookshelf at home along with Melville's *Moby Dick* and Izaak Walton's *The Compleat Angler*. Now, he says, "On that shelf of mine at home, Melville has moved a little to his right and Walton to his left, making room beside the Annotated Bibliography for the accumulated centuries of *Fishing in New Hampshire*, and Jack Noon."

John McPhee, introduction to *Henry D. Thoreau: A Week on the Concord and Merrimack Rivers*, edited by Carl F. Hovde, Elizabeth Hall Witherell, and William L. Howarth. Princeton, NJ: Princeton University Press, 2004, ix.
In a 38-page piece that is by far McPhee's longest book introduction, he writes about his 2003 retracing of John and Henry Thoreau's 1839 boating and hiking trip (Henry Thoreau's account of the trip was published in 1849). McPhee took the trip with Mark Svenvold, his son-in-law and a poet, and also involved Dick Kazmaier, a Princeton roommate who, in 1951, was the last Heisman Trophy winner to come out of Ivy League football.

McPhee's writing about the changes in the 150 years since the Thoreaus' trip is both weighty and comic. He imagines, for example, how Henry Thoreau would have experienced being on a boat in water that is now a hazard for a golf club in Lowell, Massachusetts. "He might have been slow to understand the scene we came into now: men riding in little carts and seeming to kill things on the ground," McPhee writes. The material in this introduction was also published in *The New Yorker* on December 15, 2003, and later was included in his collection *Uncommon Carriers*, published in 2006.

John McPhee, foreword to *Camp*, by Michael Eisner. New York: Warner Books, 2005, xi.
McPhee starts by saying that the Keewaydin camp in Vermont was the educational institution that had the greatest influence on him. He writes

of his many summers at the camp, and about a camp counselor who was the first editor for his writing. He traces the generations of the Eisner family at Keewaydin, including Michael Eisner, who would rise to being CEO of the Walt Disney Company and write this book about the life lessons he drew from camp.

John McPhee, foreword to *Bark Canoes and Skin Boats of North America*, by Edward Tappan Adney and Howard I. Chappell. New York: Skyhorse Publishing Inc., 2007, xiii.
For this reissue of Adney and Chappell's book, first published in 1964, McPhee writes about its importance to Henri Vaillancourt, the master craftsman of bark canoes and the leading character in McPhee's own book, *The Survival of the Bark Canoe*, published in 1975.

John McPhee, preface to *The Princeton Reader: Contemporary Essays by Writers and Journalists at Princeton University*, edited by John McPhee and Carol Rigolot. Princeton, NJ: Princeton University Press, 2011, xiii.
McPhee talks about the 75 writers from around the world—from newspapers, television, internet operations, documentary film, and elsewhere—who, like him, taught courses at Princeton under the Ferris, McGraw, and Robbins programs in the first decade of the twenty-first century.

McPhee writes with humility and wit, "Nearly all the visiting writers come for a single semester. Within this history, I am a grandfather in more ways than one, having joined the Ferris program when Jimmy Carter was governor of Georgia. All through the years, I have told incoming Ferris, McGraw, and Robbins professors that I would be happy to offer suggestions to help them plan their courses. They thanked me politely and did their own thing."

John McPhee, foreword to *Canoes: A Natural History in North America*, by Mark Neuzil and Norman Sims. Minneapolis: University of Minnesota Press, 2016, ix.
McPhee's foreword, titled "Scenes from a Life in Canoes," is a patchwork of excerpts from his previous writing about canoes, plus some

original notes on subjects like his 38 consecutive Octobers of fly casting with a friend in Lake Winnipesaukee. The authors point out that McPhee, in his eighties, still owns five canoes, about which McPhee writes, "What am I doing with five canoes?" As part of an elegant book with lovely photos and illustrations, McPhee recalls his formative experiences at Keewaydin camp in Vermont and other canoe trips that involve fishing, dams, retrieving golf balls, and more.

Digital and Audio Editions

"Readers are not supposed to notice structure. It's meant to be about as visible as someone's bones."

—JOHN MCPHEE, FROM HIS SPEECH UPON RECEIVING DEERFIELD ACADEMY HERITAGE AWARD, OCTOBER 3, 1995

More than 30 of John McPhee's books have been published in digital and audio editions. But because many of his books were originally published before digital and audiobooks were common, some have been produced years after print publication and in widely different formats. For instance, *The Headmaster*, McPhee's second book, originally published in 1966, did not come out as an audiobook until nearly 60 years later, in 2024. Edoardo Ballerini rediscovered the book years after he, like McPhee, graduated from Deerfield Academy. Ballerini, an actor and highly regarded audiobook narrator barely half McPhee's age, said that rereading the book moved him to propose and make the recording.

McPhee made many recordings of his own work before he stepped back from recording in the early 2020s. The most frequent reader of his work is Nelson Runger, who coincidentally was McPhee's classmate at Princeton, although they did not know each other at the time. After many years in public relations, Runger built a second career as an award-winning narrator of audiobooks.

Grover Gardner, one of the leading audiobook narrators in the United States, also has recorded McPhee's work, including *Oranges*,

Levels of the Game, a version of *Annals of the Former World,* and *Tabula Rasa: Volume 1.*

These books by McPhee are available in various digital formats from multiple vendors:

A Sense of Where You Are
The Headmaster
Oranges
The Pine Barrens
A Roomful of Hovings
Levels of the Game
The Crofter and the Laird
Encounters with the Archdruid
The Deltoid Pumpkin Seed
The Curve of Binding Energy
Pieces of the Frame
The Survival of the Bark Canoe
The John McPhee Reader
Coming into the Country
Giving Good Weight
Basin and Range
In Suspect Terrain
La Place de la Concorde Suisse
Table of Contents
Heirs of General Practice
Rising from the Plains
The Control of Nature
Looking for a Ship
Assembling California
The Ransom of Russian Art
The Second John McPhee Reader
Irons in the Fire
Annals of the Former World

The Founding Fish
Uncommon Carriers
Silk Parachute
Draft No. 4
The Patch
Tabula Rasa: Volume 1

Of McPhee's books, more than 20 are available as audiobooks, with the exception of some of his earliest books:

The Headmaster
Oranges
The Pine Barrens
Levels of the Game
The Crofter and the Laird
Encounters with the Archdruid
Pieces of the Frame
The Survival of the Bark Canoe
Basin and Range
In Suspect Terrain
Rising from the Plains
The Control of Nature
Looking for a Ship
Assembling California
The Second John McPhee Reader
Irons in the Fire
Annals of the Former World
Crossing the Craton (essay added in Annals of the Former World)
The Founding Fish
Uncommon Carriers
Silk Parachute
Draft No. 4
The Patch, 2018
Tabula Rasa: Volume 1

Anthologies

"Writing is selection. From the first word in the first sentence in an actual composition, the writer is choosing, selecting, and deciding (most importantly) what to leave out."

—JOHN MCPHEE, *DRAFT NO. 4* (2017), 182

McPhee's work has been included in a wide range of literary anthologies, where he has been one of the most popular American nonfiction writers. Many are "Best of" type anthologies, such as for magazine articles, essays, and travel and literary journalism, while others reflect his specialties, such as nature and sports. His anthologized pieces are from previously published writings rather than being original—with a rare exception being a memory he wrote about in a 2005 anthology on the influence of childhood reading on adult writers. For some readers, literary collections are a chance to discover McPhee's writing; for others they are an opportunity to be introduced through his work to other writers and related subjects.

Among his most anthologized writing are his "A Sense of Where You Are," about Princeton and basketball's Bill Bradley; his "Encounters with the Archdruid," on environmentalism; and the more recent and personal essay "Silk Parachute," about his mother.

He has also coedited two anthologies that include his work, both connected to Princeton University.

Here is a sampling of anthologies that include McPhee's work:

Gerald Walker, ed., *Best Magazine Articles: 1966*. New York: Crown, 1966, 219.
McPhee's entry is "A Sense of Where You Are" from *The New Yorker*. Other writers in the volume include Elie Wiesel, John Kenneth Galbraith, Tom Wolfe, and William Styron.

Herbert Warren Wind, ed., *The Realm of Sport: The Classic Collection of the World's Great Sporting Events and Personalities as Recorded by the Most Distinguished Writers*. New York: Simon & Schuster, 1966, 128.

McPhee's entry is from *A Sense of Where You Are*. Among other writers included are Robert Louis Stevenson, James Thurber, Ring Lardner, John James Audubon, Winston Churchill, Mark Twain, and John F. Kennedy. The editor of this anthology, Herbert Warren Wind, was a colleague of McPhee's at *The New Yorker*, where he was known for his specialty of covering golf.

Nat Hentoff and John McPhee, *Our Children Are Dying* and *The Headmaster*. New York: Four Winds Press, 1967.
This paperback combines the full text of two books: Nat Hentoff's portrait of Elliott Shapiro, the crusading principal of P.S. 119 in Harlem, New York, and McPhee's portrait of Frank Boyden, the headmaster of Deerfield Academy. Both pieces began as *New Yorker* profiles before being published as separate books. An introduction by Charlotte Leon Mayerson links the two educators who worked in vastly different environments: "They are the kind of teachers society must generate to save itself."

Gerald Walker, ed., *Best Magazine Articles: 1967*. New York: Crown, 1967, 262.
McPhee's entry is "Fifty-Two People on a Continent" from *The New Yorker*. Other writers include Joan Didion, Tom Wolfe, Dick Schaap, and Gore Vidal.

Hugh M. Hefner, ed., *The Twentieth Anniversary Playboy Reader*. Chicago: Playboy Press, 1974, 520.
McPhee's entry is "Centre Court" from *Playboy*. Other contributors include Gary Wills, Joyce Carol Oates, Murray Kempton, Justice William O. Douglas, and Germaine Greer.

Kenneth Brower, ed., *Guale, the Golden Coast of Georgia*. San Francisco: Friends of the Earth, 1974, 76, 78, 84.
Excerpts from McPhee's *Encounters with the Archdruid* are in this coffee-table format book about islands and wetlands off the Georgia coast. David Brower, profiled in McPhee's *Encounters with the Archdruid*, wrote the introduction and his son, Kenneth, was the editor. Rachel Carson is among the other contributors.

Evan Jones, ed., *A Food Lover's Companion*. New York: Harper and Row, 1979.
McPhee has two pieces in this anthology: on page 165 is "A Chef Named Otto Goes Shopping," adapted from his "Brigade de Cuisine" in *The New Yorker*, and on page 175 is "A Hostly Use of Oranges" from his book *Oranges*. Other writers in the book include Julia Child, James Beard, Ernest Hemingway, Enrico Caruso, Alice B. Toklas, and Marcel Proust.

Frank Bergon, ed., *The Wilderness Reader*. New York: New American Library, 1980, 347.
McPhee's excerpt is from *Coming into the Country*. Other writers in the book include John James Audubon, Henry David Thoreau, Theodore Roosevelt, John Muir, Rachel Carson, Wallace Stegner, and Edward Abbey.

Donald Hall, ed., *The Contemporary Essay*. New York: St. Martin's Press, 1984, 298.
An excerpt of McPhee's *Oranges* is in this collection of 50 essays. Other contributors include E. B. White, Eudora Welty, Walker Percy, James Baldwin, Adrienne Rich, and Joan Didion.

Sandra Loy, ed., *The Writer's Voice*. New York: Holt, Rinehart and Winston, 1985.
In this book aimed at helping writers develop their skills, McPhee is singled out along with three other writers (George Orwell, Joan Didion, and Jack Kerouac) for more extended study. Portions of *The Pine Barrens* (page 302) and *The Curve of Binding Energy* (page 307) are included.

Ann Ronald, ed., *Words for the Wild: The Sierra Club Trailside Reader*. San Francisco: Sierra Club Books, 1987, 314.
McPhee's entry is an excerpt from *Basin and Range*. In her introduction, editor Ann Ronald writes, "I perceive in McPhee's words a deep concern for man's relationship with the land, and an interest in the land's delicate future." Other writers in this anthology include Annie Dillard, Edward Abbey, Loren Eiseley, and Wallace Stegner.

FIGURE 18. In 1967, Four Winds Press published an unusual volume that combined McPhee's second book, *The Headmaster*, about Deerfield Academy's Frank Boyden, with Nat Hentoff's book, *Our Children Are Dying*, about the principal of a New York City public school.

Jeff Fischer, ed., *Maine Speaks: An Anthology of Maine Literature*. Brunswick: The Maine Writers and Publishers Alliance, 1989, 211.
McPhee's excerpt is from "North of the C.P. Line," from *The New Yorker*. Others in the book include Edna St. Vincent Millay, Henry Wadsworth Longfellow, Carolyn Chute, E. B. White, and Stephen King.

Robert Hedin and Gary Holthaus, eds., *Alaska: Reflections on Land and Spirit*. Tucson: University of Arizona Press, 1989, 107.
McPhee's excerpt is "Riding the Boom Extension," from *The New Yorker*. Other writers in the anthology include John Muir, Jack London, Harry Crews, William O. Douglas, Anne Morrow Lindbergh, Roger Tory Peterson, Peter Matthiessen, and Billie Wright.

Stephanie Mills, ed., *In Praise of Nature*. Washington, DC: Island Press, 1990, 53.
In this anthology about the environment with sections on Earth, Air, Fire, Water, and Spirit, McPhee is included in the Earth segment with an excerpt from *Encounters with the Archdruid*. Other writers included are Edward Abbey, Lewis Mumford, Rachel Carson, Saul Alinsky, and Wendell Berry.

Joseph Finkhouse and Michael Crawford, eds., *A River Too Far: The Past and Future of the Arid West*. Reno: University of Nevada Press, 1991, 127.
McPhee's excerpt is from *Encounters with the Archdruid*. Other contributors include Patricia Nelson Limerick, Wallace Stegner, and Roderick Nash.

George Plimpton, ed., *The Norton Book of Sports*. New York: Norton, 1992, 131.
McPhee's entry is "Centre Court," from *Playboy*. Other contributors include A. J. Liebling, P. G. Wodehouse, Maxine Kumin, Garrison Keillor, James Wright, Diane Ackerman, and Roger Kahn.

Tom Boswell, ed., *The Best American Sports Writing, 1994*. Boston: Houghton Mifflin, 1994, 157.
McPhee's entry is "Arthur Ashe Remembered from *The New Yorker*." Other contributors include Leigh Montville, Susan Orlean, Ira Berkow, Martha Weinman Lear, and George Plimpton.

Stephen Trimble, ed., *Words from The Land: Encounters with Natural History Writing*. Reno: University of Nevada Press, 1995, 92.
McPhee's excerpt is from *Basin and Range*. In the anthology's introduction, editor Stephen Trimble writes, "John McPhee has calculated that it takes four times as long to write about geology as it has taken him to write about anything else—first because of the research and then the translation into understanding, and finally the necessity to keep consulting with geologists for technical review." Other writers in the book include Annie Dillard, Edward Abbey, David Quammen, Sue Hubbell, Peter Matthiessen, and Barry Lopez.

Norman Sims and Mark Kramer, eds., *Literary Journalism: A New Collection of the Best American Nonfiction*. Ballantine Books, 1995, 407.
McPhee's entry is "Atchafalaya" from *The Control of Nature*. In his introduction, Sims writes, "McPhee eventually grasped his goal as a *New Yorker* writer. He recognized the power and the possibilities in nonfiction for narrative, dialogue, character sketching, metaphor. He learned to take trips with his subjects, rather than interviewing them, while seeking the matrix of a narrative." Other writers with excerpts in the book include Joseph Mitchell, Calvin Trillin, Susan Orlean, Richard Preston, Mark Singer, Jane Kramer, and Tracy Kidder.

Judith Gradwohl, ed., *Ocean Planet: Writing and Images of the Sea*. New York: Harry N. Abrams, 1995, 73.
The Smithsonian Institution helped organize this book to commemorate the 25th anniversary of Earth Day. McPhee's excerpt is from *Looking for a Ship*. The introduction of the book is by Peter Benchley, a friend of McPhee's from Princeton. Other writers include Joseph Conrad, Rachel Carson, Peter Matthiessen, Farley Mowat, Jacques-Yves Cousteau, and Ann Davison.

Scott Olsen and Scott Cairns, eds., *The Sacred Place: Witnessing the Holy in the Physical World*. Salt Lake City: University of Utah Press, 1996, 89.
McPhee's excerpt is from *Encounters with the Archdruid*. Other contributors include Richard Wilbur, Jorie Graham, Annie Dillard, and Barry Lopez.

Kevin Kerrane and Ben Yagoda, eds., *The Art of Fact: A Historical Anthology of Literary Journalism*. New York: Scribner, 1997, 485.
McPhee's excerpt is from *The Pine Barrens*. In introducing McPhee's writing, Kerrane says, "To report about nature, and about human efforts to preserve or control it, McPhee draws on exhaustive research—and on innate powers of description, lucid exposition, and easy rapport with his subjects." Other writers in the book include Abraham Cahan, John Hersey, Lillian Ross, Truman Capote, Joan Didion, Hunter S. Thompson, Ryszard Kapuscinski, and Rosemary Mahoney.

Cynthia Ozick, ed., *The Best American Essays 1998*. Boston: Houghton Mifflin, 1998, 176.
McPhee's entry is "Silk Parachute." Other contributors include Diana Trilling, Jamaica Kincaid, Oliver Sacks, J. M. Coetzee, and Saul Bellow.

Rich Youmans, ed., *Shore Stories: An Anthology of the Jersey Shore*. West Creek, NJ: Down the Shore Publishing, 1998, 206.
McPhee's entry is "The Search for Marvin Gardens," from *The New Yorker*. Other contributors include Gay Talese, Kay Boyle, Barbara Helfgott Hyett, and Robert Pinsky.

Richard Ford, ed., *The Best American Sports Writing, 1999*. Boston: Houghton Mifflin, 1999, 89.
McPhee's entry is "Catch-and-Dissect," from *The New Yorker*. Other contributors include Shirley Povich, David Halberstam, Melissa King, David Remnick, and David Mamet.

Judith Kitchen and Mary Paumier Jones, eds., *In Brief: Short Takes on the Personal*. New York: Norton, 1999, 88.
McPhee's piece is "Swimming with Canoes," from *The New Yorker*. Among the other contributors are Edwidge Danticat, Jonathan Raban, Cynthia Ozick, Frank McCourt, Ariel Dorfman, and Jamaica Kincaid.

Caryl Phillips, ed., *The Right Set: A Tennis Anthology*. New York: Vintage Books, 1999, 130.
McPhee's entry is from *Levels of the Game*. Other contributors include James Thurber, Arthur Ashe, Martina Navratilova, John Feinstein, and Alistair Cooke.

Peter Neill, ed., *American Sea Writing: A Literary Anthology*. New York: Library of America, 2000, 653.
McPhee's entry is from *Looking for a Ship*. Among the other writers included are Cotton Mather, Washington Irving, Walt Whitman, James Thurber, Rachel Carson, Peter Matthiessen, E. B. White, and Sylvia Earle.

John McPhee and Carol Rigolot, eds., *The Princeton Anthology of Writing: Favorite Pieces by the Ferris/McGraw Writers at Princeton University*. Princeton, NJ: Princeton University Press, 2001.
McPhee, coeditor of this book, wrote the preface (page v) and his entry (page 351) is "Travels of the Rock" from *The New Yorker*. Other contributors include Roger Mudd, Isabel Wilkerson, Nancy Gibbs, Deborah Tannen, Milton Viorst, James Gleick, Gina Kolata, Gloria Emerson, Samuel Freedman, Francine du Plessix Gray, and two former McPhee students, Richard Stengel and David Remnick.

John D'Agata, ed., *The Next American Essay*. Minneapolis: Graywolf Press, 2003, 7.
McPhee's entry opens the book with "The Search for Marvin Gardens" from *The New Yorker*. Contributors beside McPhee include Joan Didion, Annie Dillard, Thalia Field, Jamaica Kincaid, Barry Lopez, Carole Maso, David Shields, and Susan Sontag.

Pico Iyer, ed. *The Best American Travel Writing 2004*. Boston: Mariner Books, 2004, 175.
McPhee's entry is "A Fleet of One," from *The New Yorker*. Iyer writes in his introduction to the anthology, "I was reminded that there are many writers around—John McPhee, Peter Hessler [one of McPhee's former students] and Bill McKibben, to name but three—who can make a vacant lot come to life." Other writers in the book include Joan Didion, Adam Gopnik, George Packer, McKibben, Hessler, and Roger Angell.

Jamaica Kincaid, ed., *The Best American Travel Writing 2005*. Boston: Houghton Mifflin, 2005, 244.
McPhee's entry is "Tight-Assed River" from *The New Yorker*. In her introduction to the volume, Kincaid, a *New Yorker* colleague, writes of McPhee's essay, "I kept saying to myself, how did he do that, in wonder of the beauty of the sentences." Other writers in the book include William Least-Heat Moon, Ian Frazier, Simon Winchester, Pam Houston, and Peter Hessler.

Judith Kitchen, ed., *Short Takes: Brief Encounters with Contemporary Nonfiction*. New York: Norton, 2005, 347.
McPhee's entry is from *The Founding Fish*. The essay immediately after McPhee's is by Sandra Swinburne, titled "Essay, Dresses, and Fish," and is a tribute to McPhee's writing about fishing. Others in this collection of brief nonfiction articles include Salman Rushdie, Amy Tan, David Sedaris, and Lucy Sante.

William Deverell and Greg Hise, eds., *Land of Sunshine: An Environmental History of Metropolitan Los Angeles*. Pittsburgh: University of Pittsburgh Press, 2005, 179.
McPhee's entry is "Los Angeles Against the Mountains," from *The New Yorker*. Other writers include Paul Sabin, Jennifer Price, Jennifer Wolch, and Blake Gumprecht.

Betty Greenway, ed., *Twice-Told Children's Tales: The Influence of Childhood Reading on Writers for Adults*. New York: Routledge, 2005, 105.
McPhee's entry is "Silver Chief," an original piece later excerpted in *Draft No. 4*, a tribute to the "Silver Chief" book series, published by his grandfather and uncle, about a sled dog in the frozen north—the dog was McPhee's boyhood hero. Other writers include Penelope Lively, Barry Unsworth, W. D. Snodgrass, and Dana Gioia.

Andrew Blauner, ed., *Coach: 25 Writers Reflect on People Who Made a Difference*. New York: Warner Books, 2005, 69.
John McPhee's excerpt is about Princeton coach Butch van Breda Kolff, part of *A Sense of Where You Are*. Bill Bradley, who was the subject of McPhee's book, wrote the foreword, and other contributors include Pat Conroy, John Edgar Wideman, Christine Brennan, Andrew Solomon, Lauren Slater, and John Irving.

Wayne Grady, ed., *Dark Waters Dancing to a Breeze: A Literary Companion to Rivers and Lakes*. Vancouver: Greystone Books, 2007, 157.
McPhee's entry is "Farewell to the Nineteenth Century" from *The New Yorker*. Other contributors include William Least Heat-Moon, Kate Grenville, Mark Twain, Jill Frayne, and Nathaniel Hawthorne.

Christopher Porterfield, ed., *85 Years of Great Writing in Time*. New York: Time Books, 2008, 321.
The book covers the period between 1923 and 2008 in *Time* magazine. McPhee's entry is an excerpt from his 1961 cover story on Jackie Gleason. The introduction to the book is by Richard Stengel, the managing editor of *Time* and a former student of McPhee at Princeton. Stengel writes, "I became a *Time* writer because of one man: John McPhee. He was my writing teacher in college and had been a staff writer at *Time* for seven years before becoming an icon at *The New Yorker*. He said that if you want to learn to write, there's no better place to learn than at *Time*."

David Remnick, ed., *The Only Game in Town: Sports Writing from The New Yorker*. New York: Random House, 2010, 99.
McPhee's entry is an excerpt from *A Sense of Where You Are*. Other writers in the volume include Roger Angell, John Updike, Don DeLillo, John Cheever, and Ring Lardner.

John McPhee and Carol Rigolot, eds., *The Princeton Reader: Contemporary Essays by Writers and Journalists at Princeton University*. Princeton, NJ: Princeton University Press, 2011.
McPhee, coeditor, wrote the preface (page xiii) and his entry (page 61) is "Silk Parachute." Other writers include Greil Marcus, Felicity Barringer, Jill Abramson, Margo Jefferson, and three former students of McPhee, Joel Achenbach, Marc Fisher, and Barton Gellman.

Jane Leavy, ed., *The Best American Sports Writing of 2011*. Boston: Mariner Books, 2011, 154.
McPhee's excerpt is his article "The Patch" in *The New Yorker*. Others in the collection include Sally Jenkins, P. J. O'Rourke, and Selena Roberts.

James Marcus and the Staff of the Columbia Journalism Review, eds., *Second Read: Writers Look Back at Classic Works of Reportage*. New York: Columbia University Press, 2012, 102.
This book from the Columbia Journalism School involves journalists looking back at books that inspired them. The entry for McPhee

is excerpts from *Annals of the Former World*, analyzed by Douglas McCollam, who writes, "No work has altered my perception of the world and our place in it more than McPhee's geology tome. It has caused a shift in conscience, an alteration in the currents of my thought."

Subhankar Banerjee, ed., *Arctic Voices: Resistance at the Tipping Point*. New York: Seven Stories Press, 2012, 349.
McPhee's excerpt from *Coming into the Country* starts the "Reporting from the Field" section of this anthology about the environment, climate change, and struggles about resources. Ian Frazier, a fellow *New Yorker* staff writer and friend of McPhee, reviewed the collection in the March 7, 2013, issue of the *New York Review of Books*.

Alexander Wolff, ed., *Basketball: Great Writing About America's Game*. New York: Library of America, 2018, 40.
McPhee's entry is an excerpt from *A Sense of Where You Are*. Also in the anthology is a *New Yorker* profile by Herbert Warren Wind about Bob Cousy from two years earlier (March 23, 1963). Wind's article had almost pre-empted McPhee's profile in the magazine because top editors were worried about writing too much about basketball in a short time. Alexander Wolff, editor of this anthology, expressed appreciation that *New Yorker* editor William Shawn reconsidered and published McPhee's basketball profile too: "This excerpt showcases McPhee's ability to set a scene and deploy detail, two characteristic virtues of his work."

Other writers include Michael Lewis, David Bradley, Edith Roberts, Pete Axthelm, Kareem Abdul-Jabbar, Pat Conroy, and Melissa King.

Limited Editions

"The way to do a piece of writing is three, four times over, never once. For me, the hardest part comes first, getting something—anything—out in front of me. Sometimes in a nervous frenzy I just fling words as if I was flinging mud at a wall."

—JOHN MCPHEE, DRAFT NO. 4 (2017): 157

FIGURE 19. "Riding the Boom Extension," a 1980 article in *The New Yorker* about telephone service coming to a small city in Alaska, was published as a limited edition book by Metacom Press in Worcester, Massachusetts.

John McPhee's work has been published in several artistic, limited-edition reprints, usually signed by him and aimed primarily at book collectors.

Fair of San Gennaro. Portland, OR: Press-22, 1981.
This is a reprint of McPhee's short story that was first published in the Winter 1961 edition of *Transatlantic Review*, a literary magazine published in Europe and the United States by Joseph F. McCrindle from 1959 to 1977. It is about a woman walking in New York's Little Italy, threatened by a man as she visits the San Gennaro street festival. A hardcover with marbled paper, the edition includes an Author's

Note from McPhee that gives some background on his early writing career.

Roadkills: A Collection of Prose and Poetry. Easthampton, MA: Cheloniidae Press, 1981.
McPhee's writing in "Travels in Georgia," which first appeared in *The New Yorker*, is included in an artist's book on the theme of animals who were casualties of highway accidents. McPhee's prose is joined in the book by five poets, Gillian Conoley, Gary Snyder, Madeline DeFrees, William Stafford, and Richard Eberhart. The book, designed and with etching and wood engravings by Alan James Robinson, has a sculptural, three-dimensional front and back cover.

Riding the Boom Extension. Worcester, MA: Metacom Press, 1983.
This is a small press edition of a *New Yorker* article (August 4, 1980) about telephone service coming to a small city in Alaska, a piece later included in McPhee's collection *Table of Contents*. This is a softcover book with a French marbled paper cover. Other authors published by Metacom included highly regarded American fiction writers and poets, such as James Tate, John Updike, Ann Beattie, and Edward Gorey.

Annals of the Former World. New York: Farrar, Straus and Giroux, 1983.
This limited-edition reprint is not to be confused with the Pulitzer Prize–winning 1998 book of the same title that combined all four McPhee geology books. This slipcased two-volume edition contains the first two books in the series, *Basin and Range* and *In Suspect Terrain*.

The American Shad: Selections from The Founding Fish. Far Hills, NJ: Meadow Run Press, 2004. Illustrations by John Rice.
This hardcover volume combines selections from McPhee's *The Founding Fish*, published in 2002, with paintings by the artist John Rice. Meadow Run Press specialized in fishing and other sporting books.

2

Periodicals

"Certainly the aural part of writing is a big, big thing to me. I can't stand a sentence until it sounds right, and I'll go over it again and again."

—FROM "JOHN MCPHEE, THE ART OF NONFICTION NO. 3,"
INTERVIEWED BY PETER HESSLER, *PARIS REVIEW* 192
(SPRING 2010)

Time Magazine

After graduating from Princeton University and studying for a year in England at Magdalene College of the University of Cambridge, John McPhee spent several years in New York City writing TV screenplays and then trying corporate writing at W. R. Grace & Co. He longed to work at *The New Yorker* but continued to get nothing but rejections to his submissions.

In 1957 McPhee took a job at *Time* magazine, well known as a training ground for journalists and by far the largest American weekly newsmagazine with a circulation of three million. He started at the Time Inc. in-house newsletter, *FYI*, and he moved to a spot at *Time* in early 1958.

Time practiced a kind of group journalism that was the vision of its founder, Henry Luce, who had started the magazine in 1923. Luce believed that the best journalism was done by a team, not an individual. Until the mid-1970s, there were no bylines on stories in *Time*. Instead, reporters, researchers, and stringers around the world sent materials to writers and editors who created the stories at the New York headquarters.

FIGURES 20 AND 21. McPhee wrote nine cover stories for *Time* magazine, including about Barbra Streisand's starring role in *Funny Girl* on Broadway and about Richard Burton, who was gaining attention for his acting and his relationship with actress Elizabeth Taylor.

The lack of bylines bred a culture of anonymity, and the extent and details of McPhee's writing for *Time* have long been almost completely unknown. McPhee recalled the nine cover stories he wrote for the magazine between 1958 and 1965, but in the decades since they were never reprinted in full or received much attention. Nothing else by McPhee at *Time* was documented.

However, an annotated set of bound volumes in the *Time* archives (now held by the The New York Historical) has made it possible to definitively identify the rest of McPhee's work. Each week, someone on the *Time* copy desk, sometimes with a red grease pencil and other times with a pen, marked every story in the magazine with the initials of the writer of the story, as well as those of the editor and the researcher who worked on it.

Those bound volumes make it possible to see more than 500 stories that McPhee wrote while at *Time*. Highlights are listed below, along with brief excerpts of McPhee's writing from each story. Using the citations listed, it is possible to find the full stories, either in paper copies of the magazine or online through the *Time* search engine (https://time.com/search/?q=search). The stories are most easily searched online through the headlines given.

While McPhee wrote all the articles attributed to him, many of them also included reporting from other writers and researchers. In some cases, perhaps most notably his April 26, 1963, cover story about the actor Richard Burton, McPhee did everything. Burton, who appreciated McPhee's personality and his work on another story, insisted that McPhee alone be involved in the cover story. *Time* agreed, sending McPhee to London to interview and observe Burton and also to visit Burton's hometown in Wales. For many of his other stories, McPhee did most of the reporting and all the writing, while in some cases he never met the subject of the story and instead wrote from voluminous feeds from *Time* researchers and other reporters.

McPhee started at *Time* mostly doing the magazine's weekly "Miscellany" and "Milestones" columns, which were common assignments for new writers. He wrote almost all of those columns from March 3, 1958, until June 1, 1959, a stint longer than usual because *Time* had instituted a temporary hiring freeze soon after McPhee arrived, and that delayed the arrival of new writers to take over from him.

"Miscellany" items were almost all one sentence long, culled from oddities around the world and practically always containing a pun. (McPhee says a favorite of his was about a person who rode a bicycle on a street in Detroit and fell asleep at the handlebars: "Two Tired.") Writing the column got puns out of his system for life, he says. "Milestones" was about markers such as deaths, marriages, and divorces.

Besides the columns, as editors took measure of McPhee they assigned him to write "back of the book" pieces, first covering a range of subjects such as science, press, and sports, then moving into entertainment and the newly created Show Business department. It was fortuitous for his literary development, as writers in these sections were given significantly more freedom than those in news sections. After a while, McPhee was offered a transfer to the National Affairs department—which he called "the big rung of the ladder"—and he turned it down, preferring the opportunities where he was.

With his energy, interest, and passion for writing, McPhee thrived in the *Time* system. He wrote a large number of stories in a relatively short time and learned a great deal about the craft of writing. In addition, the magazine's headlines put a premium on cleverness and often lightness, and McPhee's work for various Princeton University publications had prepared him for that.

The Show Business section, where he settled in, was usually allotted a page or a page and a half per week, either one long piece or, more often, two or three shorter ones. For several years it was common for the entire section to be written by McPhee. His production of cover stories—nine in the span of less than four years—was high.

Time was known as a good place for talented new writers. Others coming to the magazine around the same time as McPhee included Calvin Trillin, who would go on to become a longtime colleague at *The New Yorker*; John Gregory Dunne, who would become a novelist and screenwriter, and the husband of Joan Didion; and Mitchel Levitas, later a prominent editor at *The New York Times*.

In January 1965, McPhee wrote a two-page resignation letter to Otto Fuerbringer, the powerful managing editor of *Time*. McPhee had just been hired as a staff writer for *The New Yorker*, which was publishing his breakthrough profile of Bill Bradley.

"I want to try to write things that will be, in general, much too long for the purposes of *Time*, or for any other magazine here in the building," McPhee wrote to Fuerbringer. "I have felt for quite a while that I would like to try to grow in that way as a writer." He thanked Fuerbringer for the opportunities at *Time*: "I have felt encouraged to experiment, and reach out, and do things to some extent my own way" (*Time* archives, The New York Historical, January 19, 1965). Several weeks later, on February 5, a *Time* editor sent out a note to staff, calling them to gather at the "usual place," starting at 5:30 to "raise a hail and farewell glass" to McPhee (*Time* archives, The New York Historical, February 5, 1965).

"And that was it for show business," McPhee wrote later, explaining why he stopped writing about the subject: "Not that I didn't like it. Six years was enough."

Miscellany, Mar. 3, 1958, 88.
McPhee's first contribution to "Miscellany," the column of often lighthearted items, includes:

> **Emergency.** In Indianapolis, a boy walked into the children's division of the Central Library, yelled at Librarian Elizabeth Simmons: "Hey woman, get me a book on manners."
> **Curb Service.** In Oklahoma City, E. G. Albright discovered how the city makes $125 a day in an overtime-parking crackdown: he parked his car at a spot where there was no meter, returned a short time later to find a ticket on his windshield, a meter in front of the car.

Milestones, Mar. 3, 1958, 74.
The same issue includes McPhee's initial "Milestones" column, which covers deaths. marriages, and other milestones. This week includes:

> Died. Dwight Herbert Green, 61, onetime (1941–48) Republican governor of Illinois, early famed as federal prosecutor of Al Capone, later as yes-man to the Chicago Tribune's Colonel Robert R. McCormick; of lung cancer; in Chicago. Green nominated Thomas E. Dewey for the presidency in 1944, keynoted the 1948 Republican Convention.

Cinema, "Bongo Bongo Boffo," July 21, 1958, 78.
A humorous takedown of the movie *Tarzan's Fight for Life*:

> Last week, 40 years after his first swing on a back-lot liana, Tarzan of the Apes ooo-eee-ooed the famed yodel, dropped from the treetops into his 32nd movie ... Tarzan's dialogue, over the years, has improved from a simple grunt to almost literate palaver.

The Press, "The Blushless Press," Aug. 10, 1959, 46.

In his only appearance in this section of the magazine, McPhee writes about Irish press issues:

> Roman Catholic Ireland's law and custom have long forced Irish newspapers to adopt one of the most rigorous self-censorships of any free press in the world. The taboos—stemming mostly from public moral attitude—center on indecency, concentrated coverage of crime, advocacy of birth control, and offense to the clergy . . . All of which has led to an adage that pretty accurately describes the Irish press: 'It doesn't matter what happens, as long as it doesn't get into the paper.'"

Cinema, "The New Pictures," Sept. 28, 1959, 76.
For several weeks, McPhee was the movie critic for *Time*. Here he reviews two films, including *Look Back in Anger*, the film version of an acclaimed stage play, which starred Richard Burton, Claire Bloom, and Mary Ure:

> The film's overall effect is caricature, and some of the fault is in the acting. Richard Burton turns Jimmy into a seething, snarling Elizabethan villain who seems on the point of forgetting himself and spewing out the speech of Shakespeare's Edmund.

Cinema, "The New Pictures," Oct. 5, 1959, 62.
McPhee reviews two movies, including *The FBI Story*, starring Jimmy Stewart:

> The great names of American crime cross the screen like targets in a shooting gallery: Pretty Boy Floyd, Baby Face Nelson, Ma Barker, John Dillinger and Machine Gun Kelly, the goon who screamed "Don't shoot, G-men," and dropped a new term into the language.

Sport, "Top Ten," "Man to Man," "Too Rough for Football," Nov. 16, 1959, 71.
In his first time writing about sports for *Time*, McPhee looks at the Top 10 in college football, the first professional basketball game matching Bill Russell and Wilt Chamberlain, and roughness in college football:

> Seldom in the history of basketball had so much interest been generated in a man-to-man battle . . . Boston's Bill Russell (6 ft. 10 in., 220 lbs.) has faster reactions and more experience . . . To challenge Russell's franchise among the best of the tree-tall pros, the Philadelphia Warriors' Wilt-the-Stilt Chamberlain offers 7 ft. 2 in., 250 coordinated pounds, and a broad repertory of shots: dunks, long one-handers, a soft, fadeaway jump.

Show Business, "Case History," Jan. 11, 1960, 36.
A review of a TV drama about the photographer Margaret Bourke-White's battle with Parkinson's disease:

> The TV show dramatized the moving case history that Maggie Bourke-White wrote for *Life* last spring, with some unfortunate descents to the sort of syrupy embarrassment that inevitably finds its way into TV scripts about personal struggles with sickness.

Show Business, "Passage to the Stage," Feb. 1, 1960, 52.
McPhee writes about an English stage version of E. M. Forster's novel *A Passage to India:* "Doing a stage version of E. M. Forster's novel, *A Passage to India*, is a little like trying to rewrite the Bhagavad-Gita as a sonnet."

Show Business, "Hi There, Sagittarius," Feb. 22, 1960, 76.
About Carroll Righter, Hollywood's astrologer to the stars:

> Caroll Righter has just about as much influence in Hollywood as a leading astrologer has in Thailand, where no top politician makes a move until the heavens are right. Dozens of stars will make no move (or movie) without calling Righter.

Cover story, "Comedian Mort Sahl," Aug. 15, 1960, 42.
McPhee's first cover story for *Time*, about Mort Sahl as a new kind of comedian: "With one eye on world news and the other on *Variety*, he is a volatile mixture of show business and politics, of exhibitionistic self-dedication and seemingly sincere passion to change the world." A shortened version was later published in *The Patch*, 171.

Show Business, "Sixth Sense Only," "Bye-Bye Doody," "The Treasure of the Madre," Oct. 3, 1960, 65.
A long article about the entertainer Red Skelton and shorter ones about the end of the *Howdy Doody* television show and plans for a movie about Sigmund Freud's life, directed by John Huston:

> The shuffling, pratfalling, rubber-faced, cross-eyed Skelton characters are as familiar to audiences as their own neighborhood eccentrics, but Richard Bernard Skelton himself is more eccentric than any of them. In an age of canned biographies and prefabricated flamboyance, he is one Hollywood character that no press agent yet born could possibly have invented.

> For a lot of little Americans over the past 13 years, the characters of Dickens, Milne and Grimm have been less familiar than a TV puppet named Howdy Doody.

Show Business, "Rocks on the Rocks," "The New Shows," Oct. 10, 1960, 89.
McPhee explains the popularity of a new situation-comedy series on television, *The Flintstones*, and looks at other new shows, including *My Three Sons* and *The Andy Griffith Show*:

> Called *The Flintstones*, the program uses first-rate animated cartoons in place of second-rate actors, and its approach to satire of 20th century life is by way of the Stone Age . . . The whole company is going off its rocker trying to think up Stone Age puns. Sooner or later they may have to introduce a new character called Spelunkhead, the village idiot. Mrs. Flintstone could ask her husband to please pass the basalt and pepper, and in redoing the kitchen, she could be for marble table tops, while he is for mica.

Show Business, "Baying at the Moon," Oct. 24, 1960, 64.
Reviewing David Susskind's live TV interview with Soviet Premier Nikita Khrushchev: "It could not have been a more incongruous interview—or a more fascinating sideshow—if Rumpelstiltskin had been interrogating Jimmy Hoffa, and about as much useful information resulted."

Cover Story, "The Rough Road to Broadway," Nov. 14, 1960, 64.
McPhee chronicles the out-of-town development of the much-anticipated Broadway musical *Camelot* by Alan Jay Lerner and Frederick Lowe. *Time* publisher Bernhard Auer writes his weekly note about McPhee's cover story ("A Letter from the Publisher," 17), and talks about McPhee's "61-hour, mostly sleepless writing stint."

> The road ordeal is by rewriting and cutting, by sleepless nights and interminable waiting, by cold coffee and warm highball, by panicky rumor and wild hope. Severely tested along with everyone else is the audience, which has to sit through long scenes already marked for destruction.

Show Business, "Popsie & Poopsie," Nov. 21, 1960, 61.
About Arthur Miller and Marilyn Monroe getting ready to divorce: "After four years of one of the most celebrated show-business marriages since Tom Thumb's, it was all but over between the panduriform actress and the handsome, horn-rimmed playwright."

Show Business, "Hero's Exit," Nov. 28, 1960, 61.
McPhee writes about the death of actor Clark Gable: "Although he was a thorough professional, few critics bothered to consider him as an actor. He was, simply, a hero, and everything he touched turned to Gable."

Show Business, "The Birds Go There," Dec. 26, 1960, 38.
Assessing "the most prodigious nightclub town on earth," New York City: "What New York has is jazz, man. The city has taken over the franchise from New Orleans and Chicago, and is now Coolsville itself."

Show Business, "Humor, Integrated," Feb. 17, 1961, 67.
A feature on the comedian Dick Gregory:

> A neatly dressed young comedian talks about the race problem. "Segregation is not all bad," he says. "Have you ever heard of a wreck where the people on the back of the bus got hurt?" And, on sit-ins: "I

sat at a lunch counter for nine months," he says. "When they finally integrated, they didn't have what I wanted." The audience always laughs and usually applauds the performer, who is just getting started on what may be one of the more significant careers in American show business.

Show Business, "Mail-Order Melody," Mar. 4, 1961, 70.
About the television sing-along leader Mitch Miller: "A 49-year-old man with a 20-year-old beard, Mitch Miller is something more than a jolly Shylock demanding his pound of flats."

Show Business, "Killer Diller," Mar. 24, 1961, 55.
About the comedian Phyllis Diller: "Waving an unlit blue cigarette in a holder, she pops her eyes, works her mouth into exotic shapes from figure eights to dodecahedrons, now and then poking forth a grooved tongue until she seems to be a rain-spouting functional gargoyle held up by a wildly flying buttress."

Cover story, "Playwright Jean Kerr," Apr. 14, 1961, 82.
A profile of the humorist and Broadway playwright Jean Kerr: "Almost any intern, life insurance salesman, housewife and child over five will readily recognize the style of Jean Kerr, one of the pleasantest humorists now working, a woman who can transform the ordinary vicissitudes of life into laughter, expertly turning next-to-nothing into molehills."

Show Business, "Bridge to the Old World," July 7, 1961, 53.
Previewing the new season at the Atlantic City Steel Pier: "So big and boffo that only the Atlantic Ocean can compete with it for the attention of tourists."

Show Business, "Grand Canyon East," Aug. 25, 1961, 50.
Taking measure of Radio City Music Hall (shortened version in *The Patch*, 145):

> The line of people waiting to get into the Music Hall is one of the phenomena of modern show business . . . audiences see a three-hour spectacle—roughly two-thirds movie and one-third stage show—that is anything but just another overpromoted metropolitan gyp.

Show Business, "The New Season," Oct. 20, 1961, 78.
A review, often scathing, of premieres in the new television season, including *Ben Casey* and *The Bob Newhart Show*: "'Car 54, Where Are You?' is a question that does not deserve an answer."

Show Business, "Paul the Comforter," Nov. 3, 1961, 62.
About the singer-songwriter Paul Anka: "Anka is a devoted admirer of Elvis Presley, but onstage his style consciously avoids imitation of the master . . . He neither rocks nor rolls, and his pelvis is so steady that it could house a seismograph. 'I go out there to comfort the people,' he says."

Show Business, "Caretaker's Caretaker," Nov. 10, 1961, 76.
On playwright Harold Pinter, whose play *The Caretaker*, one of his first, is the hit of the new Broadway season:

> The Caretaker is a study of the human condition at the outer limit of endurance, both funny and tragic, paradoxically baffling and plausible, gifted with the poet's touch of universality, and turned out in colloquial dialogue that is breathtakingly cadenced and exact.

Show Business, "I Believe in You," Nov. 17, 1961, 78.
About Robert Morse, star of the new smash hit on Broadway, *How to Succeed in Business Without Really Trying*: "There is probably only one Broadway actor who could turn this despicable crud into the most lovable monster since Barrie's crocodile. That actor has the part."

Cover story, "Jackie Gleason," Dec. 29, 1961, 34.
About Jackie Gleason, the actor, comedian, and writer. In his "Letter from the Publisher" (5), *Time*'s Bernhard Auer said McPhee's "assignment deserves some kind of endurance prize, for he saw his subject in a gamut of moods: testy, comradely, hostile, candid, suspicious,

trusting." McPhee later wrote in *The New Yorker* (April 7, 2014, 50) of coping with Gleason's distress about the profile by bringing *Time* Managing Editor Otto Fuerbringer to a restaurant to meet and reassure the star. A fragment of the cover story appears in *The Patch* (183): "The man inside all these textiles has a stupendous ego, and the only characters who come near him in all of fiction are Spenser's Braggadocio and Plautus' Braggart Warrior."

Show Business, "Sly Ways & Subways," Jan. 12, 1962, 58.
About the Broadway producer David Merrick gaining positive publicity for his show *Subways Are for Sleeping* by getting tributes from people with the same exact names as prominent theater critics who had panned his show:

> This one-cylinder Barnum, this tower of sneers in tasseled shoes, this Shubert Alley Catiline, this mustachioed thane of the sceptered aisle, this Greek god, this other Edam, this papier-mâché genius, this blessed plotter, this doozer producer, this publicity addict who would send his cocker spaniel to Cape Canaveral if he thought it would get into space, this man, this David Merrick has done it again.

Show Business, "Melting the Pot," Mar. 23, 1962, 73.
The meaning of Hollywood actors changing their names (collected in *The Patch*, 229):

> Some real names are out of character. Roy Rogers was Leonard Slye. Boris Karloff could not have frightened a soul as William Henry Pratt. Gypsy Rose Lee has done things that Rose Louise Hovick would presumably never do.

Cover story, "Sophia Loren," Apr. 6, 1962, 78.
On the actress Sophia Loren (a fragment appears in *The Patch*, 119):

> By her own description, Sophia Loren is "a unity of many irregularities." She has rewritten the canons of beauty . . . "Some day," she says with the earnestness of a starlet, "I hope that everyone will say I am a great actress and I will be remembered for that."

Show Business, "The Shy Man," Apr. 27, 1962, 74.
On the actor Peter Sellers, "the best light actor in the English-speaking cinema" (a shortened version appears in *The Patch*, 217):

> Sellers is the world's best mimic, equipped with an enormous range of accents, inflections and dialects—including five kinds of cockney, Mayfair pukka, stiff upper BBC, Oxford, Cambridge, Yorkshire, Lancashire, West Country, Highland Scots, Edinburgh Scots, Glaswegian Scots, Tyneside Geordie, Northern Ireland, Southern Ireland, French, Mitteleuropa, American Twang, American Drawl, American Snob, Canadian, Australian and three kinds of Indian. He fools everybody.

Show Business, "Carol the Clown," June 22, 1962, 56.
About the comedian Carol Burnett: "The biggest yuk to hit television since Sid Caesar's salad wilted is a Goofy-Cousin-Clara sort of a girl with a grin full of teeth, a manner both tentative and brash, and a talent that comes bubbling up every time she opens her big mouth, shakes a leg, or crosses an eye."

Show Business, "Old Cary Grant Fine," "The Coming Season," July 27, 1962, 40.
The lasting success of the actor Cary Grant (collected in *The Patch*, 99); a preview of the upcoming television season, where McPhee puckishly talks about new shows such as *The Beverly Hillbillies* and *The Jetsons*: "Lean, suave, incomparably tanned, he never wears makeup and has gotten steadily better looking. More or less successfully, he spends his real life pretending he is Cary Grant."

Show Business, "The Royal Floridians," Sept. 21, 1962, 70.
The bandleader Guy Lombardo, with a coming move from his long-standing New York base to Florida: "Last week the Hotel Roosevelt announced that Guy Lombardo and his Royal Canadians will not be appearing there any more. It was like Athens announcing the departure of the Acropolis."

Show Business, "On the Town," Sept. 28, 1962, 40.
Bolshoi dancers on their day off in New York City: "Except for the slightly waddling walk that characterizes ballet dancers, few Sunday strollers would recognize them as the youngsters of the Bolshoi on their day off."

Show Business, "The New Season," Oct. 12, 1962, 97.
A long preview, full of humor, of the coming television season:

> The overall impression of the new series suggests a great bowl of mentholated corn flakes . . . most of the corn is healthy, the humor and situations are pugnaciously wholesome, and the killing is largely confined to historic battlefields rather than back alleys.

Show Business, "Lawrence of Leeds," Oct. 19, 1962, 63.
A British actor ready to break out: Peter O'Toole in *Lawrence of Arabia* (a fragment appeared in *The Patch*, 216):

> His reputation as an actor grew almost as fast as his reputation as a loudmouthed roisterer. He drank hard. "I like to make things hum," he says. "I like to shout at the sun and spit at the moon." He had his nose sharpened by a plastic surgeon. His opinions did not need sharpening.

Show Business, "The New New Garland," Nov. 16, 1962, 57.
On the return of the singer and actress Judy Garland to concert performances: "She has turned near disasters into comedy skits and had brought off a remarkable performance despite a condition locally known as Chicago throat."

Cover story, "Folk Singer Joan Baez," Nov. 23, 1962, 54.
McPhee puts Joan Baez's achievements in the context of the keen enthusiasm for folk music at the time in the United States. *Time* publisher Bernhard Auer writes ("A Letter from the Publisher," 7) about the cover story by McPhee, calling him "a bright-faced and quick-tongued fellow" whose style "has acid as well as adulation in it." A shortened version of the profile is in *The Patch*, 184:

The tangible sibyl closer to hand is Joan Baez. Her voice is as clear as air in the autumn, a vibrant, strong, untrained and thrilling soprano. She wears no makeup and her long black hair hangs like a drapery, parted around her long almond face. In performance she comes on, walks straight to the microphone, and begins to sing. No patter. No show business.

Show Business, "On the Cob," Nov. 30, 1962, 76.
On the quick ascent of the new television show *The Beverly Hillbillies*: "The show is supplying an apparent demand for straightforward, unsophisticated, skillfully performed humor. 'It's my kind of corn,' says Director Whorf—'right on the cob.'"

Show Business, "In Total Demand," Dec. 21, 1962, 43.
The acclaim for the actor Anthony Quinn: "He has a face like a bloodhound that has just eaten an escaped convict ... movies are artier than ever, and the rough features of Anthony Quinn, which have long hidden a consummately skillful actor, are in total demand."

Show Business, Comedians, "His Own Boswell," Feb. 15, 1963, 78.
On a new 27-year-old comedian, Woody Allen: "These jokes come out as segments of nervous, elliptical stories. The man who tells them is a flatheaded, redheaded lemur with closely bitten fingernails and a sports jacket."

Show Business, Broadway, "Uncle Jack," Mar. 8, 1963, 60.
About the new Jack Benny show on Broadway: "His cheapskate, self-deceiving, inept, shrug-it-off, endearing and vainglorious public character has grown round him for decade after decade like layer after layer of cement, and he has long since become utterly indestructible."

Show Business, Animals, "Bum Steer," Mar. 15, 1963, 82.
On the actor and writer Buck Henry's animal hoax in Washington, DC: "The picketers hoisted their signs high and circled the White House for

seven hours straight. 'Mrs. Kennedy,' pleaded the placards, 'Won't You Please Clothe Your Horse for Decency?' SINA [the Society Against Indecency to Naked Animals] was on the march."

Cover story about actor Richard Burton, Apr. 26, 1963, 70.
In his "Letter from the Publisher" (17), Bernhard Auer writes about the cover story on Richard Burton, which McPhee reported and wrote (a shortened version of the story appears in *The Patch*, 159):

> Everyone, in short, knows who Richard Burton is, or at least what he is at the moment. He is the demi-Atlas of this earth, the arm and burgonet of men, the fellow who is living with Elizabeth Taylor. Stevedores admire him. Movie idols envy him. He is a kind of folk hero out of nowhere, with an odd name like Richard instead of Tab, Rock, or Rip, who has out-tabbed, outrocked, and outripped the lot of them. He is the new Mr. Box Office.

Show Business, Actresses, "A Firm Sense of Role," May 10, 1963, 82.
On the actress Uta Hagen in the original Broadway production of Edward Albee's play *Who's Afraid of Virginia Woolf*: "Uta Hagen comes on swearing. In three hours, she weeps, snarls, rages at her husband, expounds a boozy philosophy, talks baby talk, goes off to the kitchen to seduce a casual visitor, and turns in a performance that stains the memory but stays there."

Show Business, Hollywood, "Marilyn, My Marilyn," May 31, 1963, 47.
In the aftermath of Marilyn Monroe's death: "Under close and improving direction, her famous walk developed from something crudely virginal into something profanely sophisticated. Some unknown Corot reduced the red of her lips from a massive smear to a spot in a breathtaking landscape. Her hair, sprayed and sculpted a thousand times, softened down into a pangloss of wishful thinking, making nature say uncle."

Show Business, Television, "Good Scout," June 14, 1963, 54.
Describing Dick Van Dyke as Rob Petrie on *The Dick Van Dyke Show*:

He looks believable. He isn't aggressively glamorous or excessively cute. He is a pretty bright guy whose brain is sometimes a ball of thumbs, and he is married to an American icon [played by Mary Tyler Moore]: the steady, dependable, reliable, beautiful, clean-limbed little mother who has the sort of dewy wholesomeness that every twelve-year-old boy looks forward to in a wife.

Show Business, Actors, "The Mild One," June 28, 1963, 48.
About the actor Steve McQueen as the new John Wayne:

He is a blue-eyed Pan with croppy, disarrayed blond hair and lips that are pursed in a rubber grin. His overall look seems to say "Don't crowd me." There is a whiff of felony about him, but he is nonetheless a prototype American. With his wide ears and open face, he looks something like a young Dwight Eisenhower after sophomore year at San Quentin.

Show Business, Broadway, "The New Season," Aug. 30, 1963, 50.
A long piece about the coming season on Broadway.

Every Broadway season looks in prospect like an ingenue in a bridal gown, and in retrospect like a naked iguana. Somehow, the paper promises—the mere names, titles and themes—are always unbearably alluring; but it is much easier to develop a good idea for a show than to develop a good show, and Broadway never looks better than it does in August, just before it starts down the aisle.

Show Business, Circuses, "Brown Lake," Oct. 4, 1963, 101.
About the Moscow State Circus (a fragment appears in *The Patch*, 121):

Bears. Big bears. Little bears. Black bears. Brown bears. Mamma bears. Great strong hammer-sickle thick-coated rocket-powered Soviet bears. They eat 700 lbs. of lump sugar a day and some day their teeth will fall out, but meanwhile they have been so well trained by Valentin Filatov that they are the essential stars of the Soviet circus.

Show Business, Hollywood, "As Long as You're Up Get Me a Grant," Oct. 11, 1963, 58.
About the premier tailor in Hollywood, Sy Devore: "Sy is custom itself. He drapes David Niven aloofly and John Wayne toughly. He is the author of Bob Hope's tweeds. If Donald O'Connor wants to look like George M. Cohan, which for some reason he does, Sy cuts him a checkered vest."

Show Business, Television, "Judgment on the New Season," Oct. 18, 1963, 59.
A long review of the new television season:

> Television, which has long since replaced the crackling fire as the cozy thing to sit by of an evening, was once quite a blaze. Machine guns ratta-ta-tatted, switchblades sang, and grandmothers grunted as fists hit their mandibles. In the last couple of seasons, however, the pyrodynamics have agreeably relaxed. All that sputtered now wheezes cordially. None of this season's new series is objectionable. And a handful are quite good.

Show Business, Hollywood, "Fish Don't Applaud," Oct. 25, 1963, 67.
About the actor and comedian Bob Hope: "Bob Hope actually belongs on some sort of Mount Rushmore, his nose cantilevered on reinforcing rods near Groucho Marx's cigar and Jack Benny's bow. Hope is the longest-running one-line stand-up snap-it-out comedian in the history of show business."

Show Business, Nightclubs, "Delicious, Delectable, De-lovely," Nov. 22, 1963, 78.
About Ethel Merman at the Plaza nightclub in Manhattan:

> Then the great klaxon voice takes over. It sounds 26, or whatever the most magic laryngeal age is, and she hardly needs the frightened little mike she conceals in her brassière. Those big metallic syllables, perfectly enunciated, come forth like bullets and mow down the crowd. "I must admit," she says, "I don't exactly croon a tune."

Show Business, Repertory Theater, "West, North & South of Broadway," Nov. 29, 1963, 68.
About playwright Neil Simon (a shortened version appears in *The Patch*, 146): "Most of Neil Simon's funny lines pass the true test of comedy: out of context, they mean nothing; they rise from the fabric of incident. At 36, Simon has become Broadway's leading comedy writer."

Show Business, "Old Faces, Bogey Worship," Feb. 7, 1964, 80.
About the Harvard University craze for Humphrey Bogart and *Casablanca*.

> Bogart's side-o-mouth repartee has become the canon vernacular of Harvard Yard, and anyone who doesn't dig it is digging his social grave. Harvard boys, ordering another round of drinks, rasp: "Play it again, Sam." Raising their glasses, they say: "Here's looking at ya, kid!" And when they're getting ready to blow the joint, they ask: "Ya ready, Slim?" When they want to express arrogance or individuality, they spit: "I don't have to show you no stinking badge." That line is so popular that one group pledged to write it into examination essays, and professors were soon reading about the "stinking badge" in papers on the French Revolution.

Show Business, Singers, "The Unbarbershopped Quartet," Feb. 21, 1964, 46.
On Beatlemania: "Adults may not dig, but how could 20 million teenagers be wrong? The Beatles are fab. The Beatles are great. The Beatles are different. The Beatles are cool, cool, cool, cool, cool."

Show Business, Television, "How to Sell a Broccoli," Mar. 20, 1964, 56.
On Julia Child and her television show *The French Chef*:

> She picks up a rolling pin that could only have been made from a sequoia and crunches it down on a slab of cold butter. She lifts up a cleaver and amputates the outer wings of a goose, with a couple of chops that sound like cannon fire. She pops a chestnut into her mouth to see if it is done. She smiles and says between swallows, "Welcome to *The French Chef*. I'm Julia Child."

Cover story, Barbra Streisand, "Broadway: The Girl," Apr. 10, 1964, 62. About the actress and singer Barbra Streisand emerging in the Broadway musical *Funny Girl* (a fragment appears in *The Patch*, 192):

> Streisand establishes more than a well recollected Fanny Brice. She establishes Barbra Streisand. When she is on stage, singing, mugging, dancing, loving, shouting, wiggling, grinding, wheedling, she turns the air around her into a cloud of tired ions. Her voice has all the colors, bright and subtle, that a musical play could ask for, and gradations of power too. It pushes the walls out, and it pulls them in. She is onstage for 111 of Funny Girl's 132 minutes.

Show Business, "Waiting for Them All," Apr. 24, 1964, 52.
Sidney Poitier as the first Black actor to win the Academy Award for Best Actor:

> Everyone who has ever worked with him both likes and admires Sidney Poitier as man and actor. In bygone days, he would have been called a credit to his race. But now that his race is the human race, the semantics have changed and Poitier is merely a very good actor who has made a significant breakthrough.

Cover story on New York World's Fair, "New York World's Fair," June 5, 1964, 40.
McPhee assesses the recently opened World's Fair in New York City, which he dubbed "The World of Already," as opposed to the 1939 World's Fair in New York, which was more clearly about the future. Bernhard Auer's "Letter from the Publisher" (15) explains, "McPhee's mission was to do what no one else had done about the New York World's Fair. It had been previewed, opened, featured, highlighted and was even beginning to produce its own cliches. But there had been no intensive critique of it in the sense that, say, a theater critic reviews a play." A fragment of the cover story appears in *The Patch* (175): "The great fair succeeds, in the end, because it so abundantly contains the variety of the world. You have only to walk through it to discover continents in the corners of your eyes."

Show Business, Television, "D-Day, Ike Hour," June 12, 1964, 86.
CBS's TV show on the 20th anniversary of D-Day, with former General and President Dwight D. Eisenhower:

> Never before in history has such an immediate and permanent record been made of a general returning to the field of a great battle and describing it in his own words, while film archives supplied scenes of the actual warfare. It was something to see. It is too bad that CBS is so young. If it had existed 149 years ago, it might have invited Wellington to do a show on Waterloo.

Show Business, Readings, "Something to Write Home About," July 3, 1964, 62.
The scene at a Broadway poetry reading by Elizabeth Taylor and Richard Burton, a benefit for the acting school run by Richard Burton's foster father. McPhee writes his story in the form of a letter to "Mother" from "Agnes," with Agnes as a play on his own middle name, Angus:

> The evening was especially fun because there was so much pleasant banter between Richard and Elizabeth. Once she stopped a poem and said, "Sorry, may I start again? I got all screwed up." "I could say that in Hamlet every night," said Richard.

Show Business, Actors, "Breathless Man," July 10, 1964, 76.
About Jean-Paul Belmondo, the French New Wave film star:

> A young man slouching in a cafe chair, his socks sagging over broken shoelaces, his shirt open to the waist, his arms dangling to the floor, where his knuckles drag. A Gauloise rests in his gibbon lips, and its smoke meanders from his attractively broken, Z-shaped nose. Out of the Left Bank by the New Wave, he is Jean-Paul Bel-mondo—the natural son of the Existentialist conception, standing for everything and nothing at 738 m.p.h.

Show Business, Television, "The New Season," Sept. 25, 1964, 73.
A broad preview of the coming television season: "Let us now praise television. Its longbows, drawn since springtime, finally twanged last

week and 17 arrows flew. Wunk. Tunk. Boink. Doyng. One after another, TV's new series all hit on or near the mark."

Show Business, Actresses, "The Once & Future Queen," Oct. 9, 1964, 42. About the singer and actress Julie Andrews:

> Hollywood people would not know quite how to act with her anyway, because they see her sort so rarely. She is straightforward, amiable, eager to please, and her only eccentricity is a fondness for boiled-potato sandwiches. She wears little makeup, even when she is being photographed. She is infectiously enthusiastic. No matter how much pressure she is under, she never boils over.

Show Business, Playwrights, "Allegory of Any Place," Oct. 9, 1964, 85. On three new plays by Ray Bradbury: "As the world's best science fiction writer, author of *The Martian Chronicles* and Hollywood's *It Came from Outer Space*, Bradbury has come to think that the world has actually entered the machine-dominated sci-fi era and that the human soul is already deep in an electronic coma. Hence his plays, though they are set in the future, are actually hyperbolic allegories of the present."

Show Business, Broadway, "The Nichols Touch," Nov. 27, 1964, 86. About Mike Nichols, the prodigious young director on Broadway:

> A Nichols play is a busy, gymnastic comedy of the absurd. Characters grunt and wheeze, climb stairs, assemble rusty iron beds, ride motor scooters, lose their pants, leap off bridges, throw knives. But the procession of sight gags only emphasizes the drift of the dialogue, supporting and not replacing the language of the playwright. As he approaches character from several directions, Nichols apparently feels particularly comfortable in a tenor of intelligent slapstick.

Show Business, Singers, "She Who Is Ella," Nov. 27, 1964, 86. On Ella Fitzgerald:

> Her incredible improvising runs are effortless. She can take off from a melody, go over it, around it, through it, under it, moving at twice

the speed of nine-to-five Man, tossing in casual doodies in the abstract expressionism of sound. When other singers' jugulars would be bulging, Ella isn't even panting. She seems to breathe through her ears. Her range goes from lower owl to upper sparrow.

Show Business, "Phi Beta Football," Jan. 8, 1965, 50.
About new camera work and instant replays for pro football:

All three Cleveland touchdowns were scored on Ryan-to-Collins passes, and each time CBS instantly reran the play, showing how Collins got into the clear. If football, as many people think, has become the national sport, television has made it so. And the game's high degree of intelligibility on the screen is to a large degree due to the instant rerun device known as the isolated camera.

The New Yorker

"As I am sitting composing a sentence, my primary thought is not imagining a reader, and whether the reader is grasping this. I think that what I'm doing is trying to put it in the way that seems most effective to *me*."

—FROM "THE STRANGE CASE OF THE QUEEN-POST TRUSS: JOHN MCPHEE ON WRITING AND READING" BY DOUGLAS VIPOND AND RUSSELL A. HUNT, COLLEGE COMPOSITION AND COMMUNICATION 42:2 (MAY 1991): 200–210

John McPhee first saw a copy of *The New Yorker* in elementary school, when a friend shared his parents' copy with him. McPhee was immediately drawn to the magazine, especially the feature-length factual articles.

At age 10, McPhee made his first appearance in *The New Yorker* as writer Rogers E. M. Whitaker, who covered college football for the magazine for 31 years, mentioned him in a November 22, 1941 story about Princeton's team and its efforts to run faster. Whitaker described how McPhee, the son of the team's doctor, ran with the players during practice, wearing a Princeton jersey and carrying a miniature football.

He started dreaming of writing for *The New Yorker* when he went to high school. It took nearly two decades, with many rejection letters along the way, but eventually McPhee was hired and became one of most prolific and longstanding contributors in the history of the magazine.

By the time he enrolled at Princeton University in 1949, McPhee had begun sending finished articles to the magazine. Each one was turned down. While at Princeton he remade *The Princeton Tiger*, a humor magazine, in the mold of *The New Yorker*, including soliciting a short story from John O'Hara, an influential writer for the magazine who lived in Princeton.

Several years later, when he was on staff at *Time* magazine, handling cover stories and more, McPhee continued to try to be published in *The New Yorker*. In 1962, McPhee's latest plea to become a *New Yorker* contributor was answered by an editor, Leo Hofeller, who turned out to be a screener for the magazine's top editor William Shawn. (McPhee tells the tale in the magazine, "Tabula Rasa, Volume Two," April 12, 2021.)

Hofeller invited McPhee to submit some sample "Talk of the Town" pieces. McPhee wrote several articles, including one about a farmer growing sweet corn on the Lower East Side and another on a piece of a Dutch ship found two centuries later underground in lower Manhattan. Hofeller met with McPhee and said the stories were "pretty good," though not "very good." While none would be published, he invited McPhee to submit other ideas in the future.

Around the same time, while still working for *Time*, McPhee wrote an article, originally commissioned by *Esquire* and then rejected, about his playing on a Cambridge University basketball team while studying in England after graduating from Princeton. He then submitted it to *The New Yorker* and it became his first piece published there, on March 16, 1963. McPhee was pleased, though it unfortunately didn't clearly advance his goal of getting on staff at the magazine.

McPhee wrote to Hofeller for more advice and Hofeller again suggested sending story ideas. McPhee submitted more ideas, including a possible profile of Bill Bradley, then a star basketball player at Princeton. McPhee had seen Bradley play and was taken by his skills, work ethic, and other personal qualities, such as his determination to teach Sunday school even after Saturday night games far away.

Hofeller told McPhee to go ahead and try writing one of those pieces "but not that basketball player, we just did a profile of a basketball player" (a profile of Bob Cousy by Herbert Warren Wind, published March 23, 1963). To many people, Hofeller's answer would have been a welcome green light to do one of the other story ideas. But McPhee was determined to pursue the story about Bradley. He wrote Hofeller, thanking him and saying that he was going ahead with the Bradley piece for any publication that would be interested in it. He didn't stop there—he proceeded to write 5,000 words to Hofeller about why Bradley was so extraordinary and worthy of a profile.

To McPhee's surprise, Hofeller answered by saying that *The New Yorker* would like to read the finished piece after all, "no guarantees, of course." McPhee finished the piece months later and *The New Yorker* accepted it. He was invited to the magazine's office and introduced to Shawn for the first time. In early 1965, the Bradley story was published and McPhee was made a staff writer.

Once he became a staff writer, how did McPhee generate all his distinctive ideas for stories? "There are zillions of ideas out there—they stream by like neutrons," he says in a 2010 *Paris Review* interview. "If I went down a list of all the pieces I ever had in *The New Yorker*, upwards of ninety percent would relate to things I did when I was a kid." He says sports he played in high school (tennis, basketball, and lacrosse) led to many articles and also his 13 years at Keewaydin camp in Vermont—"I'd go on canoe trips, backpacking trips, out in the woods all summer, sleeping on the ground." Together these experiences contributed much to his writing about the environment and the outdoors.

This section includes a guide to all of McPhee's work for *The New Yorker*. Most have been full-length articles, but he also contributed to the shorter Talk of the Town section at the front of the magazine. He also wrote some "Newsbreaks," which were extremely brief and usually humorous squibs that filled out spaces between articles in the magazine.

An unusual aspect of McPhee's *New Yorker* work, speaking to its popularity, is that so many of his articles have been republished in books, and those details are given in these listings. Many of his *New Yorker* articles also have been included in anthologies, which is explored in the "Anthologies" section.

"Basketball and Beefeaters," Mar. 16, 1963, 186.
McPhee's participation in the Cambridge University Basketball Club, including how he and the team almost played a game in the Tower of London. Later included in the collection *Pieces of the Frame,* this was his first *New Yorker* article, done before he became a staff writer and after the story was rejected by *Esquire* magazine.

"A Sense of Where You Are," Jan. 23, 1965, 40.
Profile of Princeton University basketball star Bill Bradley. Later published as the book *A Sense of Where You Are.*

"Comprehensive," Newsbreak in "Talk of the Town," Feb. 12, 1966, 27 (unsigned).
Author comes across a list of telephone numbers at an acquaintance's house in Princeton.

"Big Plane," "Talk of the Town," Feb. 19, 1966, 28 (unsigned).
About the largest airplane ever designed.

Newsbreak in "Talk of the Town," Feb. 26, 1966, 29 (unsigned).
"Lady Taylor's Cake" notice at the Princeton University Store about fund-raising for an unexpected cause.

"Fifty-Two People on a Continent," "A Reporter at Large," Mar. 5, 1966, 101.
A program, developed at the Massachusetts Institute of Technology, to place highly qualified young men in civil-service jobs in emerging nations in Africa. Later included in the collection *A Roomful of Hovings and Other Profiles.*

"Coliseum Hour," "Talk of the Town," Mar. 12, 1966, 44 (unsigned).
An hour spent at the Sport and Camping Show in the New York Coliseum, including watching the star turn of professional basketball player Oscar Robertson. Later part of the book *The Patch.*

"The Headmaster," Mar. 19, 1966, 57.
Profile of Frank Learoyd Boyden, headmaster for 66 years at Deerfield Academy, a prep school in Massachusetts. Later published as the book *The Headmaster*.

Newsbreak in "Talk of the Town," Apr. 30, 1966, 39 (unsigned).
Comment from one faculty wife at the Lawrenceville School to another.

"Oranges," "A Reporter at Large," May 7, 1966, 142.
Part 1 of an article about the history, significance, and cultivation of oranges. Later became the book *Oranges*.

"Oranges," "A Reporter at Large," May 14, 1966, 144.
Part 2 of an article about the history, significance, and cultivation of oranges. Later became the book *Oranges*.

"Beauty and Horror," "Talk of the Town," May 28, 1966, 28 (unsigned).
A tour of parks and playgrounds in New York City with Commissioner Thomas P. F. Hoving.

"Girl in a Paper Dress," "Talk of the Town," June 25, 1966, 20 (unsigned).
The National Notion Association's semiannual trade show (a version in *The Patch* is greatly condensed).

"Ms and FeMs at the Biltmore," "Talk of the Town," July 2, 1966, 17 (unsigned).
The Annual Gathering of North American Mensa at the Biltmore Hotel. Later part of the book *The Patch*.

"On the Way to Gladstone," "Talk of the Town," July 9, 1966, 17 (unsigned).
The New Jersey bear that was shot by a farmer in Pottersville.

Newsbreak in "Talk of the Town," Nov. 12, 1966, 52 (unsigned).
Where George Cutsogeorge lives.

Newsbreak in "Talk of the Town," Dec. 24, 1966, 25 (unsigned).
A conversation overheard between a man and his young daughter.

"A Roomful of Hovings," May 20, 1967, 49.
Profile of Thomas P. F. Hoving, director of the Metropolitan Museum of Art. Later included in the collection *A Roomful of Hovings and Other Profiles*.

"The Pine Barrens," Nov. 25, 1967, 67.
Part 1 of an article about the rural, undeveloped land that makes up nearly 25 percent of New Jersey. Later became the book *The Pine Barrens*.

"The Pine Barrens," Dec. 2, 1967, 66.
Part 2 of an article about the rural, undeveloped land that is nearly 25 percent of New Jersey. Later became the book *The Pine Barrens*.

"Templex," Jan. 6, 1968, 32.
Profile of Temple Hornaday Fielding, travel-guide writer. Later included in the collection *A Roomful of Hovings and Other Profiles*.

Newsbreak in "Talk of the Town," Jan. 20, 1968, 23 (unsigned).
Sign beside a cemetery in Princeton, New Jersey.

"A Forager," Apr. 6, 1968, 45.
Profile of Euell Theophilus Gibbons, a leading advocate of gathering and eating wild foods. Later included in the collection *A Roomful of Hovings and Other Profiles*.

"The Lawns of Wimbledon," June 22, 1968, 32.
Profile of the head groundskeeper of the tennis courts at Wimbledon. Later included in the collection *A Roomful of Hovings and Other Profiles* and the book *Wimbledon: A Celebration*.

"Levels of the Game," June 7, 1969, 45.
Part 1 of an article about a U.S. Open semifinal tennis match between Arthur Ashe and Clark Graebner. Later became the book *Levels of the Game*.

"Levels of the Game," June 14, 1969, 44.
Part 2 of an article about a U.S. Open semifinal tennis match between Arthur Ashe and Clark Graebner. Later became the book *Levels of the Game*.

Newsbreak in "Talk of the Town," Sept. 13, 1969, 39 (unsigned).
An overhead snippet of conversation in New York City that set "the American amateur record for the long-jump split infinitive."

"The Island of the Crofter and the Laird," Dec. 6, 1969, 69.
Part 1 of an article about a small island in the Scottish Hebrides, the land of McPhee's ancestors. Later became the book *The Crofter and the Laird*.

"The Island of the Crofter and the Laird," Dec. 13, 1969, 61.
Part 2 of an article about a small island in the Scottish Hebrides, the land of McPhee's ancestors. Later became the book *The Crofter and the Laird*.

"Reading the River," Mar. 21, 1970, 126.
The Potomac Highland and Middle States Wildwater canoeing championship. Later included in the collection *Pieces of the Frame*.

Newsbreak in "Talk of the Town," Apr. 4, 1970, 35 (unsigned).
The name of a rescue boat brings to mind a Stevie Smith poem.

Newsbreak in "Talk of the Town," Apr. 18, 1970, 35 (unsigned).
Overheard in a faculty lounge at Princeton University.

"From Birnam Wood to Dunsinane," Oct. 10, 1970, 141.
A walk in Macbeth country, a journey made from Birnam Wood to Dunsinane Hill in Scotland. Later included in the collection *Pieces of the Frame*.

"Fruit of the Sea," Newsbreak in "Talk of the Town," Nov. 21, 1970, 49 (unsigned).
A supermarket shopper is startled by a sign saying a lamb chop special is "ocean fresh."

"The License Plates of Burning Tree," "Talk of the Town," Jan. 30, 1971, 20 (unsigned).
A visit to an exclusive Maryland golf club, Burning Tree. Later became part of the book *The Patch*.

"Encounters with the Archdruid," Mar. 20, 1971, 42.
Part 1 of an article about environmentalist David Brower and several of his ideological enemies. Later became the book *Encounters with the Archdruid*.

"Encounters with the Archdruid," Mar. 27, 1971, 42.
Part 2 of an article about environmentalist David Brower and several of his ideological enemies. Later became the book *Encounters with the Archdruid*.

"Encounters with the Archdruid," Apr. 3, 1971, 41.
Part 3 of an article about environmentalist David Brower and several of his ideological enemies. Later became the book *Encounters with the Archdruid*.

"Ranger," Sept. 11, 1971, 45.
Profile of George Hartzog, the director of the National Park Service, later included in the collection *Pieces of the Frame*.

"Three Gatherings," "The Talk of the Town," Dec. 25, 1971, 25 (unsigned).
The presentation of Rockefeller Public Service Awards to federal civil servants. Later became part of the book *The Patch*.

"The Conching Rooms," "The Talk of the Town," May 13, 1972, 32 (unsigned).
The Hershey company making its chocolate. Later part of the book *The Patch*.

"The Search for Marvin Gardens," Sept. 9, 1972, 45.
A visit to Atlantic City, New Jersey. Later included in the collection *Pieces of the Frame*.

"The Deltoid Pumpkin Seed," Feb. 10, 1973, 40.
Part 1 of an article about an unusual experimental hybrid airship. Later became the book *The Deltoid Pumpkin Seed*.

"The Deltoid Pumpkin Seed," Feb. 17, 1973, 42.
Part 2 of the article about an unusual experimental hybrid airship. Later became the book *The Deltoid Pumpkin Seed*.

"The Deltoid Pumpkin Seed," Feb. 24, 1973, 48.
Part 3 of an article about an unusual experimental hybrid airship. Later became the book *The Deltoid Pumpkin Seed*.

"Travels in Georgia," Apr. 28, 1973, 44.
Profile of biologist and environmental activist Carol Ruckdeschel, traveling with McPhee and Sam Candler of Georgia's Natural Areas Council. Later included in the collection *Pieces of the Frame*.

Newsbreak in "Talk of the Town," Sept. 24, 1973, 30 (unsigned).
Quote overheard on Princeton University campus about a face.

"The Curve of Binding Energy," Dec. 3, 1973, 54.
Part 1 of an article about weapons-grade nuclear material and the dangers of a homemade bomb. Later became the book *The Curve of Binding Energy*.

"The Curve of Binding Energy," Dec. 10, 1973, 50.
Part 2 of an article about weapons-grade nuclear material and the dangers of a homemade bomb. Later became the book *The Curve of Binding Energy*.

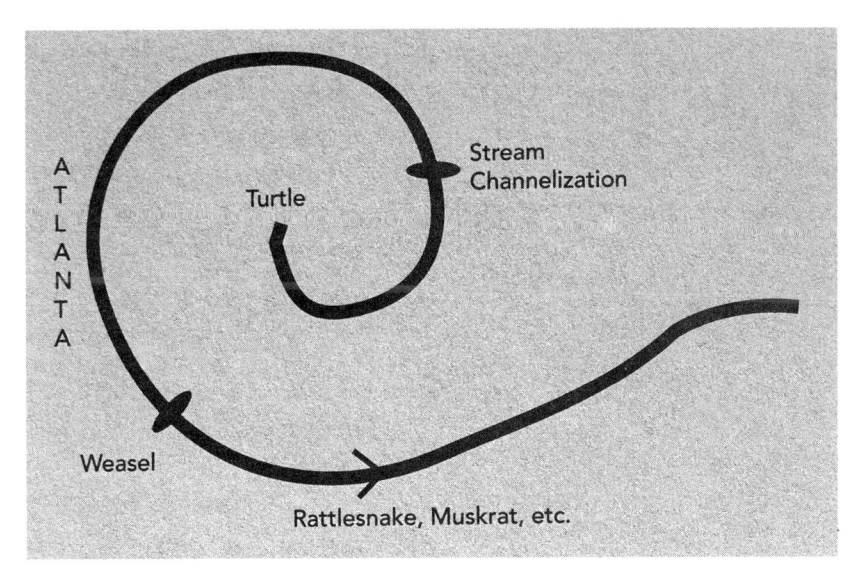

FIGURE 22. In *Draft No. 4*, McPhee included intricate drawings of structures he created to guide his writing. This one was for "Travels in Georgia," published in *The New Yorker* in 1973 and in "Structure" in *Draft No. 4: On the Writing Process.* (Copyright © 2017 by John McPhee. Reprinted by permission of Farrar, Straus and Giroux and Text Publishing Co.)

"The Curve of Binding Energy," Dec. 17, 1973, 60.
Part 3 of an article about weapons-grade nuclear material and the dangers of a homemade bomb. Later became the book *The Curve of Binding Energy*.

"Sullen Gold," "Talk of the Town," Mar. 25, 1974, 32 (unsigned).
International gold reserves stored in a cave beneath the Federal Reserve Bank in New York. Later part of the book *The Patch*.

"Firewood," Mar. 25, 1974, 81.
Firewood in New York state during an energy shortage.

"Flavors & Fragrance," "Talk of the Town," Apr. 8, 1974, 35 (unsigned).
The International Flavors & Fragrances company, where scientists create artificial flavors and fragrances for commercial use. Later part of the book *The Patch*.

"Ruidoso," Apr. 29, 1974, 83.
The 1973 All-American Futurity, a race for quarter horses held in New Mexico. Later included in the collection *Pieces of the Frame* and the basis of the movie *Casey's Shadow*.

"Police Story," "Talk of the Town," July 15, 1974, 27 (unsigned).
McPhee leaving car keys inside his locked car. Later became part of the book *The Patch*.

"'Time' Covers, NR," "Talk of the Town," Oct. 28, 1974, 40 (unsigned).
Unused cover paintings for *Time* magazine. Later became part of the book *The Patch*.

"The P-1800," "Talk of the Town," Feb. 10, 1975, 30 (unsigned).
An early computer terminal being tested at *The New York Times* by reporter Israel Shenker. Later became part of the book *The Patch*.

"The Survival of the Bark Canoe," Feb. 24, 1975, 49.
Part 1 of an article about a 150-mile canoe trip in the north Maine woods with the craftsman who made the canoes. Later became the book *The Survival of the Bark Canoe*.

"The Survival of the Bark Canoe," Mar. 3, 1975, 41.
Part 2 of an article about a 150-mile canoe trip in the north Maine woods with the craftsman who made the canoes. Later became the book *The Survival of the Bark Canoe*.

"The Atlantic Generating Station," May 12, 1975, 51.
Plans to install a floating nuclear plant off the New Jersey coast. Later included in the collection *Giving Good Weight*.

"The Pinball Philosophy," June 30, 1975, 81.
A visit with J. Anthony Lukas, Pulitzer Prize–winning writer and world-class pinball player. Later included in the collection *Giving Good Weight*.

"The Keel of Lake Dickey," May 3, 1976, 43.
A 100-mile canoe trip down Maine's St. John River. Later included in the collection *Giving Good Weight*.

"What They Were Hunting For," Sept. 27, 1976, 80.
Part 1 of an article about selecting a new site for the capital of Alaska. Later part of the book *Coming into the Country*.

"What They Were Hunting For," Oct. 4, 1976, 40.
Part 2 of an article about selecting a new site for the capital of Alaska. Later part of the book *Coming into the Country*.

"The Encircled River," May 2, 1977, 47.
Part 1 of an article about a canoe and kayak trip down a river in Alaska. Later part of the book *Coming into the Country*.

"The Encircled River," May 9, 1977, 88.
Part 2 of an article about a canoe and kayak trip down a river in Alaska. Later part of the book *Coming into the Country*.

"Coming into the Country," June 20, 1977, 43.
Part 1 of an article about Alaskans. Later part of the book *Coming into the Country*.

"Coming into the Country," June 27, 1977, 58.
Part 2 of an article about Alaskans. Later part of the book *Coming into the Country*.

"Coming into the Country," July 4, 1977, 33.
Part 3 of an article about Alaskans. Later part of the book *Coming into the Country*.

"Coming into the Country," July 11, 1977, 30.
Part 4 of an article about Alaskans. Later part of the book *Coming into the Country*.

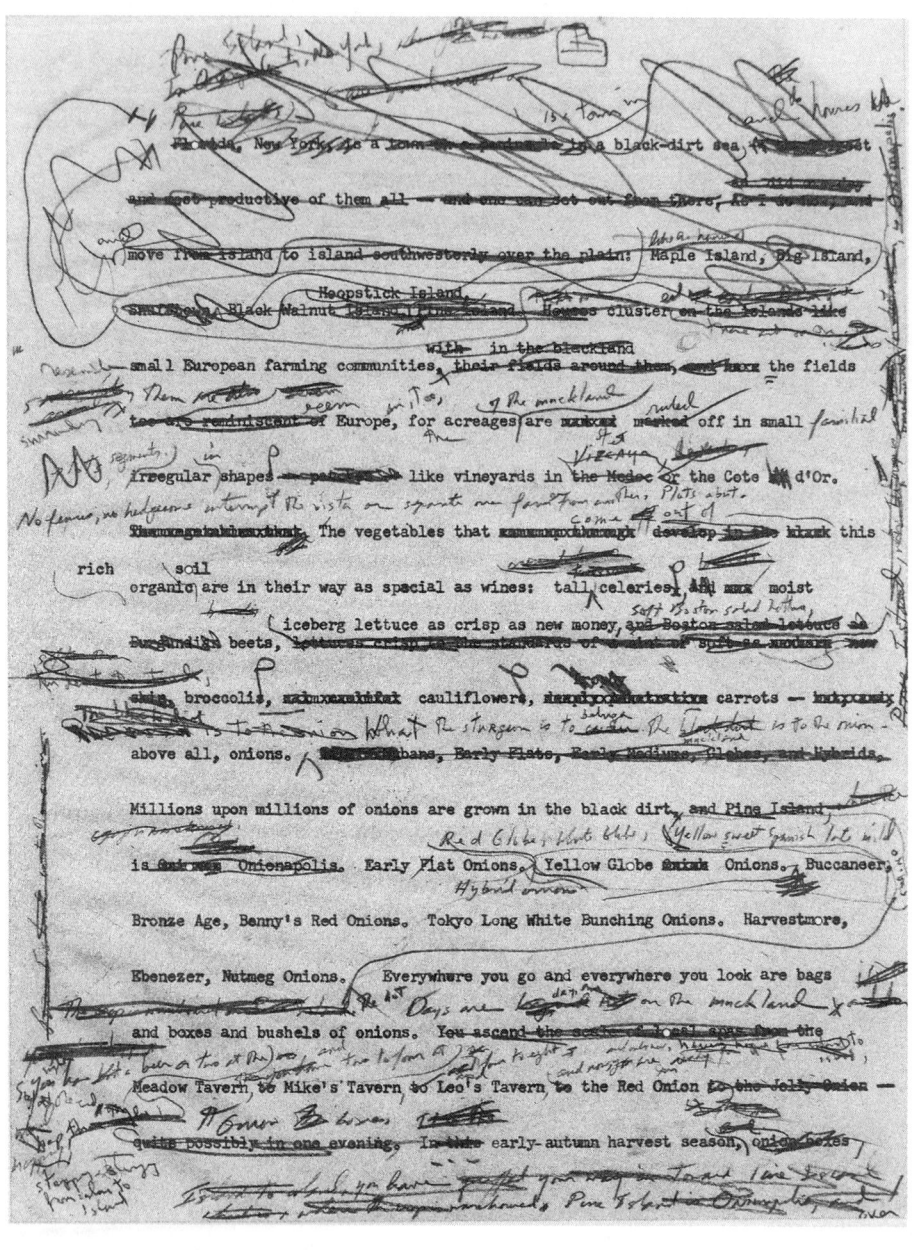

FIGURE 23. This manuscript page from the New Yorker article "Giving Good Weight," which became the title essay of one of his book collections, shows McPhee's self-editing process. The second draft of writing, McPhee says, is crucial to literary development. (Courtesy of John McPhee)

"Giving Good Weight," July 3, 1978, 36.
Open-air markets in New York City. Later became part of the collection *Giving Good Weight*.

"Brigade de Cuisine," Feb. 19, 1979, 43.
A chef, with the pseudonym Otto, at a country farmhouse inn. Later included in the collection *Giving Good Weight*.

"Dept. of Amplification and Correction," Mar. 12, 1979, 147 (unsigned).
A correction about turbot served at the restaurant Lutèce, as written about in "Brigade de Cuisine."

John McPhee and Peter Bingham, "Notes and Comment," "Talk of the Town," June 9, 1980, 31 (unsigned).
The note of a Harvard student to a family friend who tried, without success, to invite him to lunch.

"Riding the Boom Extension," Aug. 4, 1980, 36.
Telephone service comes to a small city in Alaska. Later included in the collection *Table of Contents*.

"Annals of the Former World, Basin and Range," Oct. 20, 1980, 58.
Part 1 of an article about travels with geologist Kenneth S. Deffeyes through the Great Basin of the U.S. Later became the book *Basin and Range* and is the beginning of McPhee's extended writing about geology.

"Annals of the Former World, Basin and Range," Oct. 27, 1980, 57.
Part 2 of an article about travels with geologist Kenneth Deffeyes through the Great Basin of the U.S. Later became the book *Basin and Range*.

"Minihydro," Feb. 23, 1981, 44.
The advent of small-scale hydroelectric power facilities in New York state. Later included in the collection *Table of Contents*.

"Ice Pond," July 13, 1981, 92.
An experimental cooling system being developed at Princeton University and other places. Later included in the collection *Table of Contents*.

Robert Bingham obituary, July 5, 1982, 100 (unsigned).
Obituary of *New Yorker* editor Robert Bingham. Later part of the book *The Patch*.

"Annals of the Former World, In Suspect Terrain," Sept. 13, 1982, 45.
Part 1 of an article about travels with geologist Anita Harris on Interstate 80 between New York and Indiana and her skepticism about the theory of plate tectonics. Later part of the book *In Suspect Terrain*.

"Annals of the Former World, In Suspect Terrain," Sept. 20, 1982, 45.
Part 2 of an article about travels with geologist Anita Harris on Interstate 80 between New York and Indiana and her skepticism about the theory of plate tectonics. Later part of the book *In Suspect Terrain*.

"Annals of the Former World, In Suspect Terrain," Sept. 27, 1982, 46.
Part 3 of an article about travels with geologist Anita Harris on Interstate 80 between New York and Indiana and her skepticism about the theory of plate tectonics. Later part of the book *In Suspect Terrain*.

"A Textbook Place for Bears," Dec. 27, 1982, 42.
The wild bears of New Jersey. Later included in the collection *Table of Contents*.

"Department of Amplification," Apr. 18, 1983, 137.
An invitation to visit wild bears in their dens in Pennsylvania. Later included in the collection *Table of Contents*.

"Open Man," Oct. 10, 1983, 108.
Accompanying U.S. Senator Bill Bradley as he meets voters and newspaper writers throughout New Jersey. Later included in the collection *Table of Contents*.

"La Place de la Concorde Suisse," Oct. 31, 1983, 50.
Part 1 of an article about the Swiss Army's role in Swiss society. Later became the book *La Place de la Concorde Suisse*.

"La Place de la Concorde Suisse," Nov. 7, 1983, 55.
Part 2 of an article about the Swiss Army's role in Swiss society. Later became the book *La Place de la Concorde Suisse*.

"Heirs of General Practice," July 23, 1984, 40.
Young doctors in Maine in the new medical specialty called family practice. Later became the book *Heirs of General Practice* and is also included in the collection *Table of Contents*.

"North of the C.P. Line," Nov. 26, 1984, 49.
Flights with a bush pilot who is a game warden in Maine, a man also named John McPhee. Later included in the collection *Table of Contents*.

"Annals of the Former World, Rising from the Plains," Feb. 24, 1986, 38.
Part 1 of an article about Rocky Mountain geology and geologist David Love. Later became part of the book *Rising from the Plains*.

"Annals of the Former World, Rising from the Plains," Mar. 3, 1986, 41.
Part 2 of an article about Rocky Mountain geology and geologist David Love. Later became part of the book *Rising from the Plains*.

"Annals of the Former World, Rising from the Plains," Mar. 10, 1986, 70.
Part 3 of an article about Rocky Mountain geology and geologist David Love. Later became the book *Rising from the Plains*.

"Atchafalaya," Feb. 23, 1987, 39.
The struggle to control the Mississippi River in Louisiana. Later became part of the book *The Control of Nature*.

"In Virgin Forest," "Talk of the Town," July 6, 1987, 21 (unsigned).
The primeval woods of the Hutcheson Memorial Forest in New Jersey. Later became part of the collection *Irons in the Fire*.

"Release," "Talk of the Town," Sept. 28, 1987, 28 (unsigned).
Visiting a blind English professor at Franklin and Marshall College. Later became part of the collection *Irons in the Fire*.

"Cooling the Lava," Feb. 22, 1988, 43.
Part 1 of an article about stopping a lava flow in Iceland in 1973. Later became part of the book *The Control of Nature*.

"Cooling the Lava," Feb. 29, 1988, 64.
Part 2 of an article about stopping a lava flow in Iceland in 1973, and Hawaii's struggles with volcanoes. Later became part of the book *The Control of Nature*.

"Los Angeles Against the Mountains," Sept. 26, 1988, 45.
Part 1 of an article about debris flows in the San Gabriel Mountains of Los Angeles. Later became part of the book *The Control of Nature*.

"Los Angeles Against the Mountains," Oct. 3, 1988, 72.
Part 2 of an article about debris flows in the San Gabriel Mountains of Los Angeles. Later became part of the book *The Control of Nature*.

"Altimeter Man," "Talk of the Town," Sept. 25, 1989, 48 (unsigned).
A man who specializes in hand-held altimeters. Later part of the book *The Patch*.

"Rinard at Manheim," Dec. 4, 1989, 150.
Rare automobiles at the Manheim Exotic Auction in Pennsylvania. Later became part of the collection *Irons in the Fire*.

"Travels of the Rock," Feb. 26, 1990, 108.
Repair work on Plymouth Rock, with a look at the rock's geologic history. Later included in the collections *Irons in the Fire* and *The Princeton Anthology of Writing*.

"Looking for a Ship," Mar. 26, 1990, 40.
Part 1 of an article about the fading U.S. Merchant Marine and the voyage of one of its ships along the Pacific coast of South America. Later became part of the book *Looking for a Ship*.

"Looking for a Ship," Apr. 2, 1990, 46.
Part 2 of an article about the fading U.S. Merchant Marine and the voyage of one of its ships along the Pacific coast of South America. Later became part of the book *Looking for a Ship*.

"Looking for a Ship," Apr. 9, 1990, 45.
Part 3 of an article about the fading U.S. Merchant Marine and the voyage of one of its ships along the Pacific coast of South America. Later became the book *Looking for a Ship*.

"Annals of the Former World, Assembling California," Sept. 7, 1992, 36.
Part 1 of an article about travels in California with geologist Eldridge Moores, a leading expert in global plate tectonics. Later became the book *Assembling California*.

"Annals of the Former World, Assembling California," Sept. 14, 1992, 44.
Part 2 of an article about travels in California with geologist Eldridge Moores, a leading expert in global plate tectonics. Later became part of the book *Assembling California*.

"Annals of the Former World, Assembling California," Sept. 21, 1992, 39.
Part 3 of an article about travels in California with geologist Eldridge Moores, a leading expert in global plate tectonics. Later became part of the book *Assembling California*.

"Opening the Stacks," Feb. 22, 1993, 83.
On reading *New Yorker* magazines in a canoe in New Hampshire, and the large open-stack *New Yorker* libraries all over—in people's homes.

"Arthur Ashe Remembered," Mar. 1, 1993, 57.
Tennis champion Arthur Ashe upon his death. Later became part of the book *The Patch*.

"Water War," Apr. 26, 1993, 120.
Las Vegas and its fight for water. Later part of the book *The Patch*.

"Duty of Care," June 28, 1993, 72.
Millions of old tires and ideas on how to recycle them. Later became part of the collection *Irons in the Fire*.

"Irons in the Fire," Dec. 20, 1993, 94.
Chris Collis, Nevada's livestock brand inspector, and the fight against cattle rustlers. Later became part of the collection *Irons in the Fire*.

"Disassembling California," "Comment," Jan. 31, 1994, 4 (unsigned).
About the recent earthquake in California.

"The Ransom of Russian Art," Oct. 17, 1994, 78.
Profile of an American who brought thousands of works by Soviet dissident artists to the United States in the 1960s and 1970s. Later became the book *The Ransom of Russian Art*.

"Other Snows," Jan. 22, 1996, 90.
The blizzard of 1996 and other storms. Later became part of the book *The Patch*.

"The Gravel Page," Jan. 29, 1996, 44.
Forensic geologists. Later became part of the collection *Irons in the Fire*.

"Silk Parachute," May 12, 1997, 108.
An article about McPhee's mother. Later became part of the collection *Silk Parachute* and was included in *The Princeton Reader*.

"Swimming with Canoes," Aug. 10, 1998, 33.
McPhee's childhood at summer camp and a canoe accident. Later became part of the collection *Silk Parachute*.

"Catch-and-Dissect," Oct. 19, 1998, 58.
The Alabama Deep Sea Fishing Rodeo and ichthyologist Willy Bemis.

"Farewell to the Nineteenth Century," Sept. 27, 1999, 44.
Returning rivers to their natural states. Later became part of the book *The Founding Fish*.

"Los Angeles Against the Mountains," "Takes," Feb. 21, 2000, 251.
Prompted by California storms, a reprinted excerpt of McPhee's "Los Angeles Against the Mountains" article from September 26, 1988, also published in the book *The Control of Nature*.

"They're in the River," Apr. 10, 2000, 72.
Shad fishing on the Delaware River, including the struggle with a big fish. Later became part of the book *The Founding Fish*.

"A Selective Advantage," Sept. 11, 2000, 70.
How shad behave and what it means to the fishermen who seek them. Later became part of the book *The Founding Fish*.

"Absent Without Leave," June 10, 2002, 40.
Intricacies of shad fishing and the difficulty of knowing who's at fault when they get away. Later became part of the book *The Founding Fish*.

"Sapidissima," Aug. 19, 2002, 80.
Recipes for cooking shad. Later became part of the book *The Founding Fish*.

"A Fleet of One," Feb. 17, 2003, 148.
McPhee's travels across America with a long-haul truck driver. Later became part of the collection *Uncommon Carriers*.

"The Tee Room,' Mar. 31, 2003, 49.
The plans to transform the Russian Tea Room in New York City into a golf museum.

"Whiff," "Department of Amplification," Nov. 10, 2003, 50.
How stories trying to project the future can go awry, including the plans, now shelved, for a golf museum at the site of Manhattan's Russian Tea Room.

"1839/2003," Dec. 15, 2003, 71.
Retracing Henry David Thoreau's 1839 trip on the Concord and Merrimack Rivers. Later became part of the collection *Uncommon Carriers* and the introduction to a new edition of *The Writings of Henry D. Thoreau: A Week on the Concord and Merrimack Rivers*.

"Tight-Assed River," Nov. 15, 2004, 80.
Riding barge towboats on the Illinois River. Later became part of the collection *Uncommon Carriers*.

"Out in the Sort," Apr. 18, 2005, 160.
The UPS distribution hub in Louisville. Later became part of the collection *Uncommon Carriers*.

"The Sunken City," "Talk of the Town," Sept. 12, 2005, 38.
Just after Hurricane Katrina, a reprinted excerpt of McPhee's "The Control of Nature: Atchafalaya" article from February 23, 1987, also published in the book *The Control of Nature*.

"Coal Train," Oct. 3, 2005, 72.
Part 1 of an article about riding on coal trains in Wyoming, Nebraska, and Kansas. Later became part of the collection *Uncommon Carriers*.

"Coal Train," Oct. 10, 2005, 62.
Part 2 of an article about riding on coal trains in Wyoming, Nebraska, and Kansas. Later became part of the collection *Uncommon Carriers*.

"Land of the Diesel Bear," Nov. 28, 2005, 116.
A return visit with the long-distance truck driver featured in "A Fleet of One" on February 17, 2003. Later became part of the collection *Uncommon Carriers*.

"Season on the Chalk," Mar. 12, 2007, 58.
A family trip among contemporary and former worlds on the massive chalk of Western Europe. Later included in the collection *Silk Parachute*.

"Rip Van Golfer," Aug. 6, 2007, 26.
A report from the U.S. Open golf tournament in 2007. Later included in the collection *Silk Parachute*.

"My Life List," Sept. 3, 2007, 82.
McPhee's lifetime list of exotic foods eaten, such as weasel, moose, fat behind a caribou's eye, and muskrat. Later included in the collection *Silk Parachute*.

"Checkpoints," Feb. 9, 2009, 56.
Fact-checkers at *The New Yorker*. Later included in the collection *Silk Parachute* and the book *Draft No. 4*.

"Spin Right and Shoot Left," Mar. 23, 2009, 54.
The history and growth of lacrosse, and McPhee's experience as faculty fellow for the Princeton University team. Later included in the collection *Silk Parachute*.

"One-Stop Shopping," May 25, 2009, 38.
An elite lacrosse summer camp at the University of Maryland for rising high school seniors from all over the United States.

"The Patch," Feb. 8, 2010, 32.
An essay on fishing for chain pickerel, set against the final days of McPhee's father's life. Later part of the book *The Patch*.

"Darwin and the Chilean Earthquake," Mar. 2, 2010, online only, https://www.newyorker.com/books/double-take/darwin-and-the-chilean-earthquake.
Following the February 2010 earthquake in Chile, McPhee writes about Charles Darwin experiencing an earthquake in Chile in 1835. Includes an excerpt from McPhee's 1990 *Looking for a Ship*.

"Pioneer," Mar. 22, 2010, 34.
Lacrosse coach Bill Tierney's move from Princeton to the University of Denver. Later included in *The Patch*.

"Linksland and Bottle," Sept. 6, 2010, 46.
The 2010 Open Championship at St. Andrews and the evolution of golf. Later included in *The Patch*.

"Pat Crow," Feb. 7, 2011, 25.
A tribute to Charles Patrick Crow, a longtime editor of McPhee and many other writers at *The New Yorker*, who had recently died.

"Progression," Nov. 14, 2011, 36.
On the writing process. Later became part of the book *Draft No. 4*.

"Editors & Publisher," July 2, 2012, 32.
Reflections on William Shawn and Robert Gottlieb, editors at *The New Yorker*, and Roger Straus, publisher at Farrar, Straus and Giroux. Later became part of the book *Draft No. 4*.

"Structure," Jan. 14, 2013, 46.
On the art of shaping a piece of writing. Later became part of the book *Draft No. 4*.

"Draft No. 4," Apr. 29, 2013, 32.
On writing and rewriting. Later became part of the book *Draft No. 4*.

"The Orange Trapper," July 1, 2013, 30.
A compulsion to collect golf balls. Later included in *The Patch*.

"Elicitation," Apr. 7, 2014, 50.
Techniques of interviewing and ways to elicit information. Later became part of the book *Draft No. 4*.

"Phi Beta Football," Sept. 8, 2014, 34.
The memories of McPhee, who did not play football, about football coaches and a roommate, Dick Kazmaier, who won the Heisman Trophy. Later included in *The Patch*. Unrelated to McPhee's 1953 article with the same headline in the *Newark News* about Kazmaier.

"Frame of Reference," Mar. 9, 2015, 42.
On word choice and frame of reference. Later became part of the book *Draft No. 4*.

"Omission," Sept. 14, 2015, 42.
On selection and omission in planning a piece of writing, which later became part of the book *Draft No. 4*.

"Dah Dah Doo Dah Dah Dah Dah Dah Doo Dah La Ti Mi Fa La So Fa Mi," Sept. 19, 2016, online only, https://www.newyorker.com/culture/culture-desk/john-mcphee-my-first-drink.
McPhee's first drink (at age 10), after which he practiced "Country Gardens" on the piano. Later part of the book *The Patch*.

"Direct Eye Contact," Mar. 5, 2018, 32.
Wild bears in New Jersey and McPhee's ambition to see one from the windows of his house. Later included in *The Patch*.

"Tabula Rasa: Volume One," Jan. 13, 2020, 46.
The first installment about writing projects McPhee once seriously planned, but never wrote, such as Swiss bridges and the Extremadura region of Spain. Later included in the book *Tabula Rasa: Volume 1*.

"Tabula Rasa: Volume 2," Apr. 19, 2021, 16.
The second installment of *Tabula Rasa*, including life on the seas and Peter Benchley on writing. Later included in the book *Tabula Rasa: Volume 1*.

"Tabula Rasa: Volume 3," Feb. 7, 2022, 24.
The third installment of *Tabula Rasa*, including his work as a 17-year-old night watchman at the Institute for Advanced Study and dinners with *Time* magazine owner Henry Luce. Later included in the book *Tabula Rasa: Volume 1*.

"Under the Carpetbag," Oct. 16, 2023, 22.
McPhee writes about his 60-year friendship with Bill Bradley, the former basketball star (the subject of McPhee's first *New Yorker* profile and book) and U.S. Senator.

"Tabula Rasa: Volume Four," May 20, 2024, 28.
The fourth installment of *Tabula Rasa*, include life with Wordle, the foibles of proofreading, and the surprise final exam he gave his Princeton University students.

"Tabula Rasa: Volume Five," Jan. 20, 2025, 20.
McPhee on the caribou rack in his kitchen, the day a sugar maple tree shed all its brilliant-yellow leaves in a minute or two, and his case of bleb that coincided with the birth of his first child.

3

Other Publications

"You don't want to sound like an encyclopedia or something all of a sudden. Here you are writing your book, and everything is going fine in your book, and now you suddenly sound like, you know, the Britannica. Well, avoid that. Avoid the smell of research."

—FROM "THE REPORTER AS TEACHER: A TALK WITH JOHN MCPHEE" BY HELLER MCALPIN, BARNES & NOBLE READS, SEPTEMBER 13, 2017

Newspapers and Other Periodicals

Beyond his extensive writing for *Time* magazine and *The New Yorker*, McPhee wrote nearly two dozen nonfiction articles for other magazines and newspapers. They were on a wide variety of subjects and the publications included some small ones in which he was especially interested. Several were stories that his *New Yorker* editors didn't want but that McPhee was determined to publish, such as one about the Loch Ness Monster.

John Angus McPhee, "A Princeton Man Tells Why the Comic Tiger Has Turned Serious: 'Funny Mags Are Passe,'" *New York Times*, May 25, 1952, *Sunday Magazine*, 17.
McPhee, who at the time was in college and managing editor of *The Princeton Tiger*, the school's long-established humor magazine, writes

that college humor "is a very sick man in academic America today and he is dying of an incurable disease. I call it 'Ridiculitis.'"

Two months earlier, on March 30, *The New York Times* had published a news story about "Chastened 'Tiger' Back at Princeton; Famous 70-Year-Old College Humor Magazine Returns as Serious Publication." It chronicled how McPhee and his colleagues had reinvented the humor magazine as a more serious publication. The editors of the *Times Sunday Magazine* then invited McPhee to write about the problems of college humor magazines. His article was published alongside one by Richard Lemon, chairman of the *Yale Record* humor magazine, who argues that academic humor was flourishing, except possibly at Princeton: "The Tiger's Procrustean formula for improving a situation is, apparently, to abolish it." Lemon went on to a career writing for magazines, including *The New Yorker*, the *New York Daily News*, *People Magazine* and *Entertainment Weekly*.

John Angus McPhee, "Phi Beta Football," *Newark Sunday News*, Oct. 4, 1953, 20.
McPhee writes about the intricate grading system that Princeton's football coaches created and used to analyze every play, aiming to improve the performance of players and the team.

John McPhee, "Burn Those Worthless Cookbooks," *Saturday Evening Post*, Oct. 8, 1964, 8.
McPhee says "junk" cookbooks have flooded the market without adding to knowledge of food or cooking. He tries to separate the useful from the useless as he writes archly about how he employed purposeless cookbooks as fuel for a fire.

John McPhee, "Living Off the Land," *Amerika*, Mar. 1969, 53.
This was a reprint of McPhee's writing in *The New Yorker* about Euell Gibbons, a leading advocate of gathering and eating wild foods. The publication, *Amerika*, was a Russian-language magazine published by the United States Department of State to tell Soviet citizens about American life.

John McPhee, "Good Scotch Needs Gloom, Fog, Rain, But What About Josie's Well?," *Holiday*, Jan. 1970, 66.
McPhee writes of a whisky distillery he visited in Scotland with its special "Josie's Well" as its water source. The article was reprinted in two of his collections, *Pieces of the Frame* and *In the Highlands and Islands*.

John McPhee, "Pieces of the Frame," *The Atlantic*, Jan. 1970, 42.
McPhee went on an extended trip in Scotland and Europe in 1967 with his wife and four young daughters. When they stopped at Loch Ness in Scotland, the children were keen to see the Loch Ness monster. He describes the legend: "Its sensitivity to people seems to be acute, and it keeps a wide margin between itself and mankind." The article is reprinted in the collection *Pieces of the Frame*.

McPhee writes in *The New Yorker* of November 10, 2003 ("Whiff") about how *New Yorker* editor William Shawn turned down his suggestion of Loch Ness as a subject for the magazine, which led McPhee to publish the story in *The Atlantic*: "William Shawn, this magazine's editor absolute for a great many years, used to tell his nonfiction writers that the world's worst subject was the future. Hard to tie down, the future could too easily come loose and take off on unexpected vectors . . . Reacting to a proposal of mine, he once slightly modified his position, informing me that the future was actually the second-worst subject in the world, the worst being the Loch Ness monster."

John McPhee, "Centre Court," *Playboy*, June 1971, 102.
On assignment for *Playboy* magazine, McPhee visits Wimbledon for its tennis Championships in 1970 and writes "Hoad on Court 5," an article about the tournament scene and the Australian champion Lew Hoad and other players. It was later collected in *Wimbledon: A Celebration* and also in *Pieces of the Frame*.

John McPhee, "Brandstetter and Las Brisas," *Travel + Leisure*, Autumn 1972, 52.
McPhee writes about the luxurious Las Brisas resort in Acapulco created by Colonel Frank Brandstetter, who went into the hotel business

after being born into Austrian-Hungarian nobility, then coming to the United States as a nearly penniless teenager and serving as a distinguished officer in World War II. The resort, designed for wealthy tourists, is where American astronauts went with their families after going to the moon. Other authors in this issue of *Travel + Leisure*, which included many literary figures as contributors at the time, were John Kenneth Galbraith and William Buckley on "The Politics of Skiing" and Lawrence Durrell on "The Poetic Obsession of Dublin."

John McPhee, "Tennis," *New York Times Book Review*, June 10, 1973, 1.
In the cover story of *The New York Times Book Review*'s "Summer Reading" issue, McPhee offers commentary about several current tennis books, but mostly imparts his philosophy of the game and of competition. "The thing to do with a tennis book is not to read it," he says, "but to give it away. Look it over first, then make a present of it to someone you play with whose game the book will almost certainly destroy."

Two of McPhee's regular tennis opponents responded in letters to *The New York Times* (July 22, 1973). Princeton neighbor and economics author and television commentator Adam Smith (also known as George Goodman) writes, "I am sending McPhee Vincent Lombardi's 'Run to Daylight.' 'Winning is not everything,' Lombardi said, 'it is the only thing.' McPhee subscribed to that long before Lombardi. Lombardi's teams never lost; it was just that sometimes the other team had more points when the clock ran out. Similarly, McPhee has never lost a match. He is the only player I know who, after dropping straight sets 6-0, 6-1, 6-0, has said to his opponent, 'You're not quitting now are you?'"

John McPhee, "Thrilling Sights: Love Games of Birds," *Vogue*, July 1973, 66.
McPhee got pulled into doing this article by Robert Bingham, his editor at *The New Yorker*. Bingham said a friend at *Vogue* wanted McPhee to write a "very short" story on birds for a "very long" amount of money. McPhee tried to refuse, saying he knew nothing about birds, but Bingham kept pushing him. McPhee relented and did the story mostly in the form of an interview with Bingham about his bird watching. The piece

also appeared years later in *The Patch* (page 200). McPhee, always particular about his headlines, blamed the *Vogue* editor for replacing his proposed headline with a poor one.

John McPhee, "The People of New Jersey's Pine Barrens," *National Geographic*, Jan. 1974, 52.
When *National Geographic* photographer Bill Curtsinger called McPhee out of the blue to say he wanted to do a photographic story for his magazine about the Pine Barrens in New Jersey and would he do the words, McPhee, to his own surprise, said yes right away. McPhee's deep interest in the Pine Barrens, plus Curtsinger's approach, made him willing to return to the large, rural, undeveloped area that is the subject of his 1967 *New Yorker* articles that became a well-received book. "Wild Land in the City's Backyard" was the headline for the map with the *National Geographic* story. McPhee writes about the area's history and people, accompanying Curtsinger's 20 color photographs. In 1981, Farrar, Straus and Giroux published a new, illustrated edition of *The Pine Barrens*, with additional photographs by Curtsinger and an "author's addendum" from McPhee.

John McPhee, "The Forager," *New York Times*, Jan. 10, 1976, 20.
On the op-ed page of *The New York Times*, McPhee writes an appreciation of Euell Gibbons and "his extraordinary knowledge of edible wild plants" 10 days after Gibbons died. McPhee had previously written about Gibbons, a health food advocate and writer, in *The New Yorker* (April 6, 1968). He chronicled a trip they took together in central Pennsylvania, foraging for and eating wild foods.

McPhee says his motivation for writing this opinion piece was to focus attention on Gibbons for his "special skill" and knowledge about wild food, rather than the 1970s Grape-Nuts cereal ads that turned him into "a household figure of a cartoon sort." McPhee writes, "My purpose in writing this remembrance of him is to take those GrapeNuts and blow them from here to Hawaii to get him out from under them."

On September 26, 2010, McPhee's piece about Gibbons was reprinted in a special section of *The New York Times* to celebrate the 40th anniversary of its op-ed page.

John McPhee, "An Album Quilt," *Creative Nonfiction*, No. 8, Mostly Memoir, 1997, 105.
Twenty years before "An Album Quilt" appeared in *The Patch*, McPhee gave an early version to *Creative Nonfiction*, the publication of a then-fledgling literary organization, which published this early version. It was a patchwork of items on many subjects and in the intervening years, McPhee re-edited the "Album Quilt" dramatically, dropping many items and adding others.

As a result, there are several items in this version that appear nowhere else in full form in McPhee's published writing, including "Six Princetons," about the changes to his hometown over time (which was drawn from McPhee's 25th Princeton University reunion book entry in 1978); remarks he read at a 1986 wedding rehearsal dinner for his daughter, Laura; his absent-minded behavior in 1994 on the way to a University of Kansas geology field camp; and comments he made at a Lotos Club testimonial dinner for Farrar, Straus and Giroux publisher Roger Straus in 1992 (part of this item was republished more than 20 years later in *Draft No. 4*).

John McPhee, "The Upper 1 (Alaska)," *Vogue*, Apr. 1979, 248.
In a reflective article about what he had seen in Alaska while doing the research for *Coming into the Country*, McPhee also writes also about how disorienting it was to leave Alaska and return home to New Jersey. The piece was collected in *The Patch* (page 239).

John McPhee, "Benelogue," "The Little Brown House: A Garland for Robert McGlynn," *Deerfield Publications*, May 25, 1984.
McPhee contributed to a small press publication produced on the occasion of the retirement of Deerfield Academy English teacher Robert McGlynn. McPhee was close to McGlynn when he was a student at Deerfield and afterward, often citing him as an inspiration.

McPhee recalls their first meeting in 1949, when he arrived at school two weeks after the term's start because of an injury. "Absolutely bewildered, I was standing on the dining room steps among a schoolful of strangers, when a man walked up to me said my name, and put out his hand," McPhee writes. "Words are the man . . . To be McGlynn's friend is to be given a share of his gift." Other contributors to the publication are Irish and American writers invited to speak at Deerfield by McGlynn during his more than 40 years at the school, including Seamus Heaney, Robert Creeley, Mary Lavin, and Richard Wilbur.

John McPhee, "Ten Great Science Museums: Liberty Science Center," *Discover* magazine, Nov. 1993, 95.
The Liberty Science Center opened in 1993 in Jersey City as New Jersey's first major science museum and *Discover* commissioned McPhee to review it. McPhee says his task is to be 10 years old again ("as the people I see at Thanksgiving are always ready to attest") and says his youth is "camouflaged by a gray beard." He describes his trip through the museum, describing many of the exhibits and attractions in elaborate detail. It was later included in *The Patch*.

John McPhee, "Warming the Jump Seat," *Deerfield Magazine*, Summer 1997, 20.
McPhee spent a postgraduate year at Deerfield Academy after graduating from Princeton High School and before attending Princeton University. "Deerfield Academy was my mother's idea," he writes. "Before I went to college, she wanted me out of town and more mature."

McPhee writes of developing a relationship with Headmaster Frank Boyden while at Deerfield. Boyden was also the head basketball coach. Diminutive in height but not in other ways, he rode to games with McPhee, the shortest starting player, on the fold-out jump seats of a Cadillac so others could stretch their legs. "He talked about his school," McPhee writes. "I was especially interested in what made Deerfield work, and what made Deerfield work was sitting on the other jump seat." More than 15 years later, as he started his career for *The New Yorker*, McPhee wrote about Boyden for the magazine and then developed the article into his second book, *The Headmaster*.

This article was written for a special issue of Deerfield's magazine to commemorate the school's bicentennial and was later collected in McPhee's book *Silk Parachute* (2010).

John McPhee, "Laura and Virginia," *Doubletake*, Summer 1998, 78.
McPhee describes the technique of two collaborating photographers, one his daughter Laura and the other Virginia Beahan, who use a large view camera together. "It is not unusual for Laura and Virginia to spend a whole working day driving, walking, looking for images, setting up the camera, fixing its lines with a carpenter's level, chattering under the cloth, making 'tilts and swings' and 'rises and falls,' and not exposing so much as one sheet of film. If they do all that on a given day and open the shutter once, they consider the day successful."

His essay was also an afterword in the book *No Ordinary Land* by Laura McPhee and Beahan, and it was republished as part of his *Silk Parachute*.

John McPhee, "The Ships of Port Revel," *The Atlantic*, Oct. 1998, 67.
McPhee writes about a ship-handling school on a pond in France in the foothills of the Alps that trains the skippers of large oceangoing vessels. It was later republished in his collection *Uncommon Carriers*.

John McPhee, "Nowheres," *New Jersey Monthly*, Dec. 2000, 1.
In this article, McPhee answers a travel writer who asked him why he chose to keep living in New Jersey. He ends with a line from Fred Brown, whom McPhee wrote about in *The Pine Barrens*: "I have never been nowheres I liked better than here." It was also published as the closing essay in the *Silk Parachute* collection.

John McPhee, "Passages: Farewell to the Archdruid," *Sierra*, Jan./Feb. 2001, 8.
McPhee first met the environmentalist David Brower, longtime director of the Sierra Club, in 1969. Brower was the leading figure in a series of *New Yorker* articles that became the book *Encounters with the Archdruid*. McPhee wrote this article, later also collected in McPhee's book *The Patch*, as a tribute to Brower, who had died in November 2000: "He began his mission when ecology connoted the root and shoot relationships of communal plants, and he, as much or more than anyone in the midcentury, expanded its reach and inherent power until it became the environmental movement."

John McPhee, "Designated Reader," *The Princeton Library Chronicle*, Autumn 2005, 157.

The prime reason McPhee often cited for moving from New York City back to Princeton with his wife and young daughters in the early 1960s was access to Princeton's Firestone Library. He had used it extensively as a Princeton undergraduate and knew that it would be an essential resource for the kind of fact-based writing he wanted to do. In this article he recalls how well it had worked out.

McPhee writes of using the library in between several long reporting trips to Alaska that eventually led to his bestselling *Coming into the Country*. "This great Alaskan base in the basement of a building in New Jersey," he recalls, and explains how the open stacks led him to discoveries of more and more useful books, often "a pile of books five feet high." He talks of how the library helped in years of projects, and how the growth of other Princeton University libraries increased the opportunities further.

John McPhee, "Swimming with Canoes," *Sierra Magazine*, May/June 2010, 34.

McPhee writes about his experiences at Keewaydin, the Vermont camp he attended for many summers and where his father was the camp doctor. This was first published in *The New Yorker* on August 10, 1998, and was also collected in *Silk Parachute*. McPhee tells of how he survived an overturned canoe. "Understand: I have a lifelong tendency to panic. Almost anything will panic me—health, money, working with words. Almost anything—I'm here to tell you—but an overturned canoe in a raging gorge."

John McPhee, "Writing a Strong Lead Is Half the Battle," *Wall Street Journal*, Dec. 18, 2010, C12.

Drawing from notes he used in his Princeton University writing seminar, McPhee wrote in the *Journal*'s Review section about the importance of the beginning to a piece of writing. "Writing a successful lead," he says, can "cause you to see the piece whole, to see it conceptually, in various parts, to which you then assign your materials. You find your lead, you build your structure, and you are now free to write." He adapted the article several years later in the "Structure" chapter of *Draft No. 4*.

John McPhee, "The Ignocene," *Orion*, Summer 2022, 29.
In honor of its 40th anniversary in 2022, *Orion*, a magazine focused on environmental and societal issues, asked 40 writers and 40 artists to respond to the question of when the Anthropocene—the age of time defined by man's imprint on Earth—began. McPhee was one of those invited and he responded with a poem called "The Ignocene," which was his first published poem in 70 years, since Princeton University's *Nassau Literary Review*. McPhee works into this poem a favorite Joseph Conrad passage—"vegetation rioted on the earth and the big trees were kings"—which he often used in a "greening" exercise to teach students about how to edit and condense based on what he had learned at *Time* magazine.

Time Magazine Book Reviews

"People say to me, 'Oh, you're so prolific.' God, it doesn't feel like it—nothing like it. But, you know, you put an ounce in a bucket each day, you get a quart."

—FROM "JOHN MCPHEE TROLLS THE WORLD, LANDS A SHAD" BY MARK FEENEY, BOSTON GLOBE, DECEMBER 11, 2002

Time magazine was the only place where John McPhee ever published book reviews. He, like many colleagues there, did them on a freelance basis, appreciating the extra income. His reviews are listed here.

Books, "The Purple-Prose Heart," Oct. 6, 1958, 92.
His first *Time* book review was of *Anatomy of Me*, by Fannie Hurst: "Fannie Hurst's literary career: her word power has somehow never quite kept pace with her lofty ambitions."

Books, "Grey Rides On—and On," Sept. 14, 1959, 103.
In a review of *Horse Heaven Hill*, by Zane Grey, McPhee pokes fun at one of a series of novels published under Grey's name after his death.

"Zane Grey published 44 novels while he lived. Horse Heaven Hill is No. 63 . . . the same message as all the rest on the writer's literary headstone: Here lies Zane Grey, a romantic dentist from Zanesville, Ohio, who went West as a young man. There he became a master at extracting the purple from the sage."

Books, "For Whom the Bell Tolls, Inc.," Oct. 6, 1961, 96.
Reviewing *The End of It*, an anti-war novel by Mitchell Goodman, McPhee says he "has produced an effective satire on the nature of the society that wages it."

Books, "Sophisticated Lady," Nov. 24, 1961, 82.
Reviewing *Scrap Irony*, by Felicia Lamport, a book of light poems and essays: "The pun also rises. Too much maligned as the lowest form of humor, it can soar for a brief moment. And in good hands, words can be made to jump, molt, wiggle, shrink, flash, collide, fight, strut, and turn themselves inside out or upside down." Also collected in *The Patch*.

Books, "Skits & Schizophrenia," Jan. 26, 1962, 96.
Reviewing *Captain Newman M.D.*, by Leo Rosten, a novel about a talented young army doctor working in a military psychiatric ward, McPhee says it is "a novel that suffers from cute appendicitis."

Books, "Heap o' Writin'," Apr. 27, 1962, 88.
Reviewing *A Simple, Honorable Man*, by Conrad Richter, McPhee calls it part of Richter's series of "quiet, honest novels."

Books, "This Swede," May 18, 1962, 96.
Reviewing *Jenny Lind, The Swedish Nightingale*, a biography of the Swedish opera singer, McPhee says, "Gladys Denny Schultz, author of this biography, once wrote advice to teen-agers in the *Ladies' Home Journal*, an experience that may account for the essence of nosegay that rises from too many passages in her book." Also collected in *The Patch*.

Books, "Rut: The California Trail," Dec. 28, 1962, 62.
Reviewing *The California Trail* by George R. Stewart, McPhee calls it "a proud and valuable book, researched with skill and a lifetime's attention."

Books, "Popular Science, 1805," Jan. 18, 1963, 88.
Reviewing Eric Sloane's *Diary of an American Boy* (also collected in *The Patch*), McPhee says, "Even without its fine studies of bygone craftsmanship, Sloane's book would be of value for its intimate picture of the life of American country people at the turn of the 19th century."

Books, "H Was for Halifax Then," Jan. 25, 1963, 86.
Reviewing *The Town That Died* by Michael J. Bird, about a huge 1917 explosion in the Canadian city of Halifax, McPhee writes, "During the fire and confusion of the aftermath, the horror was so intense that countless tragedies became mere anecdotes. . . . Author Michael Bird's research, according to Haligonians who survived the disaster, is accurate and well compiled."

Books, "Ace-High Straight," Feb. 28, 1964, 112.
Reviewing *The Cincinnati Kid*, McPhee writes, "Author Richard Jessup, a former merchant seaman from Savannah who once worked as a dealer in a gambling joint in Harlem, tells a cool, good story. His language is as spare as the language of the men he is writing about, but his work has the topography a novel needs."

Juvenilia

> "I think that young writers have to roll around like oranges on a conveyor belt. They have to try it all. If they are lucky, they'll fall into the right hole."
> —FROM "PROFILE: JOHN MCPHEE," BY MICHAEL PEARSON, CREATIVE NONFICTION, 1:1 (1993)

By the time John McPhee graduated from Princeton University in 1953, he had already published many pieces of writing, exploring a range of forms. Though he had been attracted to nonfiction when he saw *The*

FIGURE 24. McPhee (front row, second from left) was a member of Deerfield Academy's 1948–1949 varsity basketball team. He became close to the team's coach and the school's headmaster, Frank Boyden (standing behind McPhee), who became the subject of McPhee's 1966 book, *The Headmaster*. (Deerfield Academy Archives)

New Yorker while in grade school, McPhee spent high school and college experimenting with not only a wide variety of nonfiction, but also poetry and fiction.

As McPhee tried an assortment of kinds of writing, he also gravitated from a young age to many subjects that became the frequent topics of articles and later books by him as an adult writer, such as sports and the environment. This began in his earliest known writing, which were one-paragraph articles for his Princeton public elementary school "magazine" when he was seven, eight, and nine years old. Typical was an October 1938 piece on how to construct a canoe, where he gave instructions. Another time he wrote "One Afternoon" about an afternoon he spent on the Princeton University football field, where his father was the team physician for the university's sports teams.

Many writers start out working on their high school newspapers or yearbooks, but McPhee did not have that chance at Princeton

High School because of a strict tracking system. It reserved the newspaper and yearbook for students on the "commercial" track. McPhee was on the "academic" track, so he could not contribute to those publications.

Fortunately for his development as a writer, he had Olive McKee as his English teacher for three of his four years of high school. He has often described her class as one of his seminal writing experiences.

McKee was a great advocate of structure and planning in writing. She had her students do writing assignments three times a week. McPhee wrote in the essay "Structure" for *The New Yorker* (January 14, 2013, and collected in *Draft No. 4*): "We could write anything we wanted to, but each composition had to be accompanied by a structural outline, which she told us to do first. It could be anything from Roman numerals I, II, III to a looping doodle with guiding arrows and stick figures. The idea was to build some form of blueprint before working it out in sentences and paragraphs." As many McPhee readers (and his former students) know, it was a lesson that would stay with him always.

Beyond structure, McKee introduced her students to the practice of reading their works-in-progress aloud, and McPhee said that has helped him throughout his writing career, giving him a better sense of rhythm and word choice.

This section includes selected writing by McPhee through his graduation from Princeton University.

Deerfield Scroll

Deerfield Academy, where he spent a postgraduate year before entering Princeton, became McPhee's first formal opportunity to write for publication (beyond his childhood Keewaydin camp newspaper, where none of his writing has survived, and the story fragments he did in elementary school). He wrote several articles in the *Deerfield Scroll* that year (available through the school's archives). This writing shows many touches that would become familiar over time, such as word play and unusual word choice.

"Students Show Way to the Faculty in Overall Extra-curricular Encounters," by Johnny McPhee, *Deerfield Scroll*, Feb. 19, 1949, 3.
McPhee opens the article by saying, "Although the faculty currently enjoys a secure upper hand in the classroom, a mid-year glance at the results of the Student-Faculty competition of extracurricular nature reveals a strong trend favoring the abecedarians." He goes on to describe a number of tight student-faculty matches, including the "student shufflers" narrowly losing to the faculty in bridge, but edging ahead in chess by placing "five faculty kings in a most embarrassing position."

"Varsity Lacrosse Wins First Two Tilts with Ease," by John McPhee, *Deerfield Scroll*, Apr. 30, 1949, 4.
Covering a lacrosse match against Manhasset High School from Long Island, McPhee writes, "So the march began. Throughout the game a ceaseless procession of Deerfield scorers harried the Manhasset goal . . . The wide distribution of the scoring was a good sign to Coach Haviland, for it indicates a well balanced team." One of the scorers who McPhee mentioned was himself. He was a new player, learning the sport that would become a lifelong interest and lead to him to be the faculty fellow of the Princeton University men's lacrosse team.

At Princeton, McPhee wrote for four different publications. The first was the *Nassau Sovereign*, a monthly magazine started in 1938 by Malcolm Forbes when he was an undergraduate, before his business and publishing career. McPhee's writing in it came in the fall of 1950, close to when the *Sovereign* ceased publication.

Nassau Sovereign

"Kaz," by Johnny McPhee, *Nassau Sovereign*, Nov. 1950, 23. This issue of the *Nassau Sovereign* is only in a private collection.
McPhee, who had followed Princeton athletics, especially football, since he was a boy, had met and become friendly with Dick Kazmaier, a student in the class ahead of him. Kazmaier had a remarkable season

in 1949 (which would eventually lead to his winning the Heisman Trophy, college football's highest award, in 1951).

In the kind of profile that would become his forte, McPhee writes a detailed behind-the-scenes piece about what made Kazmaier so exceptional: "This methodical side of Dick Kazmaier is not confined to his Saturday afternoons on the gridiron, however, for he lives by a schedule. In an effort to escape the evils of 'goofing off,' he has tacked a sheet of paper to the wall of his room which bears the timetable of his weekly routine. It tells him when to study, when he can go to the movies, and when he must shut out the light and go to sleep." He then details Kazmaier's timed schedule for Friday, October 13, 1950, the day before Princeton's game against Navy, which Princeton won 20–14.

Nassau Literary Magazine

McPhee also contributed to the *Nassau Literary Magazine*, also known as *NassLit* and in recent years, *Nassau Literary Review*. It is the oldest student publication at Princeton, founded in 1842, and the second oldest undergraduate literary magazine in the country. Its issues are searchable through the Princeton University Library Papers of Princeton project (https://library.princeton.edu/collections/papers-princeton).

"Lest I Come," by John Angus McPhee, *The Nassau Literary Magazine*, Jan. 1952, 5.
This is a short horror story, about a man and a woman, full of tension. "Why did you bring me here?" she said. "Because a part of you has been here with me all along," he answered. "A part of you is in this little box." The story was also reprinted in the magazine's 1976 retrospective issue, and McPhee's work there was alongside previous *NassLit* contributors such as F. Scott Fitzgerald, Archibald MacLeish, Gertrude Stein, W. S. Merwin, Galway Kinnell, and Frank Stella.

"The Capital of the World," by John Angus McPhee, *The Nassau Literary Magazine*, May 1952, 6.
McPhee did not publish much poetry, and this poem along with two others of his in this issue are his last until the summer of 2022 (in *Orion*

magazine). In *NassLit*, McPhee's work was often in close proximity to that of George Garrett, Princeton class of 1952. McPhee and Garrett would go on to be friends for decades and Garrett won many awards for his poetry and novels and was poet laureate of Virginia. McPhee noted that this poem of his had the same title as a short story by Ernest Hemingway.

Princeton Alumni Weekly

In his senior year at Princeton, McPhee did his first professional paid writing as the "On the Campus" columnist for *Princeton Alumni Weekly* (PAW), which went to thousands of Princeton alumni. There was a competition for the columnist slot each year, and McPhee won it. His job was to bring a sense of campus life and news to alumni, and McPhee came to see it as an important chance to practice writing and have a distinct audience. He brought to the column a sharp reporter's eye, an appreciation of oddities, and a sense of humor. Here are selections from his columns that year. PAW issues for his year, from October 1952 to June 1953, are available digitally at https://library.princeton.edu/collections/papers-princeton.

"On the Campus," by John Angus McPhee '53, *Princeton Alumni Weekly*, Oct. 10, 1952, 11.
McPhee reports on the annual riots between freshmen and sophomores, and the new-style "dinks" worn by freshmen after they were given rough haircuts by sophomores: "It's not a hat, for sure; it's a *chapeau*, a Paris creation that looks something like a duffle bag. Black and bulgy, it has the orange numerals '56' set against a white background above the visor. It replaces the crew caps introduced by the present senior class and skull caps of earlier years."

"On the Campus," by John Angus McPhee '53, *Princeton Alumni Weekly*, Oct. 17, 1952, 13.
Under the headline "Zealous Island," McPhee writes of the 11-day ordeal of a Princeton undergraduate whose trip to school from Columbia in South America was sidetracked when he was held at Ellis Island because of his political views supporting the admission of Communist China to

the United Nations. Another item, "Imminent Ptomaine," was about the hot dog vendors of Nassau Street being shut down by the town's Board of Health.

"On the Campus," by John Angus McPhee '53, *Princeton Alumni Weekly*, Nov. 21, 1952, 10.
McPhee chronicles the hijinks between Harvard and Princeton students on a football weekend. He reported on a "superb" hoax issue of *The Daily Princetonian* engineered by *The Harvard Crimson*. "At first, second, and third glances, it looked genuine. Every item was obviously the result of careful scouting," he writes, and among other things, it falsely convinced at least one Princeton student that a math midterm had been postponed, leading him to miss the test. "Donkey Serenade" told of the 100-piece Harvard band waking up the Princeton campus at 6 a.m. on game day, but also being doused by water and trash.

"On the Campus," by John Angus McPhee '53, *Princeton Alumni Weekly*, Nov. 28, 1952, 11.
Reporting on an altercation that took place after a football win over Yale, where undergraduates stopped the ringing of the bell atop Nassau Hall, McPhee says it was part of a broader malady: "This attitude, this false sophistication, this apathy for Princeton's past is devitalizing the University and depriving it of its character."

"On the Campus," by John Angus McPhee '53, *Princeton Alumni Weekly*, Mar. 20, 1953, 21.
In "Flying Tiger," McPhee tells of a freshman ("wearing a red cashmere sweater, khaki pants and white buckskin shoes") who flew a small plane from Princeton headed for a date in Holyoke, Massachusetts. But he got lost and ran out of fuel, prompting an emergency landing in a cornfield in New Hampshire and front-page coverage in many newspapers.

"On the Campus," by John Angus McPhee '53, *Princeton Alumni Weekly*, Apr. 17, 1953, 13.
"Bicker," the long-standing selective process at Princeton by which students apply to private "eating clubs" for their junior and senior years,

caused controversy. "Bicker talk all but monopolized campus conversation for two weeks," McPhee writes. Efforts were being made to make sure all students had a bid from some club and that was seen as conflicting with a selective process. Stories in the *Daily Princetonian* had jumped to the national stage with an article in *Time* magazine: "As the local storm was abating, *Time* printed its *coup* and revived the furor . . . Concerning the Bicker itself, the campus is generally agreed that it needs revision."

"On the Campus," by John Angus McPhee '53, *Princeton Alumni Weekly*, May 1, 1953, 11.
McPhee reports on one of Princeton's traditions, "The Spring Riot," that every year seemed to be ignited by a different particular cause when trees bloom. This year's spark, reports McPhee, was when "a group of opportunists calling themselves 'The Friends of Joe Sugar' took advantage of Princeton's first blanket of warm air and incited a small furor designed to publicize the name of Joseph A. Sugar Jr. '54. Sugar is his friends' candidate for president of next year's senior class." Then about 800 students marched through town, also complaining about too-tight liquor laws, until a dean told them to "Knock it off!—and with that the Sugar riot dissolved."

But the wrangling wasn't over. In the days that followed, sugar lumps marked "Joe" were given away on campus and a building was decorated with his name in whitewash. And the world outside Princeton took notice, including *The New Yorker*. In its May 16 issue, a "Talk of the Town" piece ("Joe Sugar") looked at the riots and Sugar (who was elected vice president of his class). A decade later, McPhee would become a *New Yorker* colleague of the two writers who did the story, Philip Hamburger and John Brooks.

"On the Campus," by John Angus McPhee '53, *Princeton Alumni Weekly*, May 15, 1953, 11.
More student riots occurred, the second of the spring, and there was no humor this time. McPhee describes the wanderings of 1,000 undergraduates for hours in downtown Princeton, including the property damage caused and the traffic blocked, and then the students arrested, expelled,

or suspended. "Among the many unfortunate results of the riot was the treatment it was given by newspapers across the country," McPhee wrote, saying that some papers turned the riot into things it wasn't, like that it was all about sex. "Princeton received a quantity of bad national publicity, only a part of which was deserved."

The Princeton Tiger

The student publication where McPhee spent the most time and had the largest impact was *The Princeton Tiger*. First published in 1882, it was the third-oldest collegiate humor magazine in the United States. McPhee was first listed on the masthead as a staff member in the issue of April 1, 1951, the same issue when his first article, "Her Sons Will Give," appeared. By March 1952 he became the managing editor and was the leader of a transformation of the magazine. McPhee believed the magazine had become stale and stuck, and he modeled a revised version along the lines of his favorite publication, *The New Yorker*.

In *Roaring at One Hundred*, a 1983 book assessing the *Tiger* at 100 years old, McPhee is called "one of the most talented writers in The Tiger's first century" and the leader of the change to a more general magazine. "And so whatever sexual tidbits remained [there had been many, especially in cartoons] in The Tiger were expunged." The magazine is available through the Princeton University Archives.

"Her Sons Will Give," *The Princeton Tiger*, Apr. 1, 1951, 12.
A satirical, fantastical short story about the perfect roommate at Princeton: Sydney, a woman at all-male Princeton, living a secret life. The title is a reference to a lyric in "Old Nassau," Princeton's alma mater: "Her sons shall give" (after coeducation updated to "Our hearts will give"). This story by McPhee is one of the longest pieces reprinted in the 1983 centennial book about *The Princeton Tiger*.

"Dark Cloud," *The Princeton Tiger*, Mar. 26, 1952, 1.
This was McPhee's cri de coeur as the new editor of the magazine: "It has been suggested that college humor is dead. One observer noted that it was decaying. Another said that campus talent was passe. A third

claimed that raw sex had become the common denominator of successful college humor magazines... But most voices were silent—indifferent. The Tiger heard the silence, and because of it, we have changed our magazine. Some publications may be printed for the exclusive benefit of their contributor, but this one isn't."

"The new Tiger is a campus magazine," McPhee continues. "It is concerned with all things relevant to Princeton." The table of contents on the next page suggested a considerably different magazine from the past, including an article by Heisman Trophy winner and McPhee roommate Dick Kazmaier about "Pro Football's Value" (he had decided to spurn the Chicago Bears in favor of Harvard Business School), a short story by Princeton resident and *New Yorker* contributor John O'Hara (McPhee knew he lived in town and asked him for a story to publish), a story about an undergraduate who created stained glass pieces, and an article about the creative writing course of Richard Blackmur, a distinguished poet and literary critic on the Princeton faculty.

"Prutgers," *The Princeton Tiger*, May 9, 1952, 1.
An issue that aggravated McPhee and others was the university's decision to stop having janitors tidy up student rooms. He editorializes: "Eighty per-cent of Princeton's undergraduates favored the proposed optional janitor service which the Trustees crucified with dispatch... The university's constricting budget is nothing but an excuse. Actually, our governors are simply continuing a trend toward social equilibrium, a trend which (they feel) is best for Princeton. This Gilded Cage of ours is being stripped of its bars, one by one... Eventually, Princeton will be freed of all its Utopianism... it will no longer be Princeton, but good ole New Jersey State."

"On the House," *The Princeton Tiger*, Oct. 23, 1952, 2.
As Election Day approached in 1952, McPhee writes in an editorial: "*The Tiger* has received many letters advising that we 'take up the cudgel' for the 'great cause' and 'make use of the golden opportunity' that is yours as a Princeton publication" and support Adlai Stevenson, Princeton class of 1922. 'You must rise up,' said one writer, 'and acknowledge the fact that a great Princetonian, a great American, is about to become a

great President!!!' We prefer to take that one lying down . . . We are, of course, neutral. May the bald man win."

"Phi Beta Football," *The Princeton Tiger*, Oct. 23, 1952, 12.
McPhee writes an article about the sophisticated grading system that the Princeton football coach and his staff use to evaluate and improve player performance. McPhee would write a different version of this story a year later in the *Newark Sunday News* (October 4, 1953, 20). And this was the first of four times he used this headline for different stories (also the *Newark Sunday News, Time,* and *The New Yorker*).

"Spaeth on Princeton," *The Princeton Tiger*, Mar. 6, 1953, 11.
Soon before graduation and after he had stepped down as editor of the *Tiger*, McPhee wrote a profile for the *Tiger* about Sigmund Spaeth, a musicologist known for his efforts to popularize classical music. McPhee sees him as a chance to illuminate Princeton history: "Sigmund Spaeth's mind contains a wine cellar of Princetoniana, vintage 1906," the date he came to Princeton for a brief stint teaching German. He gets Spaeth to talk about various aspects of Princeton history, from the alma mater originally being sung to the melody of "Auld Lang Syne," to the eating clubs, to the epic battles that Woodrow Wilson got into as Princeton's president. Spaeth was temporarily in a New York hospital when McPhee interviewed him, and McPhee appears with Spaeth in the hospital room photo.

Also while at Princeton, McPhee was a panelist for *Twenty Questions*, a game show that was on radio and then national television. The show was created by Fred and Florence Van Deventer, a Princeton couple whose son was on the panel until he went away to college and was replaced by McPhee, whom they knew. Panelists, which sometimes included celebrity guests, tried to guess an animal, vegetable, or mineral subject in 20 questions.

Copies of only a few *Twenty Questions* shows have survived. A recording of a telecast from February 8, 1952, that included McPhee is available online: "20 Questions Game Show from the 1950's," videoarchives1000 on YouTube: https://www.youtube.com/watch?v=gVGfOTOqRG4.

Television Screenplays

"A thousand details add up to one impression."

—FROM "THE WORD MAN OF PRINCETON"
BY JOEL ACHENBACH, *PRINCETON ALUMNI WEEKLY*, NOVEMBER 12, 2014

When John McPhee came back to the United States in 1954 after a year of post-Princeton study at the University of Cambridge, he was searching for the next step in his writing. It turned out to be television screenplays, and he had a good connection for it.

McPhee's older brother, H. Roemer McPhee, who was working at the time in the White House for President Dwight D. Eisenhower, knew one of the leading TV producers of the time: Robert Montgomery. Montgomery was an unpaid advisor to Eisenhower to help on his TV appearances and he had an office in the White House. Roemer introduced his brother to Montgomery, who was the producer and on-air host of a well-regarded show on NBC, *Robert Montgomery Presents*. Montgomery's reputation in Hollywood, where he had been an actor, buoyed the Emmy-winning television show and persuaded many top actors to appear on it.

The mid-1950s were a golden age for the new medium of television, marked by a large number of live dramatic productions and creating many opportunities for writers to adapt material. Montgomery gave McPhee access to the set of the show to see how the process worked. The location was one of NBC's premier stages, Studio 8H, at 30 Rockefeller Plaza, more recently known as the set for *Saturday Night Live* since that show began in 1975.

Starting in the summer of 1955, McPhee for months watched rehearsals and studied the craft of screenplay writing. He eventually wrote five prospective episodes for the show, including two that were bought and produced, both adaptations of short stories by Robert M. Coates in *The New Yorker*, where McPhee ultimately wanted to work. Coates was a novelist, short story writer, and art critic, and in his 40 years of writing for the magazine, more than 100 of his short stories were published.

The first of the episodes based on a McPhee screenplay was "In a Foreign City," which aired October 31, 1955 (the Coates story was published in *The New Yorker* on May 14, 1955, and is collected in Coates's 1957 book, *The Hour After Westerly*). An out-of-work advertising executive's evening of too many drinks at the Princeton Club in New York (though Coates had graduated from Yale) turns into a nightmare on the streets of a city he ceases to recognize. He impulsively tries to rob a man on the street, is arrested, and then escapes.

The second McPhee episode, "The Man Who Vanished," was broadcast February 13, 1956. The Coates story on which it was based was published in *The New Yorker* on October 22, 1955, and is in the same *The Hour After Westerly* collection.

The scripts for the two produced screenplays are part of the Steven H. Scheuer Collection at Yale University's Beinecke Rare Book and Manuscript Library, which includes approximately 5,000 American television scripts dating from about 1953 to 1963.

No remaining copies of the televised version of "In a Foreign City" have been found. In the 1950s, archival practices for television programs were primitive and copies of many were taped over and otherwise lost.

However, a copy of "The Man Who Vanished" is in the collection of the UCLA Film & Television Archive and can be seen in person.

The 50-minute program starts with McPhee's credit for the "teleplay." Montgomery, as the host, reminds viewers that they had recently seen another episode written by McPhee, referring to "In a Foreign City." Montgomery says of "The Man Who Vanished," "Tonight's play is an imaginative comedy, which I think television sees far too little."

As in the original short story, the character Charlie Ballantine is central to the McPhee-adapted story. He is a seemingly normal businessman who suddenly finds himself becoming physically dim or even vanishing in the eyes of his wife, friends, and business associates. It seems that when his mind wanders, he fades out. Ballantine is played by Gene Rayburn, an accomplished Broadway and television actor who later became a successful game show host (and who donated the copy of the program to the archive).

The McPhee episode is a dramatic reimagining of Coates's story, changing the sequence significantly and building in many new characters and scenes. McPhee gives the story many new comedic touches but also makes it more of a psychological drama. One of the parts most developed by McPhee is about the fictional Cooley Clinic in Baltimore, where Ballantine goes to have his unusual condition studied. In Coates's story, the description of the clinic is sketched without great depth. McPhee spent hours talking with friends going to medical school in New York, brainstorming what that clinic and its examinations might be like. In the *Robert Montgomery Presents* version, it becomes an elaborate journey through various medical departments and the climax is when the psychiatrist, Dr. Pierce—a character McPhee invented—presents his hypothesis to his colleagues.

Dr. Pierce describes Ballantine as middle-aged and with a dull job and marriage. Speaking like a lawyer to a jury in closing arguments, he says:

> His [Ballantine's] day has obviously become a journey along the tightrope of his own frail ego with an abyss of what practically amounts to oblivion on either side.
>
> I ask you to consider, have I described anything that is unusual?
>
> I have described as well as I am able what I believe to be the essential Mr. Ballantine. Now the rest, the disappearance phenomenon with which we have been concerned, seems to be secondary and superficial.
>
> After all, when a man merely moves from a dull home to a dull office roundtrip, day after day, doesn't he figuratively or metaphorically lose his identity a bit, doesn't he in a sense disappear?
>
> Now I suggest that this is what has happened or is happening to Mr. Ballantine, particularly in his moments of dimming, fading, vanishing. He wants to escape from everything. Where to? To the past, of course. To hope again. He is an escapist, almost per se.

McPhee was impressed by the ambition of the Montgomery show, with top-flight actors and directors and expensive sets that would be used once and then destroyed. However, he did not like that when he finished his screenplay, the actors, directors, and others would then have their turn at making the final show out of it. "I wanted to make the whole shoe," he says ("John McPhee, The Art of Nonfiction No. 3," *The Paris Review*, Spring 2010, 48).

Fiction

"You are you and you consist of countless components. In your writing, all of that is going to produce something nobody else is ever going to write in that way."

—FROM AN INTERVIEW WITH JOHN MCPHEE BY JAMIE SAXON, PRINCETON UNIVERSITY OFFICE OF COMMUNICATIONS, SEPTEMBER 18, 2017

In addition to the many nonfiction newspaper and magazine articles that John McPhee wrote in high school and college, he also wrote poetry and fiction as an undergraduate (see "Juvenilia"). Ever pushing boundaries, he wrote his senior thesis in the unconventional form of a novel, titled *Skimmer Burns*.

His novel was not published and seventy years later, in the May 20, 2024, *New Yorker*, McPhee wrote about having sent it to several top New York publishers and receiving no interest. Later, he even wrote to publishing giant Alfred A. Knopf himself, seeking advice. Knopf wrote back, saying his company did not release internal correspondence, adding, "The readers' reports in the case of your manuscript would not be very helpful, and I think might discourage you completely."

McPhee had more success with some short fiction after college, writing and publishing three pieces of fiction in the 1960s. McPhee believed that young writers should experiment with different forms to find the best niche.

McPhee published his last short story in 1968, after which he decided to focus on nonfiction exclusively.

"The Fair of San Gennaro." *Transatlantic Review*, Winter 1961, 117. London: Transatlantic Review.
Also reprinted in *Stories from the Transatlantic Review*, edited by Joseph F. McCrindle. Middlesex, England: Penguin Books, 1974, 307.

This story, McPhee's first published fiction since his college years, appeared in *Transatlantic Review*, a literary magazine published quarterly in London and New York by Joseph McCrindle, an art collector and philanthropist. Contributors included prominent authors such as Samuel Beckett, Iris Murdoch, and John Updike, as well as young writers like McPhee with few or no fiction publication credits.

McPhee's story is about a young woman emerging from the New York City subway near a street fair in Little Italy, modeled on the annual San Gennaro festival that McPhee regularly attended when he lived in New York City. She is accosted by a man who threatens her with a knife and turns out to be a fugitive. As McPhee draws a vibrant portrait of the street life in and around the fair, the woman calmly and cleverly works to try to take control of the situation, building to a surprising ending.

"Eucalyptus Trees." *The Reporter*, Oct. 19, 1967, 36.
The Reporter was a biweekly news and literary magazine published in New York City from 1949 to 1968. It was the fourth largest American news magazine behind *Time*, *Newsweek*, and *U.S. News & World Report*. Known as a liberal, activist magazine, it eventually merged with *Harper's*.

In McPhee's story, Allan Gibbons works in the Industrial Development department of a company in New York City. Time, and specifically the schedule of his commuter train to and from New Jersey, is the source of much concern in his life—he is 30 and has three children. (McPhee was in his thirties when he wrote this story, had four children, and lived and often commuted from New Jersey.) McPhee makes the stress palpable. For a project about making paper for industrial and commercial purposes, Gibbons learns much about eucalyptus trees and yearns to go abroad to learn more. He finds himself up against establishment forces in his effort to get a transfer.

"Ruth, the Sun Is Shining." *Playboy*, Apr. 1968, 114.
Playboy magazine was a prestigious and well-paying publisher of fiction. Others who published stories in the magazine through the years included Vladimir Nabokov, James Baldwin, Doris Lessing, John Updike, Joyce Carol Oates, and Stephen King.

In this story, McPhee paints the scene of a husband and wife together on a small powerboat, traveling on a group of lakes in Florida. The tension in the boat between them is mirrored by the sky as an intense thunderstorm approaches. The wife is full of worries, while the husband keeps trying to reassure her by saying, "Ruth, the sun is shining."

PART II

Works about John McPhee

4

Articles

"If you invent 'facts' and sell them as nonfiction, you are a charlatan."

—FROM "JOHN MCPHEE—GIVING 'NONFICTION'
A GOOD NAME," BY STEWART DILL MCBRIDE,
CHRISTIAN SCIENCE MONITOR, SEPTEMBER 19, 1978

ASIDE FROM a modest number of book reviews, few articles were written about John McPhee before 1976. After the publication of *The John McPhee Reader* and then the bestselling *Coming into the Country*, however, he received a wave of attention, including profiles in many of the country's top publications.

Yet in the 1980s, 1990s, and into the 2000s, the number of articles about McPhee again became smaller as McPhee focused on continuing his research and writing and was reluctant to do much publicity for his books. He was unusual in declining to ever have a photo on his dust jackets, and he politely turned down many opportunities to be interviewed.

Since the start of the 2010s, the number of articles on him rose again as McPhee, with his travel for research subsiding, accepted more publicity requests. Many publications saw *Draft No. 4*, *The Patch*, and *Tabula Rasa: Volume 1* as fitting chances to assess his career.

This is a selective guide to significant articles about McPhee and his work, including a description of the subjects covered in them.

FIGURE 25. McPhee, shown camping on a gravel bar in Alaska, conducted much of his research in the wilderness for what became *Coming into the Country*. (Brad Snow and Lilly Allen Collection, Alaska and Polar Regions Collections, University of Alaska Fairbanks)

Israel Shenker, "The Annals of McPhee," *New York Times,* Jan. 11, 1976, New Jersey section, 20.
Shenker, a former colleague of McPhee's at *Time* magazine who became a scholarly, stylish writer at *The New York Times,* wrote one of the first profiles of McPhee, appearing in the paper's Sunday New Jersey section. He recounted McPhee's long quest to work for *The New Yorker* and how he became "a star of the first magnitude. He is superb at casting life into new perspectives. Flair, ingenuity, style, a fresh eye—all are there."

Ann Waldron, "Grinding Out Perfection," *The Philadelphia Inquirer Today* (Sunday magazine), July 11, 1976, 20.
"McPhee is, in a way, a writer's writer," says Waldron, former book editor of the *Houston Chronicle*. Her article focuses on his process in drafting his books.

Edmund Fuller, "John McPhee: Dripping It Out," *Wall Street Journal*, Nov. 30, 1977, 14.
Fuller, the *Wall Street Journal* chief book critic, visited McPhee in Princeton. Noting his "boundlessly diversified range of curiosity," he reviews McPhee's recent success with *Coming into the Country* and how he achieved it: "He craves a way to produce a truly enormous amount—fast, but it comes back to 'dripping it out.'"

Jeannette Smyth, "John McPhee of *The New Yorker*," *Washington Post*, Mar. 19, 1978, L1.
The lede: "A solitary man, McPhee. He is the best journalist in America." This Style section article profiles McPhee near the peak of the success of *Coming into the Country* and looks at his personality: "McPhee very much fits the old 'Front Page' ideal of reporting as shoe leather, guts, luck and an endless pedant's grind of information-gathering."

Art Carey, "Good at What 'Only a Nut' Does," *The Philadelphia Inquirer*, June 15, 1978, D1.
Starting with a description of McPhee wearing a "garish, orange-and-black, tiger-motif" sports jacket for his recent 25th reunion at Princeton, the writer talks about McPhee's modesty in light of his bestselling success with *Coming into the Country*. "I've been amazed, amused, flabbergasted, pleased and surprised by it," McPhee says.

Stewart Dill McBride, "John McPhee—Giving 'Nonfiction' a Good Name," *Christian Science Monitor*, Sept. 19, 1978, B6.
The focus is on McPhee's inventions in nonfiction: "Mr. McPhee has proved that reportage can be art, that facts can deliver more than information, and that real characters can live on a page as vividly as fictitious ones." The profile also includes one of the first extended descriptions of the Princeton University writing seminar McPhee began teaching in 1975.

One of the largest controversies involving McPhee's writing involved his February 19, 1979, profile in *The New Yorker*, "Brigade de Cuisine" (later collected in his *Giving Good Weight* book). McPhee wrote about the artistry of a master chef who, in a small restaurant outside New York City, made many of the best meals McPhee had ever eaten.

There were two flash points. First, McPhee and *The New Yorker* allowed the publicity-shy chef to be anonymous with the pseudonym of "Otto" and for the name and location of the restaurant to be undisclosed. The magazine bent its usual rules and allowed the fact-checking to be done primarily by McPhee and not in detail by the magazine's usual fact-checkers. Second, chef Otto suggested that frozen fish was served at the legendary French restaurant Lutèce in New York City. It was a claim that Lutèce's chef/owner, Andre Soltner, said was false, and which McPhee and the magazine later corrected.

McPhee's story set off a frantic race in the press to identify Otto and the restaurant. Within several days, the restaurant critic for *The New York Times* and its wine writer solved the mystery and panned the restaurant and chef (Mimi Sheraton and Frank J. Prial, "'Otto' Tracked Down in Pennsylvania," *The New York Times*, February 24, 1979, 18).

The story reverberated for a long time across the U.S., showing the reach of McPhee and *The New Yorker*. Bob Greene, a syndicated columnist based in Chicago, recounts McPhee's story and says that the chef was the victim of "the sensation of the New York media community" and "a feeding frenzy." Bob Greene, ("A 'Hydrogen Bomb' Falls, and a Little Guy Loses His Solitude and His Will," *Los Angeles Times*, March 9, 1979, C7).

Melvin Maddocks, longtime editor and writer for *The Christian Science Monitor*, said McPhee was an "elegist" and "Mr. McPhee found in Otto the perfect metaphor for the writer. He perceives Otto, not as a chef but as a fellow artist, patiently gathering ingredients as a reporter assembles facts, searching out the one appropriate seasoning as a writer looks for the *mot juste*, then adding everything—flavor, texture, aroma, appearance—for one capping effect" (Melvin Maddocks, "Otto— Chewy Snails or a Legend in His Thyme?," *The Christian Science Monitor*, March 12, 1979, 26).

David W. McCullough, *People, Books & Book People*. New York: Harmony Books, 1981, 119.
McCullough was an editor for the Book-of-the-Month Club and interviewed prominent authors for many years. This book includes McCullough's conversations with McPhee and more than 90 other writers. Drawn from a 1976 visit to McPhee's office that McCullough says has "a nice sense of academic clutter," McPhee talks about his work on "Oranges," "The Survival of the Bark Canoe," and his process with *The New Yorker*.

William Safire, "Hide That Agenda," *New York Times*, Sept. 16, 1984, Sunday Magazine, 18.
For 30 years, William Safire wrote a weekly language column in *The New York Times Magazine*. This installment was mostly about McPhee's use of the words "agenda" and "hidden addendum" in the same article, which was "Heirs of General Practice" in *The New Yorker* on July 23, 1984.

Bob Sipchen, "Mountains from Molehills: Speck by Speck, Writer John McPhee Compiles Scary Tale of L.A.'s Slippery Geology," *Los Angeles Times*, Aug. 6, 1989, J1.
The article is about McPhee's research in Los Angeles that contributed to his *New Yorker* article and book on *The Control of Nature*: "He came as 'a foreign correspondent,' here to cover with a fresh eye the theme he examines in each of three sections in his new book: the battle between humanity and nature."

David W. Chapman, "Forming and Meaning: Writing the Counterpoint Essay," *Journal of Advanced Composition*, Winter 1991, 73.
A rhetorical analysis of McPhee's September 9, 1972, *New Yorker* article "The Search for Marvin Gardens," about Atlantic City (collected in his book *Pieces of the Frame*) as a "counterpoint essay." McPhee's article combines an account of a Monopoly game with descriptions of actual locations made famous by the game. Chapman, an English professor at Samford University in Alabama, wrote, "The counterpoint structure

forced students to look for a purpose in the essay—not a stated thesis, but one implied by the form itself."

Douglas Vipond and Russell A. Hunt, "The Strange Case of the Queen-Post Truss: John McPhee on Writing and Reading," *College Composition and Communication*, May 1991, 200.
The authors, professors at St. Thomas University in New Brunswick, Canada, do a close examination of specific writing choices McPhee made in his *New Yorker* article "In Virgin Forest," published July 6, 1987, and collected in *Irons in the Fire*. They also interview McPhee about his writing and discuss the term "queen-post trusses" that appeared in the piece.

Michael Kowalewski, ed., *Temperamental Journeys: Essays on the Modern Literature of Travel*. Athens: University of Georgia Press, 1992.
McPhee is the subject of a chapter in this anthology, "The Wilds of New Jersey: John McPhee as Travel Writer" (164) by David Espey, a professor at the University of Pennsylvania, about how much of McPhee's work involves travel, and whether he qualifies a travel writer. "A century after Thoreau, McPhee accurately exemplifies Thoreau's notion of the ideal traveler," Espey writes.

Michael Pearson, "Twenty Questions: A Conversation with John McPhee," *Creative Nonfiction*, No. 6, The Essayist at Work, 1996, 103.
Pearson, an English professor at Old Dominion University who published a biographical study of McPhee in 1997, spends a day with McPhee in Princeton discussing his writing process (McPhee says he does occasional tape recording when handwritten notes won't work), his reading of reviews ("I read them ... But I can't say that I've read anything in a review that caused a great swerve in my writing"), and how he views himself as a writer ("I'm not one of the new journalists. I'm an old journalist. I have some sympathy for the term 'creative nonfiction,' however ... It's an attempt to recognize something, that a piece of writing can be creative while using factual materials, that creative work can respect fact").

Norman Sims, "John McPhee," *Dictionary of Literary Biography, American Literary Journalists*. Detroit: Gale Research, 1997.
In a thorough narrative about McPhee's writing career from his youth through his twenty-third book, *The Ransom of Russian Art* in 1994, Sims writes, "McPhee proves the value of 'ordinary life' in literary journalism, but his writing techniques and style are far from ordinary."

Dan Cryer, "The Unmistakable John McPhee," *Newsday*, June 2, 1997, B4.
Cryer, *Newsday*'s book critic, visits with McPhee after the publication of *Irons in the Fire* and writes about the process that creates "immaculate prose that makes the name McPhee synonymous with intelligence and grace."

Lee Gutkind, "From the Editor: Anatomy of 'An Album Quilt' Excerpt," No. 8, *Mostly Memoir*, 1997, 1.
The head of the new Creative Nonfiction organization and journal recalls McPhee's participation in a summer writers conference and gives a preview of McPhee's "An Album Quilt."

Mark Feeney, "John McPhee Trolls the World, Lands a Shad," *Boston Globe*, Dec. 11, 2002, C1.
On the publication of *The Founding Fish*, Feeney writes about McPhee's first book since winning the Pulitzer Prize: "McPhee's geological undertaking, ultimately comprising five books, marginalized him to a degree ... Yet at the same time, the geology books are his greatest achievement."

Norman Sims, "'Essence of Writer': John McPhee's Early Training," a chapter in *Coming into McPhee Country: John McPhee and the Art of Literary Nonfiction*, edited by O. Alan Weltzien and Susan N. Maher, University of Utah Press, 2003.
Sims, who wrote several essays about McPhee, takes a detailed and insightful look at his development as a writer from a young age: "His literary journalism depends on the creation of a distinctive voice and an

effective architecture, qualities that enliven our interest no matter what subject McPhee takes on."

Peter Kaminsky, "First, You Have to Catch the Fish," *New York Times*, May 14, 2003, F1.
McPhee's *The Founding Fish* lands on the cover of *The New York Times* food section. Kaminsky, a food writer and outdoors columnist for the paper, goes shad fishing on the Delaware River with McPhee and Ed Cervone, a fishing friend of McPhee's, and then has a meal of the day's catch cooked by Cervone's wife, Marian.

Candace Braun, "Princeton Author John McPhee's Book Chosen as Book of the Year for N.J.," Jan. 28, 2004.
The Pine Barrens, published 36 years earlier, is named a "One Book New Jersey" book of the year, in libraries and other educational forums around the state. "John McPhee's *The Pine Barrens* is one of the very few examples I know of a book that is not only a joy to read, but is also a work of art that made a real difference in the real world," says Carleton Montgomery, executive director of the Pinelands Preservation Alliance.

Robert S. Boynton, *The New New Journalism: Conversations with America's Best Nonfiction Writers on Their Craft*. New York: Vintage Books, 2005.
McPhee is not interviewed in this collection but is a large presence in the book, starting with him being mentioned in the introduction. Then his influence is discussed by writer Susan Orlean, a *New Yorker* colleague, and especially by two former Princeton students of his, Richard Preston and Eric Schlosser, who says of McPhee, "I wouldn't have been a writer without him."

Howard Berkes, "The 'Unreadable' Thing: John McPhee on the Craft of Writing," National Public Radio, Nov. 15, 2006, Society for Environmental Journalists, https://www.sej.org/publications/journalismmedia/the-unreadable-thing-john-mcphee-on-the-craft-of-writing.

Berkes, NPR's rural affairs correspondent, visits McPhee after publication of *Uncommon Carriers*. "McPhee is now 75 and I wonder how many words and characters he has left in him. I try to figure out a polite way to ask about the stories and books to come," Berkes writes. McPhee replies, "I'm not going to stop doing this. I'm just trying to figure out what I'm going to do next. Y'know, you always start with a small thing and see where it grows."

George Vecsey, "Observing a Lacrosse Pioneer, McPhee Style," *New York Times*, May 26, 2011, B15.
The sports columnist George Vecsey writes about the pioneering lacrosse coach Bill Tierney, who left his successful career at Princeton to go to the University of Denver—from the point of view of McPhee, a friend of Tierney's and the faculty fellow for the Princeton men's lacrosse team.

Touré, "Tennis by the Book," *New York Times Book Review*, July 1, 2011, 27.
In a fanciful piece about "this year's Intertemporal Tennis Writer's Classic," author Touré tells how McPhee and his "Levels of the Game" fared against competition that included Red Smith, Vladimir Nabokov, and David Foster Wallace.

Adam Hochschild, "Why's This So Good?," No. 61: John McPhee and the Archdruid, Nieman Storyboard, Oct. 2, 2012, https://niemanstoryboard.org/stories/whys-this-so-good-no-61-john-mcphee-and-the-archdruid/.
This story also appears as the chapter "A Literary Engineer" in *Lessons from a Dark Time and Other Essays* (Berkeley: University of California Press, 2018), 224.

Hochschild assesses McPhee's work, particularly in *Encounters with the Archdruid*. Compared to "new journalists" of the 1960s and 1970s, such as Tom Wolfe, Gay Talese, and Hunter Thompson, Hochschild writes, "More lasting, I think a grand pointillist mural of our time and place, as expressed in the lives of an encyclopedic range of people, will be the work of John McPhee."

Martha McPhee, "Run, Daddy, Run," Martha McPhee website, Jan. 7, 2013, https://marthamcphee.com/2013/01/07/run-daddy-run/.
The novelist and English professor Martha McPhee, John McPhee's youngest child, writes about the family trip in 1967 to England, Scotland, and Spain that made travelers of her and her sisters.

James Osborne, "A Long Pinelands Trek," *Philadelphia Inquirer*, Mar. 4, 2013, B1.
In a panel discussion, two former New Jersey governors and environmental activists assess the role of McPhee, his *New Yorker* articles, and his book *The Pine Barrens* in the preservation of more than a million wilderness acres in New Jersey.

William Fiennes, "A Classic of Tennis Writing," *The Guardian*, June 28, 2014, https://www.theguardian.com/books/2014/jun/28/john-mcphee-levels-game-more-great-sportswriting-tennis-william-fiennes.
"John McPhee's book about the 1968 US Open semi-final is a thrilling nonfiction adventure in which tenses and sentences are the star players," William Fiennes writes in the *Guardian*. Fiennes assesses McPhee's work of 45 years earlier, in *Levels of the Game*, focusing on the strength of McPhee's writing and structure.

Issues in Science and Technology, "Imagining Deep Time," National Academy of Sciences, Fall 2014, https://issues.org/imagining-deep-time/.
The concept of "deep time" connected to geology, of time on a scale far beyond human experience, was introduced in the eighteenth century; however, the term wasn't coined until McPhee used it in the 1980s in *Basin and Range*. One of the outgrowths of McPhee's use of the term was an exhibition from August 2014 to January 2015 at the National Academy of Sciences in Washington, DC, which referenced McPhee's invention of the phrase.

Joel Achenbach, "The Word Man of Princeton: Writer, Mentor, Professor for Life," *Princeton Alumni Weekly*, Nov. 12, 2014, 1.
Joel Achenbach, a former student of McPhee's who covers science and politics for *The Washington Post*, writes about the impact of McPhee's

long-running student seminar at Princeton. He recalls many of McPhee's insights, and he adds the reactions of other former students who have been heavily influenced by McPhee.

David Shenk, "A Thankless Task," *New York Times Book Review*, Feb. 22, 2015, 33.
Shenk, the author of several books, writes about whether acknowledgments are essential in books. He cites McPhee as an example of a writer who eschews acknowledgments in his books. "Do I think John McPhee (a personal hero) isn't grateful to his friends, assistants, colleagues and librarians?" Shenk writes. "Not at all. I suspect, rather, that he considers the book something of a sacred object, and sees acknowledgements as pedestrian, a perhaps-useful-but-still-not-necessary-distraction."

George Estreich, "John McPhee's Geology: The Art of the Sentence," *Tin House*, Dec. 4, 2015, https://tinhouse.com/the-art-of-the-sentence-john-mcphees-geology/.
Estreich explores how McPhee's writing style gives meaning in his complex geology books.

"Forty Years Later, an Alaska Conversation About *Coming into the Country*," KTOO TV, Jan. 2017, 85-minute video recording. https://www.ktoo.org/video/coming-into-the-country/
In 2017, 40 years after *Coming into the Country* was published, Juneau-based public television station KTOO tracked down many people featured in McPhee's book to talk about how the state had changed and the impact of the book.

Wyatt Williams, "After Oranges," *Oxford American*, Summer 2017, 98, https://main.oxfordamerican.org/magazine/item/1233-after-oranges.
Fifty years after McPhee's *Oranges* was published, Williams, a critic and essayist, says he "drove to Florida to look for the oranges McPhee wrote about," re-examining the orange industry and culture in the state. "Young writers—those of us still looking for a subject to open the world the way oranges did for McPhee—need books to aspire to, guides off in the distance, green fruit glowing on the high branches of a tree," he says.

Charlie Euchner, "John McPhee's Step-by-Step Approach to Narrative Nonfiction," The Elements of Writing.com, Sept. 15, 2017, https://theelementsofwriting.com/mcphee/.
Euchner, a teacher and author, distills McPhee's writing into a series of steps, using comments and experiences from McPhee throughout.

Sam Anderson, "The Mind of John McPhee: A Deeply Private Writer Reveals His Obsessive Process," *New York Times*, Oct. 1, 2017, *Sunday Magazine*, 28.
In a highly readable, broad profile, Anderson uses the just-published *Draft No. 4* and a visit to Princeton to explore McPhee's career and his personality. "McPhee's work is not melancholy, macabre, sad or defeatist," Anderson writes. "It is full of life. Learning, for him, is a way of loving the world, savoring it, before it's gone."

Richard K. Rein, "On the Trail of Princeton's Literary Lion John McPhee," *U.S.1 Princeton Info*, Oct. 17, 2017, https://www.communitynews.org/princetoninfo/.
Rein, a longtime editor and writer in the Princeton community, takes an extended look at McPhee's career and writing philosophy, using McPhee's writings and that of others who have written about him.

Kerri Arsenault, "Wishing I Were John McPhee," *Literary Hub*, Nov. 15, 2017, https://lithub.com/wishing-i-were-john-mcphee/.
A far-ranging conversation with McPhee about his approach to creating narrative fiction. "McPhee said I must transition," Arsenault writes, "between the world I 'move around in all day long' and go 'across that membrane and into writing' every day."

Sean Gregory, "Author John McPhee Still Finds Wonder in the Outdoors, Chocolate and Circus Bears," *Time*, Dec. 17, 2018, https://time.com/5472309/john-mcphee-writer-interview/.
A writer from *Time* magazine visits McPhee in Princeton to talk about his career, his latest book, *The Patch*, and his Princeton seminar.

Ashley Anderson, "Teaching Experimental Structures through Objects and John McPhee's 'The Search for Marvin Gardens,'" *Assay: A Journal of Nonfiction Studies*, Spring 2019.
Anderson, an instructor in the English department at the University of Missouri, talks about McPhee's Marvin Gardens essay (published in *The New Yorker* September 9, 1972, and collected in *Pieces of the Frame*) and how his "experiment with structure" worked or ran into problems with students in her course on nonfiction prose.

Margo Bresnen, "Writing in the Time of Coronavirus: John McPhee's Legendary Course Goes Virtual," Princeton University, Mar. 26, 2020, https://www.princeton.edu/news/2020/03/26/writing-time-coronavirus-john-mcphees-legendary-course-goes-virtual.
In the spring of 2020, Princeton University shifted to remote instruction due to the COVID-19 pandemic, and so did McPhee's Creative Nonfiction writing seminar. This story describes McPhee's first online class, including the day's guest and former student David Remnick, editor of *The New Yorker*, who discussed writing and played his guitar from his New York City apartment.

Jonathan Russell Clark, "How Reading John McPhee's Book on Tennis Helped Me Write About Skateboarding," Literary Hub, Feb. 9, 2022, https://lithub.com/how-reading-john-mcphees-book-on-tennis-helped-me-write-about-skateboarding/.
Clark, a literary critic, applies lessons from McPhee's *Levels of the Game*, about a U.S. Open semifinal tennis match between Arthur Ashe and Clark Graebner, to his own writing of a book about skateboarding. "His work helped me find my way into my own," Clark writes. "He helped me get started, which any writer will tell you is a great boon."

"Object Lesson," *Deerfield Magazine*, Winter 2023, 96.
McPhee wrote his second book, *The Headmaster*, about Frank L. Boyden, who led Deerfield Academy for 66 years. After the book was published in 1966, McPhee, who attended Deerfield as a postgraduate

student, donated to the school his research materials for the book. This magazine's two-page spread, drawn from the school's archives, gives a rare look at McPhee's techniques for research and writing.

Chris Vognar, "John McPhee Calls His New Book an 'Old-People Project.' Consider the Alternative," *Los Angeles Times*, July 13, 2023.
McPhee talks about *Tabula Rasa: Volume 1*, and how the process of producing the items in it has been more fun than his previous writing. These pieces, he says, are "very short. You get into one and out the other side before you know what happened. It's just been a very pleasant and utter contrast to the grousy curmudgeon who was there before." Vognar writes, "So far, it's worked out for him—and for us."

Nathan Taylor Pemberton, "Legendary Author John McPhee on Procrastination, Dread, and His Endless Final Project," *GQ*, Aug. 14, 2023. Pemberton talks with McPhee about his career, his choice of subject matter, how he got along with the people he profiled, and his writing habits. McPhee says he's never missed a deadline because he has never had one: "I've never had pressure from anybody but actually myself."

5

Interviews

"Sometimes it's only a paragraph. Sometimes it's several thousand words. The idea is to get a lead that is honest and relevant. It should shine like a flashlight far down into the piece."
—FROM "MOUNTAINS FROM MOLEHILLS" BY BOB SIPCHEN, *LOS ANGELES TIMES*, AUGUST 6, 1989

PARTICULARLY IN the years before his dramatic success with *Coming into the Country*, John McPhee spent most of his time doing research, which often involved travel and then writing. He was protective of his time and he developed a reputation at times as reclusive. His pace in producing *New Yorker* articles and books was remarkably fast, yet his public profile was low.

After *Coming into the Country* and the accomplishments that followed, McPhee received many more requests for interviews. He agreed to only a small number of those invitations and the pattern would not change until the late 2000s and the 2010s, as his travel schedule became less intense and his writing became more reflective.

This section is a selective guide to interviews McPhee has given, available either in print or online, and it outlines the subjects discussed. McPhee's interviews were often a master class about the process of research and writing.

JOHN MCPHEE FARRAR, STRAUS & GIROUX
COMING INTO THE COUNTRY Photo credit: Thomas Victor

FIGURE 26. McPhee's publicity photo for *Coming into the Country*, taken in 1977 by Thomas Victor, a prominent literary photographer.

Thomas Brady, "New Yorker's McPhee Overcame Rejection," *Philadelphia Inquirer*, Apr. 20, 1977, Q2.
In an interview in advance of a talk in Princeton about *Coming into the Country*, McPhee discussed aspects of his writing career, such as how he takes notes, his switch from a typewriter to a computer, and the role of literary agents.

Stephen Singular, "Talk with John McPhee," *New York Times Book Review*, Nov. 27, 1977, 1.
In an article that accompanied Edward Hoagland's review of *Coming into the Country* on *The New York Times Book Review* cover, this interview includes McPhee talking about his writing process and how he found stories of interest. He discusses how various profile subjects reacted to his writing—for instance, canoe builder Henri Vaillancourt "had the graciousness to say nothing" after McPhee wrote about a difficult journey with him. McPhee speaks about the influences on his work, starting with Shakespeare, and his reputation as a hardworking and long-suffering writer ("No writer likes writing").

"All Things Considered," National Public Radio, 1978, 22-minute audio recording, https://www.npr.org/2006/06/24/5508293/john-mcphee-a-reporters-reporter.
McPhee talks about *Coming into the Country*, how he focuses on people and profiles, his work in the field doing research, how he uses language, and the discounted book of his that he found in Bermuda.

Jeffrey Shear, "McPhee: Getting Started Is the Hard Part," *Philadelphia Inquirer*, Jan. 22, 1978, 13G.
McPhee talks about when a relationship goes bad with someone he's writing about; how he has chosen subjects to write about, including his Alaska project; and his writing process.

Terry Gross, "Fresh Air," National Public Radio, Aug. 11, 1989, 22-minute audio recording, https://freshairarchive.org/guests/john-mcphee.
Terry Gross interviews McPhee on his new book, *The Control of Nature*. McPhee discusses what led him to write that book, whether he has ever "bailed out" of a subject he's researching, and how he feels about traveling for research versus doing the writing. He also discusses organizing his notes, his attempt to literally tie himself to a chair in order to write more, and why he does so few interviews.

Jared Haynes, "The Size and Shape of the Canvas," *Writing on the Edge*, Spring 1994, 109.
In the first of a two-part interview with Jared Haynes, who taught writing at the University of California, Davis, McPhee speaks about a variety of subjects: how he still wonders (at age 62) if he could make a living as a writer; the influence of Olive McKee, his high school English teacher; how he struggled with writing several books, such as *The Survival of the Bark Canoe* and *Basin and Range*; and how he got the ideas to write many articles that became books, such as *The Control of Nature* and *Looking for a Ship*.

Jared Haynes, "The Size and Shape of the Canvas," *Writing on the Edge*, Fall 1994, 109.
In the second of a two-part interview with Haynes, McPhee discusses how he handles taking notes, including whether he uses a tape recorder; how he knows when he is ready to start writing; setting up a work space for writing; revising drafts using a pencil; the importance of reading work out loud, such as when his wife, Yolanda, told him about a section, "That doesn't work at all"; why he chose not to have a glossary in his geology books; and a detailed description of his Princeton student seminar.

Claudia Dreifus, "A Conversation with John McPhee, A Writer Takes a Turn Reading Sermons in Stone," *New York Times*, Nov. 17, 1998, F5.
McPhee is interviewed in the *Science Times* section, mostly talking about geology and the just-published *Annals of the Former World*. McPhee says how his study of geology had changed his view of the world. He also gives a geologic description of his Princeton office and speaks about why some see geology as a slightly inferior science.

Ira Flatow, *Science Friday*, National Public Radio, June 1999, transcript or 45-minute audio recording, https://www.sciencefriday.com/segments/john-mcphee-geology/.
In 2021, *Science Friday* host Ira Flatow replayed his 1999 interview with McPhee, recorded shortly after he won the Pulitzer Prize for *Annals of*

the Former World. McPhee talks about the origins of the geology project and how he learned about geology. He then takes calls from listeners about *Annals* and previous books of his.

Jared Haynes, "Ideas Stream By: An Interview with John McPhee," *Writing on the Edge*, Spring 2004, 110.
Picking up with McPhee from an interview 10 years earlier, Jared Haynes asks what has happened in that time. McPhee talks about why he wrote about geology and also fishing and shad, about his most difficult interviewees, when and how to use a tape recorder, and how the computer changed his writing process.

Howard Berkes, "John McPhee: A Reporter's Reporter," June 24, 2006, 15-minute audio recording and then 7 minutes in four other sections, https://www.npr.org/2006/06/24/5508293/john-mcphee-a-reporters-reporter.
McPhee gives an audio tour of his Princeton University office, talks about his *Uncommon Carriers* collection, why he went on a cross-country truck trip, whether he feels accepted by those he interviews, and how he comes up with metaphors. Also included are short audio clips with McPhee's comments on "choosing his subjects," "sounding out his words," "Princeton and beyond," and "interviewing and shyness."

"Re-Assembling California: A Conversation with John McPhee," Davis, CA, Nov. 12, 2003, 27-minute recording, https://www.youtube.com/watch?v=vLwd_giY9dg
https://escholarship.org/uc/item/0t46b8pp.
A moderated conversation between McPhee and Eldridge Moores, the geologist at University of California, Davis, who is featured in *Assembling California*. In a program sponsored by the Pacific Regional Humanities Center, McPhee discusses why he is writing about geology, his experience working with scientists, and his trips with Moores. Moores discusses what it is like to cooperate with a writer and to be a major subject in a book.

Peter Hessler, "John McPhee, The Art of Nonfiction," *Paris Review*, Spring 2010, 39.
Hessler, a former student of McPhee's at Princeton and a fellow staff writer at *The New Yorker*, conducts a wide-ranging interview. McPhee talks about his high school English teacher, the importance of reading work aloud (and the time he read 60,000 words to an editor), his first impressions and experiences with *New Yorker* editor William Shawn, how he finds ideas for stories, why structure in writing is not mechanical but freeing, and why he stops writing at 7 p.m.

"The Pine Barrens: The Past, the Politics, and the Future," Mar. 3, 2013, 64-minute audio and video recording, https://www.youtube.com/watch?v=uZovx0j15vY.
McPhee is a panelist in a public discussion about the New Jersey Pine Barrens, sponsored by the Morven Museum and including former New Jersey governors Brendan Byrne and Jim Florio and others. McPhee talks about the origins and reporting for his 1968 book on the Pine Barrens and his relationship with Byrne, who was a central figure in their preservation.

"John McPhee's Legacy," *The New Yorker Radio Hour*, July 8, 2016, 20-minute audio recording, https://www.wnycstudios.org/podcasts/tnyradiohour/segments/john-mcphees-legacy.
McPhee is interviewed by David Remnick, the editor of *The New Yorker* and a former student of McPhee's at Princeton. McPhee discusses why he decided to be a writer, how he organizes his research notes and uses them in writing, why he chose geology as a subject, how he has felt time pass in his career, and how he gets through the difficulties of writing.

"Hoops Hour with Henderson—John McPhee '53," Oct. 3, 2016, Princeton, NJ, 63-minute audio recording, https://art19.com/shows/princeton-tigers/episodes/a7e350bd-5311-4f45-a703-af303a0c82e8.
McPhee is a guest on the podcast of Princeton University basketball coach Mitch Henderson. McPhee talks about his connections to Princeton athletics, competing on the *Twenty Questions* quiz show while at

Princeton, former Princeton basketball coach and friend Pete Carril, bicycling, Princetonians he's worked with, and his book *Levels of the Game*.

"The Wright Show," 2017, 66-minute audio and video recording, https://www.youtube.com/watch?v=Qytux831HIQ; https://bloggingheads.tv/videos/47738.
Robert Wright, a writer and former McPhee student, has McPhee as a guest on his audio and video podcast. McPhee declined to be shown on camera, related to his view that writers shouldn't get between their books and readers. McPhee discusses his recently published *Draft No. 4*, his feelings about New Journalism, structure in writing, the importance of the lead in a story, and categories of stories in which he is not interested.

"John McPhee: Great Writers, Great Readings," Hofstra University, Long Island, NY, 2017, 70-minute audio and video recording, https://www.youtube.com/watch?v=cYDdhR_GPp4.
Hofstra University English professor Kelly McMasters interviews McPhee. He talks about *Draft No. 4* and reads selections from it, discusses the practice of finishing research before starting writing, structure in writing, and finding the right title for a piece. McPhee's daughter Martha, a novelist and Hofstra professor, introduces the program.

Alaska call-in radio show about *Coming into the Country*, Alaska Public Media, Jan. 24, 2017, 59-minute audio recording, https://alaskapublic.org/2017/01/20/coming-into-country/.
As part of commemorating the 40th anniversary of McPhee's *Coming into the Country* being published, Alaska Public Media hosted an interview and call-in show with McPhee, with a radio host and people around the state asking him about the book and Alaska.

Heller McAlpin, "The Reporter as Teacher: A Talk with John McPhee," *Barnes & Noble Reads*, Sept. 13, 2017, https://www.barnesandnoble.com/blog/reporter-as-teacher-john-mcphee/.
McAlpin, a book critic and a former student of McPhee's at Princeton, talks to McPhee about why he writes more personally in *Draft No. 4*, his

class at Princeton and its impact on the students and him, what creative nonfiction is, the importance of not sounding like an encyclopedia, and what "greening" is.

Studio 360 With Kurt Andersen, Public Radio International (PRI), "John McPhee's Rules for Writing," Sept. 14, 2017, 19-minute audio minute recording, https://slate.com/culture/2017/09/john-mcphee-gives-writing-tips-and-actor-b-j-novak-explains-why-he-loves-fuller-house.html.
The writer Kurt Andersen talks to John McPhee about his *Draft No. 4*, covering such topics as whether McPhee is surprised by which of his students have succeeded, his self-professed shyness, the differences in writing between fiction and nonfiction, and why he has stayed in Princeton so long. Also included are recorded comments by some of McPhee's former students from Princeton: David Remnick, Rick Stengel, Jenny Price, and Joel Achenbach.

"What I Think: John McPhee," Princeton University Office of Communications, Sept. 18, 2017, https://www.princeton.edu/news/2017/09/18/what-i-think-john-mcphee.
Jamie Saxon of Princeton's communications office interviews McPhee about writing and his Princeton course. Four former students from McPhee's writing class—Jim Kelly, Jessica Lander, Eric Lander, and Lilith Wood—talk about him and the course.

"An Hour with John McPhee," *The Colin McEnroe Show*, Connecticut Public Radio, Sept. 28, 2017, 54-minute audio recording, https://www.ctpublic.org/arts-and-culture/2021-07-07/an-hour-with-john-mcphee.
In conversation with the radio host Colin McEnroe, McPhee talks about "disappearing" to achieve a comfort level with people he writes about, how he gently teaches about subjects with his writing, using "I" in writing, and structure.

Lily Rothman, "John McPhee on Writing, Reading and How Working in Magazines Has Changed," Time.com, Oct. 18, 2017, https://time.com/4983145/john-mcphee-draft-no-4-time-interview/.
Rothman, an editor at *Time*, speaks to McPhee on the publication of *Draft No. 4*. He talks about his years at *Time* and what the process of writing a story was like when he was there, as well as the culture of the magazine.

"Can You Teach Good Writing? We Ask One of the Greats," EdSurge, Sept. 18, 2018, https://www.edsurge.com/news/2018-09-18-can-you-teach-good-writing-we-ask-one-of-the-greats.
Jeffrey Young, a former student of McPhee's at Princeton, interviews him about teaching writing. McPhee talks about his writing course and why he continued to teach it, the teacher who most shaped him, and what it takes to be a good writing teacher.

Raffi Joe Wartanian, "Into Another World: An Interview with John McPhee," *Columbia Journal*, Oct. 25, 2018.
In this literary magazine produced by the Columbia University MFA Writing Program, McPhee talks about his father and fishing, his writing routine, what he says to writers in their twenties, and why lacrosse has grown in popularity.

Paul Holdengraber, "John McPhee's Album Quilt," *Library Talks* podcast, New York Public Library, Dec. 2, 2018 (event at library was Nov. 26, 2018), 92-minute audio recording. https://www.nypl.org/blog/2018/11/26/john-mcphee-ep-243.
As part of the "LIVE from NYPL" series, Paul Holdengraber, founder and director of The New York Public Library's cultural series, spoke with McPhee. He starts by asking McPhee for a seven-word bio and then asks him what he means by "crop rotation" about the energy he gains by not writing while he is teaching. McPhee also talks about the structure of *The Patch* and its Album Quilt, the importance of libraries, and his love for dictionaries. Holdengraber then reads a long letter from the New York Public Library archives from McPhee to Robert Silvers, coeditor of the *New York Review of Books*, about Silver's reluctance to

publish a McPhee article about geology. The program ends with McPhee reading about Alaska.

"Martha McPhee and John McPhee on the Writer's Process," Arcadia Books, Spring Green, WI, July 30, 2020, 55-minute audio and video recording, https://www.youtube.com/watch?v=0AmglS6KTVI.
During the early months of the COVID-19 pandemic, John McPhee and his daughter Martha McPhee, a novelist, have an online conversation with James Bohnen, the owner of a Wisconsin bookstore. Both talk about their books, the writing process, and the importance of perseverance. Martha McPhee also talks about her relationship with her father and his love of words.

Ann Tashi Slater, "On Going into the Zone," *Tricycle: The Buddhist Review*, Dec. 6, 2022, https://tricycle.org/article/john-mcphee/.
Slater, a magazine and fiction writer and a former student of McPhee's at Princeton, talks to him about his writing process, the choices he has made that have determined his path, and improving the "muscle memory" of writing.

John Austin and Julia Elliott, "Tete-a-Tete: John McPhee '49," *Deerfield Magazine*. Winter 2023, 24.
In conversation with the current head of school at Deerfield Academy and a writer there, McPhee—who attended the prep school for a postgraduate high school year and later wrote his second book, *The Headmaster*, about Frank L. Boyden, the school's legendary headmaster—talks about the impact of Boyden and Deerfield on him, and his writing career.

Scott Simon, *Weekend Edition Saturday*, National Public Radio, July 15, 2023, 8-minute audio recording and transcript, https://www.npr.org/2023/07/15/1187929941/writer-john-mcphee-on-his-book-tabula-rasa.
Simon interviews McPhee about his *Tabula Rasa: Volume 1*. McPhee says "the idea is that the slate is clean because I never wrote these pieces" before. Simon reads a passage in the book about contemporary cliches and McPhee talks about the importance of "frame of reference."

6

Book Reviews

"Nonfiction writers go out not knowing what to expect. In a way you're like a cook foraging for materials, and in many ways, like a cook, you're only as good as your materials."

—FROM "PROFILE: JOHN MCPHEE" BY MICHAEL PEARSON, *CREATIVE NONFICTION*, VOL. 1, NO. 1, 1993

JOHN MCPHEE'S first few books were scarcely reviewed at all, not unusual for an author new to the scene. But interest in his books grew in the late 1960s and early 1970s, and then McPhee's visibility multiplied dramatically in 1977 with his bestseller, *Coming into the Country*. He became one of the most reviewed authors of his time.

McPhee's reviewers also became a who's who of top literary circles. In addition to the chief book critics at leading publications, influential writers who reviewed his work included Edward Hoagland, Larry McMurtry, Susan Brownmiller, Robert Coles, Diane Johnson, Wallace Stegner, Doris Grumbach, and Evan S. Connell.

This list of reviews is selective and intended to incorporate the main strands of commentary about McPhee's books.

McPhee's work has received overwhelmingly positive reviews throughout his career, but there have been criticisms too, and they are represented here.

This list also reflects geographic diversity and includes publications from the American West, where so many of McPhee's books were set, especially those on geology.

Still, as the listings show, book reviews have long been highly concentrated in large American cities and particularly in the Northeast. This trend has become more pronounced in recent years as many publications, especially newspapers, have reduced or eliminated book reviews. *The New York Times*, which has been the most frequent reviewer of McPhee's work, has long been the premier American book review source and its position has grown more dominant over time.

Besides newspapers and magazines, reviews in some science and technology journals are included to show how McPhee was regarded in the specialized areas that he wrote about.

A Sense of Where You Are

Rex Lardner, "Shoot That Ball!," *New York Times Book Review*, Nov. 28, 1965, 71.
In *The New York Times*, a staffer at *Sports Illustrated* wrote one of the only known newspaper reviews of McPhee's first book. He said it "is immensely well-written, inspiring without being preachy, and contains . . . the clearest analysis of Bradley's moves, fakes and shots that have appeared in print."

Kirkus Reviews, Sept. 1, 1965, https://www.kirkusreviews.com/book-reviews/john-mcphee/a-sense-of-where-you-are/.
The book review magazine said of McPhee's book: "What a rare sports book! The story of Princeton's phenomenal basketball superstar, Bill Bradley, constantly takes the reader right in the middle of the action. Seldom has court psychology been better explained, while revealing at the same time a player's temperament."

The Headmaster

Joseph G. Herzberg, "End Papers," *New York Times*, Nov. 26, 1966, 33.
"The fine portrait Mr. McPhee draws of an individualist's individual."

John McKey, "Giant Without Peer," *Boston Globe*, Dec. 4, 1966, D14.
"John McPhee stands in the first rank of professional journalists . . . 'The Headmaster' is a record of a lifetime's striving [by Frank Boyden] to

create perfection—a striving conducted with zest, vision, humor and an unbelievable capacity for work."

Oranges

Harry Gilroy, "End Papers," *New York Times*, Mar. 8, 1967, 43.
"Anyone with the same passion for reading about oranges that John McPhee has for writing about them will find this a diverting book... This book is quite a marmalade."

Pamela Marsh, "Citric Insouciance," *Christian Science Monitor*, Mar. 29, 1967, 9.
"Mr. McPhee proves a most agreeable instructor, employing a light, casual style—so easy to read, so hard to write... Mr. McPhee's pages contain a plethora of fascinatingly useless tidbits."

Mary Corddry, "Oranges Made Fun," *Baltimore Sun*, May 21, 1967, D5.
"Mr. McPhee restores the image of the orange with such effect that the very word remains a poetic symbol."

The Pine Barrens

Earl Schenck Miers, "Land of the Jersey Devil," *New York Times Book Review*, May 12, 1968, 18.
"It will be a long time before another book appears to equal the literary quality and human compassion of this one. Among books of its type, it could be a classic."

David Appel, "The Pine Barrens: Jersey Wilderness," *Philadelphia Inquirer*, May 19, 1968, 7.
"It is reportage of a superior quality... He makes a strong plea for their [the Pine Barrens'] preservation."

A Roomful of Hovings and Other Profiles

G. H. Pouder, "Capturing the Essences," *Baltimore Sun*, Jan. 19, 1969, D5.
"His range of interest, his light touch, and his passion for research are admirably suited to a device [the profile] which is largely American in both style and journalistic technique."

"Little Aristocracy," *Time*, Jan. 31, 1969, 78.
"A classicist in technique, McPhee is nonetheless a romantic in his tastes. He relishes dash and flair."

Pamela Marsh, "The Lively Snippet, the Appetizing Trifle," *Christian Science Monitor*, Feb. 1, 1969, 9.
"With a bore's persistence he seizes a subject, shakes loose a cloud of more detail than we ever imagined we would care to hear on any subject—yet somehow he makes the whole procedure curiously fascinating."

Levels of the Game

Wilfrid Sheed, "Levels of the Game," *New York Times Book Review*, Nov. 2, 1969, 36.
The well-known essayist says, "The visual reproduction of the match is excellent, and you can easily follow the rallies without twisting your neck . . . McPhee likes to study humanity one at a time."

Robert Lipsyte, "Sports of the Times: Sports Books for Christmas," *New York Times*, Dec. 4, 1969, 72.
"A brilliant explication of a tennis match at Forest Hills . . . This may be the high point of American sports journalism."

Carolyn F. Ruffin, "Tennis in a Writer's Net," *Christian Science Monitor*, Dec. 24, 1969, 13.
"Mr. McPhee's book is a compact sociology. It has the tone of a coolly executed drama about intertwined loyalties. And it scores well on all levels."

FIGURE 27. In *Levels of the Game*, McPhee presents a dual biography of tennis stars Arthur Ashe and Clark Graebner. (Jacket design by Janet Halverson)

The Crofter and the Laird

Edmund Fuller, "An Intriguing Return to Scottish Origins," *Wall Street Journal*, June 24, 1970, 14.
"McPhee, who dwells in Princeton and inhabits a sophisticated, cosmopolitan world, clearly feels the pull of isolated communities and hardy, self-reliant life styles."

Jeanne Rose, "For Exiled Scots Who Dream of Hebrides," *Baltimore Sun*, July 5, 1970, SD5.
"He has written a gem of insight and grace, which manages to capsule the spirit, the beauties and the heavy problems of Highland Scotland into very small space."

Neil Millar, "His Heart's in the Hebrides," *Christian Science Monitor*, July 9, 1970, 15.
"Coolly, cleanly, unromantically, honestly, we are shown a hard-faring life and a firm Highland people."

Encounters with the Archdruid

Edmund Fuller, "Of Honest Men Who Disagree," *Wall Street Journal*, Aug. 11, 1971, 8.
"The importance of this lively book in the unmanageably proliferating literature on ecology is in its confrontation between remarkable men who hold great differences of opinion with integrity on all sides."

Phelps Dewey, "A Conservationist Meets His Enemies," *San Francisco Chronicle*, Aug. 29, 1971, 158.
"McPhee's description of the results of those volatile encounters makes fascinating reading, and offers a better insight into both sides of three major conservation battles."

Benjamin Marble, "'Archdruid': A Study of Ecomania in America," *Los Angeles Times*, Nov. 28, 1971, X8.
"It beautifully illustrates the paradox of good men following their best instincts, advocating diametrically opposite courses of action."

Wimbledon: A Celebration

Burke Wilkinson, "Grenades on the Grass," *Christian Science Monitor*, May 24, 1972, 11.
"There is none of the cumulative drama of a narrowing field . . . Rather, he gives us a pen portrait, stroke by stroke, of what Wimbledon is like."

Michael Olmert, "The Wimbledon Scene: Twynam, the Tournament," *Washington Post*, June 25, 1972, BW4.
"McPhee's art has been to conceal a great deal of inside information in a quickly moving narrative—a technique that seems to turn his readers into instant experts on the subject at hand."

The Deltoid Pumpkin Seed

Christopher Lehmann-Haupt, "Christ Through Air Power," *New York Times*, July 13, 1973, 33.
"There really isn't that much to the story when you think about it objectively ... Still, Mr. McPhee takes the story of this flying pumpkin seed and makes it seem as momentous as the first trip to the moon."

Paul West, "It's a Bird! It's a Plane! It's Aereon!," *Washington Post*, July 14, 1973, D4.
"Even his [McPhee's] digressions are imperative (especially on rigid airships), feeding needed aeronautical lore into the text without fanfare."

[Unsigned], "'Pumpkin Seed' a Whatchamacallit Sort of Book," *Los Angeles Times*, Sept. 23, 1973, O16.
"The obsession of the Aereon builders, inspired or wrongheaded or both, illuminates an important corner ... The reader catches a long glimpse of what being human is about."

The Curve of Binding Energy

Sandra Schmidt Oddo, "How to Not Make an Atomic Bomb," *New York Times Book Review*, June 23, 1974, 4.
"John McPhee has an eye and an ear and a typewriter that operate like the camera and full crew of a documentary film study ... 'The Curve of Binding Energy' is a documentary that carries an imperative far more important than its vehicle."

Richard Rhodes, "A Do-It-Yourself Atom Bomb? It's Closer than You Think," *Chicago Tribune*, June 30, 1974, F3.
Rhodes, who would later write the Pulitzer Prize–winning *The Making of the Atomic Bomb*, says, "McPhee's work, as always, is superb; he has got onto a subject that most Americans long ago chose to stop thinking about, and his research and his conclusions are impeccable."

FIGURE 28. *The Curve of Binding Energy* is McPhee's exploration of the world of Theodore B. Taylor, a physicist and designer of atomic bombs who turned to protecting against them. (Jacket design by Janet Halverson)

Philip Morrison, *Scientific American*, Sept. 1974, 201.
"This is a faintly dangerous book, glittering, original, awry."

Pieces of the Frame

Margaret Manning, "Of Biologists and the Loch Ness Monster," *Boston Globe,* June 22, 1975, 65.
"This is para-journalism, para-cultural-and-sociological commentary quite lacking in the livid hyperbole which drenches the work of writers like Norman Mailer and Tom Wolfe."

Edward Hoagland, "From John McPhee and Craftsmanship," *New York Times Book Review*, June 22, 1975, 3.
Hoagland, a writer sometimes compared to McPhee because of writing styles and subjects (and both were Deerfield Academy alumni, although they didn't know each other at the school), praises McPhee here as "probably the most versatile journalist in America." He also urges him to take more chances, "blast out" and "seek his fortunes on higher ground."

Bruce Allen, "Pieces of the Frame," *Chicago Tribune*, June 29, 1975, F1.
"The writer's 'frame' is a necessary organizing device. It is also a cage. John McPhee knows both these truths together and lets that double knowledge flow vigorously, lifegivingly through every territory he explores."

The Survival of the Bark Canoe

Christopher Lehmann-Haupt, "Traveling the Natural Way," *New York Times*, Nov. 27, 1975, 31.
"From the moment we enter the field of Henri Vallencourt's obsession, we are drawn irresistibly to the taper of thwarts, the laminating of stempieces, the goring of bark."

Simon Li, "Let Him Entertain and Teach," *Philadelphia Inquirer*, 13–16.
"In his 12th book, McPhee, who lives and works in Princeton, turns the magnifying glass of his careful reporting, extraordinary descriptive powers, and limpid prose on the Indian birch-bark canoe."

The John McPhee Reader

Larry McMurtry, "Classically Crafted Reportage," *Washington Post*, Dec. 27, 1976, B6.
Larry McMurtry, a noted novelist and essayist, says of McPhee: "He is good not merely at reporting facts, but at establishing the characters of the individual people." He claims McPhee was yet to write a bad book, and adds, "it would be satisfying, now and then, if McPhee's enthusiasm for his subjects was a little less muted by an impersonal style."

Robert Kirsch, "Artful Craft of John McPhee," *Los Angeles Times*, Mar. 10, 1977, F5.
"He is a good writer because he uses the language imaginatively and intelligently, allows the conscious and unconscious parts of his mind to work together . . . is not afraid to experiment with time and narrative and more than anything is willing to avoid specializing."

Spencer Brown, "The Odor of Durability," *The Sewanee Review*, Winter 1978, 146.
Spencer Brown, a poet, reviews McPhee's *Reader* alongside E. B. White's new book of essays: "McPhee and White are not really alike except in one way: in the preface to *Lyrical Ballads* Wordsworth said he sought 'a certain colouring of imagination, whereby ordinary things should be presented to the mind in an unusual aspect' . . . The poet's prosy formulation states what these two distinguished prose writers have consistently achieved."

Coming into the Country

John Leonard, "Books of the *The Times*," *New York Times*, Nov. 25, 1977, 88.
"Mr. McPhee gives us the places, faces, voices and choices in a prose tuned so fine that its rhythms take over the reader's head . . . He came out of the bush with a marvelous book."

Edward Hoagland, "When Life Begins Over," *New York Times Book Review*, Nov. 27, 1977, 1.
In McPhee's first appearance on the cover of *The New York Times Book Review*, Hoagland writes: "McPhee has not always been a risk-taker, had published several books that were essentially magazine articles between book covers . . . But here, presumably, he made his will, took the gambit . . . And since it is a reviewer's greatest pleasure to ring the gong for a species of masterpiece, let me say he found it."

Susan Brownmiller, "An Alaskan Mother Lode," *Chicago Tribune,* Dec. 18, 1977, F1.
The author of the bestseller *Against Our Will* and other books writes, "McPhee is incapable of writing a dull sentence, and he never stoops to doing an across-the-table interview with one of his subjects."

Benjamin DeMott, "Two Reporters at Peace and War," *The Atlantic,* Jan. 1978, 91.
A prominent cultural critic writes about McPhee's book and *Dispatches* by Michael Herr, saying McPhee "has become the name of a standard by which ambitious magazine journalism is now judged ... What is really in view in *Coming into the Country* is a matter not usually met in works of reportage—nothing less than the nature of the human condition."

Robert Coles, "Alaska, The State That Came in from the Cold," *Washington Post,* Jan. 22, 1978, F1.
The author and child psychiatrist wrote, "John McPhee's approach, justly celebrated, brings us to the dramatic terrain ... [McPhee] has enough confidence in his angle of vision, and the subtlety and competence of his writing, to shun large statements, portentous generalizations."

Diane Johnson, "Ah, Wilderness," *The New York Review of Books,* Mar. 23, 1978.
The novelist and longtime contributor to *The New York Review of Books* reviews two new books by *New Yorker* writers McPhee and Jane Kramer (*The Last Cowboy*). She says of McPhee, "An outdoorsman, romantic but also astute and accepting, he understands the wilderness, he appreciates naivete, and he also see who will sell out whom."

Ronald Weber, "Letting Subjects Grow: Literary Nonfiction from the New Yorker," *The Antioch Review,* Autumn 1978, 486.
Weber, a critic specializing in the study of nonfiction, also writes about McPhee and Jane Kramer's books together and says, "*Coming into the Country* seems to me to stand apart from McPhee's earlier work as far

more ambitious and artful, a distinguished work of literary nonfiction while yet retaining the broad form of the journalistic report."

George Core, "The Eloquence of Fact," *Virginia Quarterly Review*, Autumn 1978, 733.
Core, editor of *The Sewanee Review*, reviews *Coming into the Country* alongside *The John McPhee Reader* and the *Essays of E. B. White*: "John McPhee's compass has more points and greater breath than any journalist today . . . His commitment to character is fictive in its comprehensiveness and intensity, and his scenes are more powerful than most contemporary fiction."

Philip G. Terrie, "John McPhee's 'The Encircled River,'" *Western American Literature*, Spring 1988, 3.
In a detailed analysis of "The Encircled River," the first part of McPhee's Alaska book, Philip Terrie says: "We can see especially well how McPhee is constructing a narrative not only about nature but also about inner discovery. In no other essay or book has McPhee allowed his own character to become such a vital part of his writing."

William Bonney, "The Frontier as Commodity," *Interdisciplinary Studies in Literature and Environment*, Spring 1993, 81.
In a negative review of *Coming into the Country*, published more than 15 years after the book's first publication, William Bonney, who was an English professor at University of Alaska and then Mississippi State University, writes that McPhee's book "is little more than still another opportunistic effort to realize profit by selling the fugitive term 'frontier' to American consumers."

Giving Good Weight

Anatole Broyard, "Fuzz on the Peaches," *New York Times*, Nov. 17, 1979, 21.
"Mr. McPhee's usually limber prose congeals when he describes the chef [in "Brigade de Cuisine"] . . . It sounds as if Mr. McPhee needs to get back into the open air."

Barry Siegel, "'Good Weight': Coming into McPhee Country," *Los Angeles Times*, Dec. 2, 1979, M19.
"His newest collection of *New Yorker* pieces is not as rich or varied as his best collection, 'Pieces of the Frame,' but it should do nothing to diminish McPhee's reputation."

William Brashler, ". . . and Craftsmanship from the New Yorker," *Chicago Tribune*, Jan. 6, 1980, E3.
"McPhee is a gentle, simple writer who lets his subject carry him. His writing is sparse, but precise, without cadenzas or diversions added to show himself off."

Basin and Range

Evan Connell, "The Lay of the Land: How the West Was Made," *Washington Post*, Apr. 19, 1981, *Book World*, 4.
The author, who often wrote about the American West, says of McPhee's first geology book, "His tone is affable, his meandering appropriate and the tutorial intent of *Basin and Range* is commendable—for surely nobody could measure the width or depth of our ignorance."

Caroline See, "The New Geology Served on the Rocks," *Los Angeles Times*, Apr. 27, 1981, F8.
The novelist, nonfiction writer, and book critic writes: "Once you surmount the initial shock of the topic, it's not so bad. McPhee, a benign fanatic as opposed to a 'popularizer,' doesn't condescend to his reader as much as invite him repeatedly to share in his own fascination."

Stephen Jay Gould, "Deep Time and Ceaseless Motion," *The New York Review of Books*, May 14, 1981.
Gould was for many years an influential evolutionary biologist who taught at Harvard. He writes of McPhee's book: "Where McPhee's style works—and it usually does—he triumphs by succinct prose, by his uncanny ability to capture the essence of a complex issue, or an arcane trade secret, in a well-turned phrase . . . But granite is granite, whether

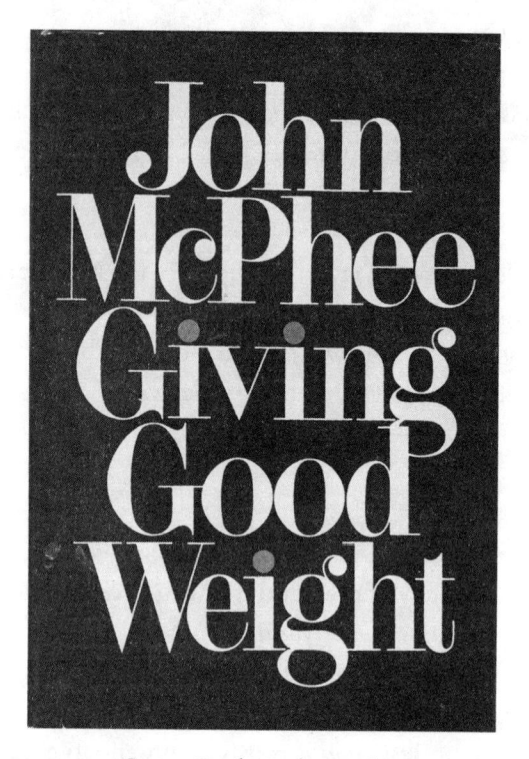

FIGURE 29. *Giving Good Weight*, a collection of McPhee articles from *The New Yorker*, was published in 1979. (Jacket design by Lawrence Ratzkin)

formed in the Cambrian or yesterday. McPhee presents too much descriptive history."

Paul Zweig, "Rhapsodist of Deep Time," *New York Times Book Review*, May 17, 1981, 1.
The poet and critic writes in another *New York Times Book Review* cover for McPhee: "In 'Basin and Range,' the perspectives and expertise of geology become a language for the drama of time. The result is a fascinating book."

Charles Petit, "If You're Tired of Gaping Witlessly at Weird and Wonderful Geography . . .," *San Francisco Chronicle*, May 17, 1981, 198.
"This is possibly the greatest contribution of this book. Many writers and scholars have explained how brief is the period man has existed on

earth. McPhee makes the newness of our arrival emphatic, pummeling the reader with descriptions of eras, ages, and epochs."

In Suspect Terrain

Michiko Kakutani, "The Writing in the Rocks," *New York Times Book Review*, Jan. 30, 1983, 1.
McPhee's second geology book is also on *The New York Times Book Review* cover, and Kakutani writes, "At his best, Mr. McPhee imparts these facts with such fluency and good humor that his lessons in history and technology are painless, if not fun . . . Such observations, unfortunately, are rarer in 'In Suspect Terrain' than in 'Basin and Range.'"

Margaret Manning, "In Suspect Terrain," *Boston Globe*, Feb. 6, 1983, B10.
"The average person doesn't know enough to understand a lot of the scientific talk, but that is not an excuse for avoiding it. You will learn, which is the best reason for reading anything."

Wallace Stegner, "Good Digs: Geology and John McPhee," *Los Angeles Times*, Feb. 27, 1983, N1.
The novelist and environmentalist writes about McPhee's book: "A travelogue across country and through time, 'In Suspect Terrain' is a most instructive book. No one who has read it will ever travel Interstate 80 between Indiana and New Jersey without seeing, beyond or below the present countryside, the dim coasts of the Ordovician or Devonian."

Philip Kopper, "McPhee Takes on the Wrinkles in Geology," *Philadelphia Inquirer*, Mar. 6, 1983, R5.
"In his fascinating fashion, as always, McPhee uses immediate subjects—Anita [Harris] and the Appalachians here—as departure points for variously vivid, diverting, lyrical and instructive asides."

Pamela Marsh, "Rocks Smile While Geologists Argue," *Christian Science Monitor*, Mar. 11, 1983, 17.
"I think he [McPhee] is daring us. Okay, he seems to be saying, you say you care about the extraordinary, dramatic way your world was built

billions of years ago, so prove it—if you can. And off he goes refusing to talk down to us, insisting that we stick with him."

La Place de la Concorde Suisse

Susan Dooley, "La Place de la Concorde Suisse," *Washington Post*, Apr. 8, 1984, *Book World*, 6.
"No one who reads *La Place de la Concorde Suisse* will ever again gaze at an Alp without imagining what's inside: fighter planes ready to take off from hidden hangars carved out of the mountains; defense centers with miles of underground corridors, hospitals and storerooms full of food and fuel—in short a defense system that covers the whole country."

Jonathan Steinberg, "Neutral and Armed to the Teeth," *New York Times Book Review*, May 6, 1984, 41.
Jonathan Steinberg, a historian and expert on Switzerland, writes, "[John McPhee] has written a strange, often very beautiful, and ultimately ambiguous little work . . . Mr. McPhee puts his reader inside Switzerland with elegance and insight. After reading his book, nobody need complain that Switzerland is a bore; it's not."

Bruce Colman, "A Prickly Principle for National Defense," *San Francisco Chronicle*, May 20, 1984, 179.
"We find again his [McPhee's] delight in skillful people . . . He is still our best writer at conveying landscapes, and his love for place names and what they can tell us about geography and society is intact."

Jon Goddard, "Switzerland Ready to Protect at Any Cost," *Cincinnati Enquirer*, Aug. 26, 1984, D23.
"John McPhee's latest book, *La Place de la Concorde Suisse*," has the feel, elegance and timeliness of a fine Swiss watch."

Table of Contents

Christopher Lehmann-Haupt, "Books of the Times," *New York Times*, Sept. 27, 1985, C27.
"Backward progress is the theme of the eight pieces . . . they bring news of old professions being rediscovered, of obsolete technologies becoming viable again, of endangered animal species repopulating their old habitats, and of people finding new ways to live in what remains of North American wilderness."

Noel Perrin, "Uncommonly Nice Pioneers," *New York Times Book Review*, Oct. 13, 1985, 26.
"A little more attention to the difference in possibilities between magazine articles and a book of essays might have made this good collection even better. I'm not wishing Mr. McPhee had done more rewriting . . . I am wishing the book had a touch more coherence."

Doris Grumbach, *Morning Edition*, National Public Radio, Nov. 13, 1985.
The novelist and literary critic says, "This is a kind of sampler, a fine way to come upon McPhee's impeccable prose and always unexpected and unusual subject matter . . . The longest piece, 'Heirs of General Practice,' is a masterpiece of reporting."

Rising from the Plains

James Trefil, "Rising from the Plains," *Los Angeles Times*, Nov. 9, 1986, U12.
"Every bed of rock, every outcropping, has its story to tell about some era in the distant past. I know of no author who is better able to give us a feeling for the land we live on than McPhee."

Evan S. Connell, "Snapshot of a Billion Years," *New York Times Book Review*, Nov. 23, 1986, 14.
"You need not have passed Geology 101 to enjoy 'Rising from the Plains,' but it might help . . . Nevertheless, this instructive account of the geologic West and frontier West is a delight."

Timothy Bay, "In the Wilds of Wyoming," *Baltimore Sun*, Dec. 21, 1986, 11J.
"The geology in the book can be daunting . . . It takes patience sometimes to pick one's way through such verbal outcroppings of the geologist's language as branchiopods, amphibolites and anorthosites. But in the end, the patient reader is well rewarded."

Bill Sniffin, "'Rising from the Plains' Is a Classic Wyoming Book," Cowboystatedaily.com, Oct. 23, 2019, https://cowboystatedaily.com/2019/10/23/rising-from-the-plains-is-classic-wyoming-book/.
This review on a local Wyoming website—written more than 30 years after McPhee's book was first published—speaks to the book's lasting appeal: "ranks as one of the most interesting and most important books ever written about Wyoming . . . McPhee writes in a style that vividly lets you imagine the extreme rising of mountain ranges, the descent of valleys, and the rolling together of various land masses."

The Control of Nature

John Wilkes, "Nature's Irresistible Force," *San Francisco Chronicle*, July 23, 1989, 265.
"His [McPhee's] unhurried, droll style contrasts nicely with the tension of his subject matter. He chronicles his subjects' quiet but intense lives with unusual empathy, as well as meticulously researched understanding and unobtrusive wit."

Jack Miles, "McPhee on Debris," *Los Angeles Times*, July 30, 1989, 302.
"Fewer, even among the best popularizers of science, attempt as he does in this piece to combine scientific synthesis with a description of engineering in action—and then to situate the engineer in a vivid and deeply instructive human context . . . we all have a lot of environmental thinking ahead of us. McPhee offers a unique clue to how we should proceed."

Christopher Lehmann-Haupt, "Oh, to Still the Floods and Quench the Fires," *New York Times*, Aug. 3, 1989, C21.
"Too often, his [McPhee's] narrative seems to meander simply for the charm of its meandering. But finally it meanders to a telling conclusion . . . This is what Mr. McPhee ends up capturing so tellingly. The odds are overwhelmingly on uncaring nature's side. Yet humans, inevitable losers, go on imagining that they are in control."

Nicolaus Mills, "Altering the Course of Nature," *Newsday*, Aug. 6, 1989, C15.
"What is the solution? . . . McPhee never says, and that in the end is the problem with this book. It avoids coming to terms with the very questions it so deftly raises."

Stephen J. Pyne, "A War Against the World," *New York Times Book Review*, Aug. 6, 1989, 1.
Another *New York Times Book Review* cover: "The book is a fascinating, if sometimes disjointed, report from three revealing battlefields in humanity's global war against nature . . . If the stories bear witness to the ultimate triumph of nature over human engineering, they also testify to the triumph of art over nature."

Looking for a Ship

William W. Warner, "The Call of the Running Tide," *Washington Post*, Sept. 9, 1990, J1.
"The strength of *Looking for a Ship*, as in so many of McPhee's 20 previous books, rests in the author's quick hand in gaining the trust of his subjects and bringing them fully alive with a remarkable economy of dialogue and description."

Paul Theroux, "At Sea with McPhee," *New York Times Book Review*, Sept. 23, 1990, 3.
The noted travel writer says, "Economy is a virtue in magazine writing. In a book it can seem like meagerness and insufficiency . . . I would have

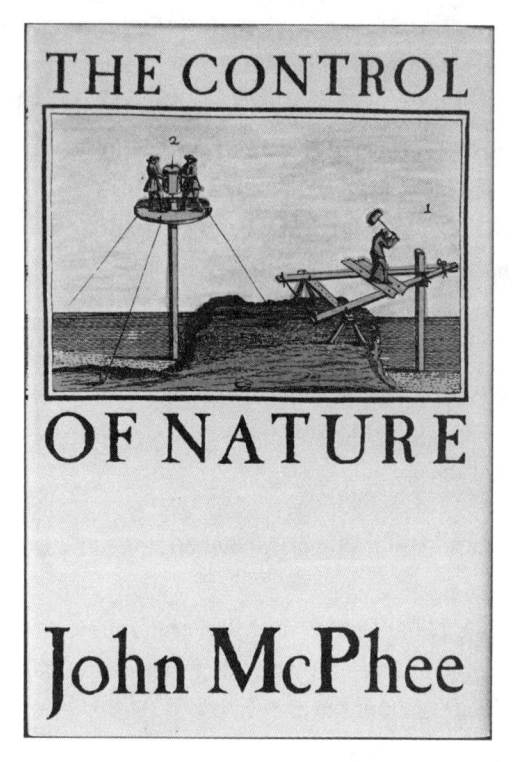

FIGURE 30. In *The Control of Nature*, published in 1989, people in Louisiana, Iceland, Hawaii, and Los Angeles try to manage nature. (Jacket design by Cynthia Krupat)

preferred 'Looking for a Ship' to sprawl more . . . I wanted more. That might sound like criticism. I mean it as praise."

Lesley Krueger, "At Sea in a Disappearing World," *The Globe and Mail* (Canada), Nov. 10, 1990.
"Up on the bridge and down in the engine room, he logs the voyage with wryness and precision. And since these happen to be old Yankee seafaring virtues as well as *New Yorker* ones, the book is a perfect marriage of style and subject."

Richard F. Shepard, "In Search of Seafaring, or Whatever Is Left of It," *New York Times*, Dec. 25, 1990, 26.
"The chapters do not sail as does the ship from one point to another; each picks up at a different position and takes a different aspect of maritime living . . . It is a charming sort of garrulity and puts one in mind of a most articulate old sea dog who has swallowed the anchor and sits on a waterfront bollard telling his lubberly acquaintances about what happens out there."

Colonel Lane C. Kendall, "Looking for a Ship," *U.S. Naval Institute Proceedings*, July 1991, 95.
"*Looking for a Ship* is a fine product of a highly skilled literary craftsman . . . For those concerned for the future of the U.S. Merchant Marine, it is a thought-provoking presentation. For the general reader, it is simply an excellent book."

Assembling California

Page Stegner, "On the Rocks," *Los Angeles Times Book Review*, Jan. 31, 1993, 1.
"The assembling of California is more than a comprehensible story, it is a fascinating drama. OK, the reader may wish to know a bit less about gabbros, pillow basalts and plagiogranites . . . But this is a biography of the earth (as we understand it today). It has its own schizo personality, and is flamboyant enough on its own, as any survivor of the Loma Prieta earthquake will testify. It's well worth getting to know a little better."

Peter Stack, "California's Grand Geological Adventure," *San Francisco Chronicle*, Jan. 31, 1993, 4.
"'Assembling California' is one of the most entertaining and informative travel guides ever written about the Golden State. It's just that the travelers are immensely different, taking millions of years to amble a foot here, a yard there. Thanks to McPhee's bright, intelligent writing, it's all truly awesome."

David Rains Wallace, "Shaky After 100 Million Years," *New York Times Book Review*, Mar. 7, 1993, 9.
"'Assembling California,' is a good book, like all of Mr. McPhee's works, but not quite as good as earlier volumes of the 'Annals' . . . Mr. McPhee maintains a certain ironic detachment toward the environmental issues that often arise with geology. In 1993, this attitude begins to seem anachronistic."

T. H. Watkins, "The State of Flux," *Washington Post*, Mar. 7, 1993, *Book World*, 5.
"Much of McPhee's journey through the earth's dynamics has been complex, unpredictable, discursive and sometimes idiosyncratic to the point of eccentricity, held together less by the discipline of narrative than by the stylistic inventiveness of the prose and the importance of the theme the books have explored. But it has been a hell of a ride, and I, for one, am sorry to see it end."

The Ransom of Russian Art

Harlow Robinson, "He Who Smuggles Must Learn to Party," *New York Times Book Review*, Dec. 18, 1994, 24.
"Unfortunately, Mr. McPhee never alights on any one artist or idea for very long. There is a jumpy, almost unfinished quality to the writing here, as though the author could not quite find the key either to Mr. Dodge or to the nonconformist art scene . . . Mr. McPhee is undone by his cheerful American optimism and his desire to explain things rationally."

Marion Botsford Fraser, "Finding McPhee in Russian Art," *The Globe and Mail* (Canada), Jan. 21, 1995.
"This is not a likely McPhee subject, and in a sense the subject has wrested control away from McPhee . . . It lacks that rooting, grounding, in-place quality that is a McPhee motif . . . I kept waiting for that shift into familiar McPhee gear, and it didn't happen."

Penelope Mesic, "The Art Remover," *Chicago Tribune*, Feb. 5, 1995.
"McPhee's style is like a pane of perfectly transparent glass that celebrates everything that is rational, useful and knowable. But here he almost prankishly applies himself to the obscure, the contradictory, the flamboyant, the lurid."

David Remnick, "Notes from the Underground," *The New York Review of Books*, Mar. 2, 1995.
"McPhee's latest work, *The Ransom of Russian Art*, a profile of an eccentric art collector, has the same qualities of precision and praise as in *A Sense of Where You Are*... *The Ransom of Russian Art* is not unlike Chekhov's longer stories—funny and true. Score one for 'parajournalism' and, especially, for McPhee, its master."

The Second John McPhee Reader

John Motyka, "Books in Brief," *New York Times Book Review*, June 30, 1996, 21.
"The method throughout is vintage McPhee: fact is piled on fact in a steady accretion of telling detail that is rarely less than absorbing in the accumulation. Somehow, whatever the subject, the narrative drive never fails, and we are immersed in the stories; judicious selection and editing are helpful in this regard."

Tom Bailey, "The Second John McPhee Reader," *Interdisciplinary Studies in Literature and Environment*, Summer 1998, 130.
"Those works which could offer the greatest challenge to the editors, the four in *Annals of the Former World*, have been selected by McPhee himself... These four books are important for ecocritics to try to come to terms with, and McPhee's own selections from them are a good enough reason to buy this book."

Irons in the Fire

Susan Salter Reynolds, "In Literary Pursuit of Rustlers, Rock Hounds and Others," *Los Angeles Times*, Apr. 4, 1997, E3.
"This appealing style ... provides an escape for the mind, the hearts and the senses. It gives a reader something to pour himself into. It is a grand old form, and McPhee stays light on his feet within it."

Kate Shatzkin, "McPhee's 'Irons'—Journey with Fact," *Baltimore Sun*, Apr. 6, 1997, 4F.
"In their best moments, these seven pieces evoke a sense of mystery and quiet adventure that will hook any reader intrigued with the interplay of man and earth. Unlike some of McPhee's collections, which have been criticized for lack of cohesion in theme, these essays have as a common subject journey-making."

David Espey, "John McPhee Back Out in the Field," *Philadelphia Inquirer*, Apr. 20, 1997, Q8.
"When the factual world can be as absorbing and dramatic as McPhee makes it, who needs fiction?"

Annals of the Former World

Sarah Kerr, "Like Water from a Stone," *Slate*, June 10, 1998, https://slate.com/culture/1998/06/like-water-from-a-stone.html.
"Sentence by sentence, this book has more finely tuned prose than anything I've read in ages. Which is, as it turns out, its main shortcoming. Things written sentence by sentence often lack a larger energy ... For all McPhee's expertise at crafting a narrative, it feels unnecessarily bloated ... Above all, there's a sense of strain—of McPhee working hard to make all these facts sing."

David Quammen, "Rocks of Age," *New York Times Book Review*, July 5, 1998, 9.
Quammen, a writer specializing in science and nature subjects, says, "As in any McPhee work, there are gemlike sentences, richly rhythmic

paragraphs, nicely burnished synecdoches, metaphors as pungent as wasabi and, behind those felicities, vast amounts of painstaking research. Is all this enough to make 'Annals of the Former World' a formidable and compelling book? Well, sorry: in my view, no. Why not? Because . . . it's virtually bereft of anything else. There's no argument, no urgency, no passion, no sense of larger purpose or emergent meaning, no point to the whole—beyond the bland point that geology is interesting."

The *Times* published (July 26, 1998, *Book Review*, 4) a letter rebutting Quammen's review from Sara Lippincott, a former fact-checker at *The New Yorker* who worked on McPhee's geology articles. Lippincott disputes Quamman's claim that *Annals* had no "larger purpose." She also contradicted Quammen's complaints about the lack of a bibliography in the book, saying that seminal papers and books, and their authors, were credited in the book's text.

John Skow, "Romancing the Stones," *Time*, July 6, 1998, 90.
"In the [*New Yorker*] magazine, attenuated among the Jag and Audi ads, these journeyings seemed dark, intriguing and geologically long, but in book form the same field reports were sunlit, brilliant and short . . . McPhee, whom this reviewer has known for 40 years [since they were colleagues at *Time*], is the most methodical of intuitive writers, or the most intuitive of methodicals."

Rob Laymon, "Eloquence Fills a Tome of Geological Weight," *Philadelphia Inquirer*, July 19, 1998, Q9.
"McPhee makes it all work. He somehow makes his nearly 700 pages of geological discourse sound like the archetypal drama of the planet . . . Everywhere in this book one finds the joy not just of geology, but of what language can do with rocks and the study of rocks."

David L. Ullin, "A Planet's Progress," *Chicago Tribune*, Aug. 2, 1998, M1.
"McPhee's magnificent study provokes in us an abiding appreciation of how everything is connected, down to the smallest, most ancient fossil still embedded in the earth."

Roy Porter, "Rock 'n' Roll," *Los Angeles Times*, Aug. 16, 1998.
"Tripling as a geology primer, an autobiography and a panorama of the nation, bejeweled with splendid vignettes and set-pieces, 'Annals of the Former World' offers a view of America like no other. It is the outpouring of a master stylist."

Gordon P. Eaton, "Annals of the Former World," *Science*, Oct. 30, 1998, 885.
"John McPhee's *Annals of the Former World* is sound armchair science at its most pleasurable. It is a highly informative and enormously satisfying read . . . I believe the book can be an equally rewarding read for lay person and geologist alike."

The Founding Fish

Candus Thomson, "McPhee on Shad—There's a Whole World of Fanatics," *Baltimore Sun*, Oct. 13, 2002, 12F.
"McPhee . . . cheerfully admits to being one of the obsessed. That blind spot—and his editor's reluctance to reel his author in—is what keeps this book from being all it could be, which is shorter. It's a shame, too, because stretches of the book are as powerful as the creatures themselves and their instincts to return to the place of their birth."

Craig Nova, "In History's Current," *Washington Post*, Oct. 27, 2002, *Book World*, 9.
"This book is good fun and exceedingly informative, and its heart is surely in the right place . . . Yet there is also something here that elevates *The Founding Fish* into another realm: an all-consuming vision of how the fish interacts with its world and ours."

Michael S. Rosenwald, "McPhee Reels in the Perfect Story," *Boston Globe*, Nov. 10, 2002, E8.
"In his hands, 'The Founding Fish' is not a book about fish. It's about passion; a quirky saga of fish swimming through history."

FIGURE 31. In *The Founding Fish* (2002), McPhee writes about American shad, using a blend of personal, natural, and United States history. (Jacket design by Gretchen Achilles)

Robert H. Boyle, "A Sense of Where They Are," *New York Times Book Review*, Dec. 8, 2002, 16.
"In sum, 'The Founding Fish' is that rarest of works, a fishing book that is far more than a fishing book. It is a mini-encyclopedia, a highly informative and entertaining amalgam of natural and personal history, a work in a class by itself."

Uncommon Carriers

David L. Ulin, "Heavy Mettle," *Los Angeles Times*, May 28, 2006, R9.
"Here we have McPhee's worldview in a nutshell: that understanding is in the details and that we must be patient, careful enough, attentive

enough to see . . . What McPhee is after here, as he has been throughout his writing life, is a sense of order, of the way the world works, the means by which things get done."

Adam Hochschild, "Trains, Planes and Automobiles," *New York Times Book Review*, June 18, 2006, 12.
"We often read about people in glamorous professions—surgeons, actors, musicians, writers—but so seldom about those who do the jobs we all depend on, those who transport raw materials on river barges, or haul the coal that generates electricity."

Robert Braile, "McPhee's 'Carriers' Is Transporting," *Boston Globe*, June 26, 2006, B7.
"After more than four decades of literary journalism, he [McPhee] still draws from its altruistic tenets, however passe others may consider them. He has chosen a fascinating, important subject, how America works, each and every day, in ways that we take for granted and should not. He has allowed that subject to speak for itself, through its people and places, continually finding magic in the ordinary."

Witold Rybczynski, "Shipping News," *The New York Review of Books*, Aug. 10, 2006.
Rybczynski, a noted architect and writer, says, "Thanks to McPhee's elegant prose and his close observation, we learn a great deal about the machines, but even more about the people . . . McPhee has previously written about the natural environment, but his subject here is man overcoming natural forces."

Dan Cupper, "Train Time at 'The New Yorker,'" *Railroad History*, Spring–Summer 2006, 92.
"One way that McPhee makes dry technological stories come alive is by telling the story through the narratives of people, and he's done that here . . . He also uses correct terminology, something that will come as a surprise to many railroad-knowledgeable readers who are accustomed to finding errors and oversimplifications in the popular press."

Silk Parachute

Susan Salter Reynolds, "John McPhee's New Book Gets Personal," *Los Angeles Times*, Feb. 28, 2010, E1.
"There's a fault line opening in John McPhee. After 28 books and countless essays, he is giving us, bit by bit, a more personal sense of who he is."

Tim McNulty, "John McPhee's Evocation of Family, Friends and Places," *Seattle Times*, Mar. 6, 2010.
"We're fortunate McPhee has written as much—and as well—as he has. For readers who have always wanted a more personal glimpse, 'Silk Parachute' should be floating your way."

Danny Heitman, "Silk Parachute," *Christian Science Monitor*, Mar. 9, 2010, 22.
"How long the McPhee tradition will endure is anyone's guess. But for now we have 'Silk Parachute,' a testament to a kind of literary journalism that will, with any luck, have both its standards and its standard-bearer for years to come."

Elizabeth Royte, "At Close Range," *New York Times*, Mar. 18, 2010, 9.
"Readers hungry for details—how he developed his voice, his sensibility, his 'inn-terr-esst'—will gobble up these essays. Readers who shrug, 'Eh?', may simply enjoy the scope of McPhee's intellectual curiosity and his great gnashing of words . . . In the age of blogging and tweeting, of writers' near-constant self-promotion, McPhee is an imperative counterweight, a paragon of both sense and civility."

Draft No. 4

Ben Yagoda, "A Master Class in Creative Nonfiction," *Wall Street Journal*, Sept. 2, 2017, C9.
"Assent, demur or file away for future reflection, Mr. McPhee's observations about writing are always invigorating to engage with. And 'Draft No. 4' belongs on the short shelf of essential books about our craft."

Parul Sehgal, "The Gloom, Doom and Occasional Joy of the Writing Life," *New York Times*, Sept. 13, 2017, C3.
"His new book, 'Draft No. 4,' a collection of essays on craft, is a sunny tribute to the gloomy side of writing . . . But reading McPhee makes you realize that perhaps writers wax about craft because it's the easiest part of writing to talk about. It's much harder to account for the flashes of inspiration, the slant of seeing, the appetite for the world—to know it down to its core—that keep you coming back to McPhee."

Malcolm Harris, "Who Can Afford to Write Like John McPhee?," *The New Republic*, Sept. 13, 2017.
"When McPhee starts getting into the labor conditions he has experienced during his career [at *The New Yorker*], we move solidly into 'must have been nice' territory . . . The bosses are loose with time, attention, discretion, and money . . . I would recommend *Draft No. 4* to writers and anyone interested in writing, but no one should use it as a professional guide uncritically or they're liable to starve."

John Warner, "John McPhee's 'Draft No. 4' Offers Illuminating View of What It Means to Write," *Chicago Tribune*, Oct. 11, 2017.
"If anyone needs to know what it's like to write, I can simply point to 'Draft No. 4' and McPhee's descriptions of searching for the proper structure or opening points . . . If someone asked me what it takes to become a writer, I am tempted to tell them to learn to think and act like McPhee, but this would be wrong. The trick is to learn to think and act as genuine version of oneself. Let 'Draft No. 4' serve as inspiration, not a how-to."

Brooke Allen, "The Prancing Pen," *The New Criterion*, Oct. 2017, 68.
"Many of McPhee's guidelines are sound, but surprisingly often he fails to follow his own tenets. Much is made, for instance, of the all-consuming 'search for the mot juste,' and he advises aspiring writers not 'to choose a polysyllabic and fuzzy word when a simple and clear one is better . . .' but McPhee himself is addicted to the polysyllabic and the fuzzy."

Corby Kummer, "Get Me Rewrite!" *New York Times Book Review*, Nov. 12, 2017, 13.
"Writers looking for the secrets of his stripped-bark style and painstaking structure will have to be patient with what is a discursive, though often delightful, short book."

Eric Ormsby, "Shooting Forth Light: How to Write in the New Yorker," *Times Literary Supplement*, Apr. 6, 2018.
"John McPhee's suggestions may seem unduly schematic to some. He acknowledges that his approach may not be ideal for novelists and poets; he leaves little room for serendipity. But any writer can benefit from his emphasis on structure, on the value of established fact, on the dogged quest for the best word."

The Patch

Willy Blackmore, "A Writerly Life Explored in Artful Patches," *Los Angeles Times*, Dec. 2, 2018, F8.
"As a book, 'The Patch' is by no means the story of a life from beginning to end—A Memoir—but is maybe a more honest and effective way of stitching together the memories of a life, the structure in a way acknowledging that a neat beginning, middle and end is part of the artifice of writing."

Craig Taylor, "Easy to Come By, Hard to Explain," *New York Times Book Review*, Dec. 23, 2018, 14.
"At first it looks like a revelation in looseness . . . but my hunch is that 'The Patch' is surreptitiously structured, un-unplanned. After years of elevating his prose with patience and organization, the craftsman just can't help himself. I suspect it's all he knows."

Alex Abramovich, "John McPhee's Ways of Seeing," *Bookforum*, Dec. 2018/Jan. 2019, https://www.bookforum.com/print/2504/john-mcphee-s-ways-of-seeing-20435.

"It's a rare gift, to be able to see as well as McPhee sees, and to be given the time that it takes to describe the connections between things so clearly . . . 'What's a hundred years?' McPhee has asked, elsewhere. 'Nothing. And everything . . . It makes the idea of some kind of heritage seem touching, seem odd.' Perhaps. But in his own quiet, meticulous way, McPhee's built a body of work that will stand."

Stephen Goodwin, "The Portrait Master: Known for Rendering Others, a Writer Turns His Attention Inward," *The American Scholar*, Winter 2019.
"McPhee has always been drawn to odd, idiosyncratic, obsessive people who happen to possess a unique talent or way of moving through the world; and in *The Patch*, perhaps his most personal book, it is clearer than ever that McPhee himself is one of their number."

Tony Daniel, "The Twilight of Master Essayist John McPhee Is Beautiful," *The Federalist*, June 28, 2019, https://thefederalist.com/2019/06/28/twilight-master-essayist-john-mcphee-beautiful/.
"McPhee also stealthily and inexorably imparted to me what good writing was. You can't come away from a McPhee essay without having developed better taste . . . Maybe the greatest quality of McPhee as a writer is that he goes forth. He gets off the damn East Coast. He explores places he doesn't understand. He befriends people who are absolutely nothing like him or anybody he grew up with."

Tabula Rasa: Volume 1

Robert Wilson, "Good Writing Never Gets Old," American Scholar, Summer 2023, https://theamericanscholar.org/notes-and-outtakes/.
"McPhee has always been the perfect *New Yorker* writer, and not only because of his sterling prose style and his ability to dig a story out of terrain that others might overlook—firewood, for instance, or oranges. As a Princeton townie who is both enamored of and slightly superior to New York and its excesses, he falls within the magazine's long

tradition of starry-eyed outsiders, starting with its first editor, Harold Ross . . . Since *Tabula Rasa* begins and ends in the middle of things, future volumes seem more than possible. May we all live to read them."

Jim Kelly, "Giving His Own Good Weight," Air Mail, July 1, 2023, https://airmail.news/issues/2023-7-1/giving-his-own-good-weight. Kelly, a former student of McPhee's at Princeton and former Managing Editor of *Time* magazine, says: "His talent at turning any subject that interests him into writing that is fresh and compelling is unmatched . . . What *Tabula Rasa* really is about is John McPhee, now 92, and, along with his last couple of books, it is as close to an autobiography as we will get."

Mark Oppenheimer, "In 'Tabula Rasa,' John McPhee Looks Back at Books Not Written," *Washington Post*, July 7, 2023, https://www.washingtonpost.com/books/2023/07/07/john-mcphee-tabula-rasa-review/. "Few of the subjects discussed in '*Tabula Rasa*' call out for longform treatment; McPhee's instincts (and editors) steered him well. But there are still pleasurers to be had in these 50 short chapters. Minor league McPhee is still major league writing. It's not faint praise to say he is still more pleasingly consistent than any other writer working. There is never a dud metaphor, never a cliché."

Michael Pearson, "Tabula Rasa: Volume 1," *New York Journal of Books*, July 11, 2023, https://www.nyjournalofbooks.com/book-review/tabula-rasa-volume-1.
Pearson, who has written extensively about McPhee, says, "For McPhee, Princeton is like Twain's Hannibal, the locus of his imagination. And some of the tales in Tabula Rasa have a Tom Sawyer–like feel to them, narrating the sweet and funny adventures of a pre-adolescent boy who knew every back alley and open window on [the] Princeton campus . . . McPhee is a writer with a generous heart and sharp self-deprecatory sense of humor. *Tabula Rasa* is no blank slate. It is the story that tells the reader much about McPhee the writer, the man, and the teacher."

Tom Seymour Evans, "Loose Ends," *Times Literary Supplement*, Aug. 18/25, 2023, https://www.the-tls.co.uk/articles/tabula-rasa-john-mcphee-book-review-tom-seymour-evans/.

"All memoirs seek to cheat death, but few do it so brazenly as *Tabula Rasa* . . . In other hands the set-up could seem rickety—old-timer anecdotes spun as concept memoir—but in the context of the author's back catalogue it carries a sly heft."

Noah Rawlings, "Annals of an Alternate World: On John McPhee's 'Tabula Rasa,'" Sept. 15, 2023, https://lareviewofbooks.org/article/annals-of-an-alternate-world-on-john-mcphees-tabula-rasa/.

"*Tabula Rasa*'s most profound theme is not place, however, but death—the ultimate blank slate. Early on, McPhee cheekily presents his book as a means of keeping death at bay. He is a nonagenarian Scheherazade, staying alive each night by telling a new story . . . Death occurs in *Tabula Rasa* as an unavoidable preoccupation, a bell tolling at regular intervals . . . There will be time, until there is not. In preserving a record of his unfinished stories, McPhee does honor to those of the dead."

7

Books

"I'm an old man. And to keep writing is to keep going, to keep living."
—FROM "WRITER JOHN MCPHEE ON HIS BOOK
'TABULA RASA,'" SCOTT SIMON, NATIONAL
PUBLIC RADIO *WEEKEND EDITION*, JULY 15, 2023

JOHN MCPHEE has been the subject of two book-length studies.

Michael Pearson, *John McPhee*, Twayne's United States Authors Series, No. 674. New York: Twayne Publishers, 1997.
This 128-page book is a combination of biography and critical study, going from McPhee's early years growing up in Princeton through the publication of 21 of his books, ending before his *Irons in the Fire* collection and the *Annals of the Former World* volume that won the Pulitzer Prize.

Author Michael Pearson, who was an English professor at Old Dominion University, writes in a somewhat academic style, but covers a broad span of material in a creative way, including all the basic elements of McPhee's biography and literary story. A highlight is his chapter on "The McPhee Hero," discussing the common threads in how McPhee tells the stories of individual lives.

Pearson interviewed McPhee five times between 1992 and 1995 and includes material from those conversations and many other sources.

FIGURE 32. *Coming into McPhee Country* includes 14 essays about aspects of McPhee's writing by professors and literary journal editors.

The book is part of the publisher's series of "critical introductions" to several hundred major writers.

O. Alan Weltzien and Susan N. Maher, eds., *Coming into McPhee Country: John McPhee and the Art of Literary Nonfiction.* Salt Lake City: University of Utah Press, 2003.
This book was developed following a program devoted to McPhee at the 1999 Western Literature Association (WLA) meeting in Sacramento, California. Using material from the session and going well beyond it, this is the first and so far only comprehensive anthology discussing McPhee's work. The authors are all professors or editors of literary journals.

The book is organized in three sections: "The Evolving Writer," "McPhee and the Natural World," and "The Writerly Challenges of McPhee." It includes 14 thematic essays on topics such as McPhee's writing about nature, his style in portraying individuals, and how a professor used McPhee's *The Control of Nature* to teach.

Study Guide: The Control of Nature John McPhee. Middletown, DE: SuperSummary, 2020.
A study guide was published for McPhee's book *The Control of Nature* more than 30 years after the book was first published in 1989, again showing the staying power of his work.

This volume provides a condensed study guide to the McPhee book, for classes and other uses, summarizing the chapters, key terms, and main figures.

8

Theses

> "As an interviewer, I don't think I come on very strongly, and I think that's an advantage. I'm shy, and I get into people's worlds."
>
> —FROM AN INTERVIEW WITH JAMIE SAXON, PRINCETON UNIVERSITY OFFICE OF COMMUNICATIONS, SEPTEMBER 18, 2017

JOHN MCPHEE's work has been studied throughout the academic world in terms of his techniques and theory of writing, as well as specific subject areas, including the environment (*The Control of Nature*), food (*Oranges*), and land use (*Coming into the Country*).

Here are publicly available theses that are completely or in large part about McPhee's work:

John Beard, "Inside the Whale: A Critical Study of New Journalism and the Nonfiction Form" (PhD dissertation, Florida State University, 1985).
A critical examination of the work of McPhee, Tom Wolfe, Norman Mailer, and Hunter S. Thompson.

Elizabeth Giddens, "John McPhee's Rhetoric of Balance and Perspective" (PhD dissertation, University of Tennessee, Knoxville, 1990).
Giddens writes about how McPhee balances journalistic fair-mindedness with a persuasive aim that has rhetorical impact. She talks

about how McPhee's work, though widely popular, has been the subject of little scholarly study yet (as of 1990) and how that dearth of attention could be traceable to McPhee's modesty.

Matthew Shinobu Main, "Zones of Confluence: Alaskan Non-Fiction and the Environment" (master's thesis, University of Alaska Anchorage, 2019).
Main examines part of McPhee's *Coming into the Country* to explore cultural consciousness in Alaska.

Lia Oppedisano, "The Impossible Moment: Shape-Shifting Nonfiction and Magical Realism Influences" (master's thesis, Harvard University, 2016).
Oppedisano looks at how McPhee uses surprise and confounds expectations in his writing.

George Roundy, "Crafting Fact: The Prose of John McPhee" (PhD dissertation, University of Iowa, 1984).
This dissertation, believed to be the first done about McPhee, explores his stylistic techniques. Roundy includes an account of his first meeting with McPhee in 1979 where he learned of McPhee's "profound respect, almost a reverence, for facts," and also his preoccupation and fascination with structure.

Holly E. Schreiber, "Representations of Poverty in American Literary Journalism" (PhD dissertation, Indiana University, 2015).
McPhee's *The Pine Barrens* is analyzed.

Paul F. Sharke, "Samuel Florman and Literature of Technology" (master's thesis, New Jersey Institute of Technology, 1998).
McPhee's *The Control of Nature* is the subject of Sharke's study.

James N. Stull, "Self and the Performance of Others" (PhD, University of Iowa, 1990).
Stull discusses McPhee's "pastoral vision."

Brian Turner, "Rhetorics of Assent: A Rhetorical Analysis of 'Good Reasons' Arguments for the Environment in the Nonfiction of Jonathan Schell, Wendell Berry, and John McPhee" (PhD dissertation, University of Alberta, 1992).

The author praises the rhetorical effectiveness of McPhee's work, primarily focusing on his work about nature and the environment.

PART III
Miscellany

9

Readings and Speeches

"Sooner or later, you have to have a sense of structure, or all you've got is a bowl of spaghetti. It's just the basic idea of thinking things out before you do it."

—FROM "AUTHOR JOHN MCPHEE STILL FINDS WONDER IN THE OUTDOORS, CHOCOLATE AND CIRCUS BEARS" BY SEAN GREGORY, TIME MAGAZINE, DECEMBER 6, 2018

AS HIS success and public profile grew, John McPhee was in increasing demand for public readings and speeches. Besides his individual appearances, he also did a decade-long occasional series of readings around the country with his wife, Yolanda, based on his *Rising from the Plains* book published in 1986.

This is a sampling of his readings and speeches.

John McPhee, "Deerfield Academy Heritage Award Presentation," Deerfield, MA, Oct. 3, 1995.
Available through the Deerfield Academy archives, either as a transcript or 39-minute audio recording.
McPhee, who was honored as a Deerfield Academy graduate "whose professional and personal achievements represent a special contribution to the betterment of society," was invited to the school in western Massachusetts to accept the award. He speaks of his inspiration to write

The Headmaster in 1966, which was his book about Deerfield and its longtime head, Frank Boyden. He also discusses how to structure one's writing, using part of *Coming into the Country* as an example, and how he got involved in writing about geology.

John McPhee, *Rising from the Plains* reading, Colgate University, Hamilton, NY, Apr. 11, 1996, 74-minute audio recording, https://digitalcollections.colgate.edu/node/6852.
As part of a nationwide series of readings from his *Rising from the Plains*, McPhee, along with his wife, Yolanda Whitman, read for Colgate University students and faculty. He is introduced by Leila Philip, a former student of his at Princeton who was then an English professor at Colgate. The reading includes Whitman reading from the journals of Ethel Waxham, a teacher in early twentieth-century Wyoming whose previously unpublished journals figured prominently in McPhee's book about the West and geology.

John McPhee, discussion session with students, Colgate University, Hamilton, NY, Apr. 11, 1996, 59-minute audio recording. https://digitalcollections.colgate.edu/node/6989.
McPhee, who visited Colgate to read from *Rising from the Plains*, spends an hour with a class of undergraduate students answering their questions about writing, including how to know when to stop doing research and start writing, the importance of first writing a lead and knowing where the piece will end, and why he generally leaves out his thoughts and opinions.

John McPhee and Eldridge Moores, Geological Society of America annual meeting, Denver, CO, Oct. 2002, https://www.geosociety.org/awards/02speeches/PSA.pdf.
McPhee receives the Public Service Award from the Geological Society of America for his writing about geology. Eldridge Moores, a professor at the University of California, Davis, and a major figure in McPhee's *Assembling California*, says in presenting the award: "John has made geology a household word." In his acceptance speech, McPhee thanks the

geological community for its "unending patience in teaching me, guiding me, encouraging me, and correcting me in a project that must have seemed quixotic."

"Elliott Bay Books Presents: John McPhee," Seattle, WA, June 26, 2006, 48-minute audio and video recording, https://archive.org/details/SMA_9039.
In a program at the Seattle Public Library, the bookstore Elliott Bay Books hosts John McPhee for a reading from *Uncommon Carriers*, followed by a question-and-answer session with the audience. McPhee talks about why he did a cross-country trip with a truck driver, how he organizes his writing, his use of the internet, and how he finds the people he profiles, such as Bill Bradley.

Peter Hessler, "John McPhee with Peter Hessler, Reading," Lannan Foundation, Santa Fe, NM, Nov. 10, 2010, 58-minute audio and video recording for an introduction of McPhee's reading, plus a 27-minute audio and video recording of a conversation between Hessler and McPhee, https://lannan.org/media/john-mcphee-with-peter-hessler.
Hessler, a former student of McPhee's at Princeton and a fellow staff writer at *The New Yorker*, introduces McPhee, who reads parts of several pieces from *Silk Parachute*. McPhee then tells Hessler about fact-checkers at *The New Yorker*, why he is more personal in his writing in *Silk Parachute*, how *The New Yorker* has changed, and how he finds subjects.

"John McPhee at Politics and Prose," Washington, DC, Mar. 29, 2011, 46-minute audio recording, https://archive.org/details/JohnMcpheeAtPoliticsAndProse.
This recording comes from an appearance by McPhee at the Politics and Prose bookstore in Washington, DC. After he reads from *Silk Parachute*, he answers questions from the audience, speaking about which nonfiction writers influenced him most as a young person, fact-checking, thoughts about documentary film, and how he gets people to "reveal their souls."

National Book Critics Circle Awards, New York City, Mar. 15, 2018, https://www.c-span.org/video/?441611-1/2018-national-book-critics-circle-awards.

Stacey Vanek Smith speaks at the 28-minute mark, John McPhee at the 35-minute mark. Audio and video recording.

Text of McPhee acceptance speech:

https://www.bookcritics.org/2018/03/23/john-mcphee-accepts-the-sandrof-award-for-lifetime-achievement/.

McPhee receives the lifetime achievement award from the National Book Critics Circle. He is introduced by author and NPR host Stacey Vanek Smith, a former student of his at Princeton, who talks about his impact as a teacher and a writer. In his acceptance speech, McPhee discusses what is creative about nonfiction and pays tribute to *New Yorker* editor William Shawn.

10

Book Dedications

"A writer grows on the volume of what the writer writes. People standing around, over drinks, talking about writing, isn't writing. Writing is when you go off on your own, close the door and fight it out with the blank screen or paper."

—FROM "AUTHOR JOHN MCPHEE STILL FINDS WONDER IN THE OUTDOORS, CHOCOLATE AND CIRCUS BEARS" BY SEAN GREGORY, *TIME* MAGAZINE, DECEMBER 6, 2018

BOOK BY book, these are John McPhee's dedications.

A Sense of Where You Are: To Harry Roemer McPhee [his older brother]

The Headmaster: To Robert McGlynn [a Deerfield Academy English teacher who was a friend and mentor]

Oranges: For Pryde [his first wife]

The Pine Barrens (original edition): For Pryde and for her father Charles Mitchell Brown [his first wife and his father-in-law]

A Roomful of Hovings and Other Profiles: Mary Ziegler McPhee [his mother]

Levels of the Game: For Bill Bradley [the Princeton basketball star about whom he wrote his first book]

The Crofter and the Laird: To Pryde [his first wife]

Encounters with the Archdruid: To Robert Bingham [his longtime editor at *The New Yorker*]

Wimbledon: A Celebration: We [with photographer Alfred Eisenstaedt] dedicate this book to Robert Twynam [the head groundskeeper of the All England Club]

The Deltoid Pumpkin Seed: For Jenny [one of his daughters, a writer and translator]

The Curve of Binding Energy: To William Shawn [editor of *The New Yorker*]

Pieces of the Frame: For Yolanda [his second wife]

The Survival of the Bark Canoe: To John Kauffmann [a friend who helped inspire several books]

Coming into the Country: For Martha [one of his daughters, a novelist and professor]

Giving Good Weight: For Laura [one of his daughters, a photographer]

The Pine Barrens, a special edition with photographs: For Kate and Yolanda [the wives of photographer Bill Curtsinger and McPhee]

Basin and Range: For Sarah [one of his daughters, an art historian and professor]

In Suspect Terrain: To Bill Howarth [a Princeton faculty colleague, who wrote the introduction to the *John McPhee Reader*]

La Place de la Concorde Suisse: For my daughters in their Wanderjahre [a French, German, and Scandinavian term for years of travel or journey]

BOOK DEDICATIONS 197

Table of Contents: For Laura Anne and Roemer [his sister and brother]

Heirs of General Practice: For my mother in memory of my father, Harry R. McPhee, M.D. 1895–1984

Rising from the Plains: For Yolanda Whitman [his wife]

Outcroppings: To the memory of Ethel Waxham Love 1882–1959 [the author of previously unpublished writing about early twentieth-century Wyoming that he used in *Rising from the Plains*]

The Control of Nature: For Vanessa, Katherine, Andrew, and Cole [his stepchildren]

Looking for a Ship: For Yolanda [his wife]

Assembling California: To Kenneth Stover Deffeyes [a Princeton geology professor who advised him on his geology books]

The Ransom of Russian Art: For Roger Straus [cofounder and chairman of Farrar, Straus and Giroux, McPhee's longtime publisher]

The Second John McPhee Reader: In memory of Anne Sullivan [a vice president at Farrar, Straus and Giroux who was killed after being struck by a bus on a New York City street in 1995]

Irons in the Fire: Laura [one of his daughters, a photographer]

Annals of the Former World: Yolanda Whitman [his wife]

The Princeton Anthology of Writing: For almost half a century, distinguished writers have taught at Princeton on visiting appointments made possible by two individuals to whom this book is gratefully dedicated: Harold W. McGraw Jr., of the Princeton Class of 1940, chair emeritus of McGraw-Hill, who endowed the McGraw Seminars in 1984, in recognition of the importance of writing in all disciplines. Edwin F. Ferris, former *New York Herald* journalist and Princeton alumnus of the Class of 1899, whose bequest in 1957 established the Ferris Professorship in Journalism.

The Founding Fish: For George Hackl, of the Roebling Flats, of Chicken Island and the New York Eddy, of Portofino and Trans-Keld, of High Lee, Middle Lee, and sine qua non, The Patch. For Ronnie and Alan Lieb, without whom not much. For Jim Merritt, the master.

[Hackl is longtime companion for fishing in New Hampshire; the Liebs ran a restaurant in Pennsylvania that McPhee wrote about for *The New Yorker*, and he calls Jim Merritt, a friend and writer about fishing subjects, his "ichthyotherapist." The locations are all connected to McPhee and fishing, including the special spot in New Hampshire, The Patch, that gave his book its name 16 years later in 2018.]

Uncommon Carriers: To Sam Candler, of the Boarskin Shirt, of Cemocheckobee Creek, of the Shad Alley and the Coal Train, all aboard [a longtime friend with whom he traveled in Georgia and other places]

Silk Parachute: For My Grandchildren, Isobel, Jasper, Leandro, Livia, Nicholas, Oliver, Rebecca, Riley, Tomasso

The Princeton Reader: This book is dedicated to the extraordinary writers who have taught at Princeton University since the beginning of the journalism seminars in 1964 and to our generous benefactors: Edwin F. Ferris, Princeton Class of 1899, former *New York Herald* journalist and owner and founding editor of the *Scranton Times*, whose bequest in 1957 established the Ferris Professorship in Journalism. Harold W. McGraw, Jr., Princeton Class of 1940, chief executive of McGraw-Hill from 1975 to 1983, who endowed the McGraw Seminars in recognition of the importance of writing in all disciplines. Joyce Michaelson, who created the Robbins Professorship in 2000 with a gift from the E. Franklin Robbins Trust, in honor of her late husband, William G. Michaelson, Princeton Class of 1959, and their daughter, Robin L. Michaelson, Princeton Class of 1989.

Draft No. 4: For Gordon Gund, who doesn't miss a word, and For Yolanda Whitman, who is unreluctant to say when words are missing, and To half a thousand Princeton students, who have heard it all before. [Gund is a businessman and friend of McPhee's who went blind and to whom McPhee would read his work aloud; Whitman is McPhee's wife; the students were in his Princeton University writing seminar.]

The Patch: For My Grandchildren, Ayane, Isobel, Jasper, Leandro, Livia, Nicholas, Oliver, Rebecca, Riley, Tomasso

Tabula Rasa: Volume 1: For and To Yolanda Whitman [his wife]

11

John McPhee's Editors at *The New Yorker* and Farrar, Straus and Giroux

"I never have the feeling, *Oh, this is gonna be a terrific story, I can't miss.* I think it's rational to feel that what you're writing isn't very good as you go along, because how else are you gonna improve it? I'm always nervous when I'm writing."

—"LEGENDARY AUTHOR JOHN MCPHEE ON PROCRASTINATION, DREAD, AND HIS ENDLESS FINAL PROJECT," BY NATHAN TAYLOR PEMBERTON, GQ, AUGUST 14, 2023

WITH HIS longevity as a writer, John McPhee has had many editors at *The New Yorker* and Farrar, Straus and Giroux. The overlap of editors at *The New Yorker* reflects that McPhee usually received editing from both the editor of the magazine as well as another staff editor.

The New Yorker

William Shawn, 1965–1987
Robert Bingham, 1966–1982
Patrick Crow, 1982–1998
Robert Gottlieb, 1987–1992

John Bennet, 1998–2016
David Remnick, 1998–present
Deidre Foley-Mendelssohn, 2017–2019

Farrar, Straus and Giroux

Harold Vursell, 1965–1970
Thomas Stewart, 1970–1976
Patricia Strachan, 1977–1988
Linda Healey, 1988–1992
Elisheva Urbas, 1992–1998
Paul Elie, 1998–2011
Alex Star, 2012–present

12

Film Adaptation

"I think writing is a suspension of life in order to recreate it, and the life you suspend is your own."

—FROM "THE ANNALS OF MCPHEE," *NEW YORK TIMES*, BY ISRAEL SHENKER, JANUARY 11, 1976

MANY OF John McPhee's books and articles have been considered as subjects for film adaptations. Although some of his books, including *Levels of the Games*, were optioned several different times, only one film has been made from McPhee's writings: *Casey's Shadow*, a 1978 film starring Walter Matthau and Alexis Smith. It was based on McPhee's article "Ruidoso," in the April 29, 1974, *New Yorker* and later collected in the book *Pieces of the Frame*. Ray Stark, one of the most successful producers in post–World War II Hollywood, read the story and then pursued it as a movie.

McPhee had no role in the adaptation, which was written by Carol Sobieski (who was later nominated for an Academy Award for her adaption of Fannie Flagg's *Fried Green Tomatoes*). McPhee says he did not even want a credit.

The film received a positive review from the chief movie critic of *The New York Times*, Vincent Canby (March 17, 1978). The screenplay "manages to touch almost all of the bases one expects in a horse movie, but it does so without condescension," Canby writes. Gary Arnold, movie critic for *The Washington Post*, writes, "'Casey's Shadow' is a beautiful title and a surprisingly appealing and stirring movie."

FIGURE 33. McPhee's "Ruidoso" article in *The New Yorker* about a race for quarter horses in New Mexico became a 1978 movie, *Casey's Shadow*, starring Walter Matthau and Alexis Smith.

Despite not wanting to be involved in the making of the film, McPhee was curious to see the result. After watching the movie at a theater near Princeton with his wife and children, he wrote in *Draft No. 4* that he bent down to look for some coins he had dropped under his seat. He says he was distracted until he heard a roar—his family cheering his credit for writing the story that the film was based upon.

13

Books by Former Students

"The best teacher of writing is writing itself. Writers grow slowly. They don't spring like something out of the ear of Zeus. They do it one sentence after another, through time."

—"TETE-A-TETE: JOHN MCPHEE '49,"
IN CONVERSATION WITH DEERFIELD ACADEMY
HEAD OF SCHOOL JOHN AUSTIN AND WRITER
JULIA ELLIOTT, *DEERFIELD MAGAZINE*, WINTER 2023

JOHN MCPHEE says he never planned to teach, yet it became a large part of his life and literary legacy.

He jumped in when Princeton University asked him in late 1974 to be a last-minute replacement for the writer Larry L. King, who had resigned. McPhee continued his course, first called "The Literature of Fact" and later "Creative Nonfiction," for nearly 50 years as a Ferris Professor of Journalism. He received the Princeton President's Award for Distinguished Teaching in 1999.

Through his teaching, McPhee nurtured a network of what became hundreds of former students. Many became authors themselves, carrying forward writing principles McPhee had taught, while others followed different creative pursuits and brought his ideas into other fields.

McPhee offered his course in the spring term of the academic year starting in 1975, planning in conjunction with his own writing schedule. For many years he taught for two consecutive spring terms and then

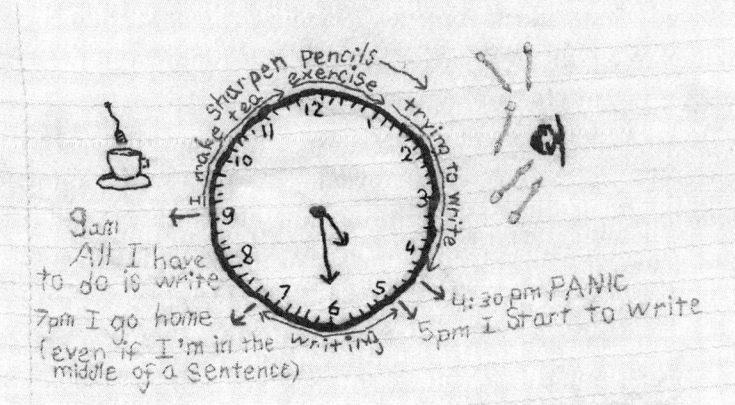

[Clock diagram with annotations:]
sharpen pencils
make tea / exercise / trying to write
9 am
All I have to do is write
7pm I go home (even if I'm in the middle of a sentence)
writing
4:30 pm PANIC
5pm I start to write

WHAT SEEMED SO FASCINATING WAS THAT 1000's OF WORDS COULD BE HUNG ON A STRUCTURE — OR COULD INVERSELY, COLLAPSE WITHOUT IT   BANG!

[Timeline diagram:]
born — high school — build houses — EARTHQUAKE — get married — do this or that → human time
geologic, geographic time

Humans = smallest unit of time is 1 sec
Geologists = smallest unit of time they can really think in is a million years

"IF YOU FREE YOURSELF FROM THE CONVENTIONAL REACTION TO A QUANTITY LIKE A MILLION YEARS, YOU FREE YOURSELF A BIT FROM THE BOUNDARIES OF HUMAN TIME, AND THEN IN A WAY YOU DO NOT LIVE AT ALL, BUT IN ANOTHER WAY YOU LIVE FOREVER."

FIGURE 34. Diana Buri Weymar, a former student in McPhee's Princeton University writing seminar, became a textile artist who created and exhibited *The John McPhee Sampler*, a set of hand-embroidered pages threaded with text from his articles on the craft of writing. (Courtesy of Diana Weymar)

took a year off, though he later switched to teaching every year. He capped the class at 16 and usually 60 to 80 students applied for admission. In early years it was open to all undergraduate classes and he also accepted a few graduate students (including Sheryl WuDunn, who went on to earn a Pulitzer Prize for international reporting). Eventually it became a course for sophomores only.

When McPhee taught, he suspended his own writing. He said the experience of teaching, which he enjoyed for its back-and-forth with students, was also a useful break for him. "Then I go back to writing with fresh vigor and I'm writing through summer, fall and January," he says. "I think I've written and published more, over the years, than I would have had I not spent those semesters teaching. Teaching and writing have been symbiotic for me" (Princeton University communications story, Jamie Saxon, September 18, 2017).

McPhee's academic office on the Princeton campus, for many years in a tower of the Gothic-style Guyot Hall, which housed the geosciences department, was where he held private conferences with students to talk in-depth about their writing, an essential part of his course. Princeton has never offered a journalism major or degree, and McPhee's office was long an epicenter for nonfiction writers on campus.

In addition to his reference books, maps, and other material, McPhee's office contained something special: shelves filled with hundreds of books written by his former students, sent and inscribed with expressions of appreciation to him.

From when he started teaching the course in 1975 through spring 2020 (after which he moved into an advisory role for the writing program) McPhee taught 544 Princeton students. Of those, 125 or nearly a quarter of them have published at least one book since graduation. Many have won awards for their books and often have published more than one—up to 30 for one former student (Francine Mathews, a mystery novelist who publishes under the name Stephanie Barron as well as her own).

Some of McPhee's students have pursued nonfiction, and others have written novels, memoirs, mysteries, and children's books. Many have cited McPhee and his class as an inspiration, such as Jordan Salama, a 2017 McPhee student whose book *Every Day the River Changes: Four*

Weeks Down the Magdalena was chosen in 2022 as the book for all Princeton's first-year students to read before coming to campus.

Many former students say they have kept their writing assignments from the McPhee class with his handwritten comments as a sort of talisman. The first assignment, in which students paired up in alphabetical order and wrote profiles of each other, led to many lasting friendships. Guest speakers, including regular visits for many years from the colorful Roger Straus, who was the founder of McPhee's publisher, Farrar, Straus and Giroux, have been long remembered. Years later, former students recall specific advice from McPhee, and he has stayed in touch with many students for decades afterward. Many cite his words in phone calls, letters, or emails as crucial encouragement, especially when they came in early years after Princeton.

Beyond the former students who have followed in McPhee's footsteps as book writers, others have gone on to different writing and editing careers. Dozens have become magazine and newspaper writers, and several have been the top editors of magazines (including David Remnick of *The New Yorker* and two top *Time* magazine editors, Jim Kelly and Richard Stengel). Many have contributed to *The New Yorker* and other leading publications.

Others have taken creative efforts in other directions, such as Alex Gansa, the creator and executive producer of TV's *Homeland*; Sam Gravitte, a singer-songwriter who starred in *Wicked* on Broadway; Joanne Shen, a filmmaker, director, and producer; and Janani Sreenivasan, a comedian and humor writer. Diana Buri Weymar, a textile artist, has exhibited a variety of projects, including *The John McPhee Sampler*, hand-embroidered pages threaded with text using McPhee's words sewn onto fabric that looks like lined notebook paper.

Beyond McPhee's students individually staying in touch with him, there have been group tributes. When the 16 members of the class who were alumni of the McPhee course in 2015 celebrated a Princeton reunion in 2022, they wrote "Reflections on 'Creative Non-Fiction'" and gave McPhee a bound book called *The McPhee Project*.

Claire Ashmead, who put the tribute book together, says of McPhee's influence, "We have taken his lessons into our careers, not just within the writing industry but into medicine, mathematics, theater, law. We thank our lucky stars we took his seminar—and I know I'm not alone in calling up or emailing to ask for advice. Like many extraordinary teachers, I imagine he is only aware of one one-millionth of the gratitude we his students feel. So I felt it was important to make 'The McPhee Project' as a way of saying: This class matters to all of us, and it matters to all of us in a daily way. Not because you write for *The New Yorker* or because we write for a living, but because you are a great teacher and mentor and friend. And that has shaped our lives."

For all the intensity of McPhee's connection to his Princeton students, his impact on writers has also been much wider. In his introduction to *The Second John McPhee Reader*, David Remnick writes, "Actually, only a small percentage of McPhee's students studied with him at Princeton; he has been for dozens and dozens of non-fiction writers what Robert Lowell used to be for poets and poet wannabes of a certain age: the model."

What follows is a list of former McPhee students who have published books, with a record of their first book. Some of them had collaborators on their books and their names are given in parentheses including a "with" annotation.

>Achenbach, Joel. *Why Things Are: Answers to Every Essential Question in Life.* New York: Ballantine Books, 1991.
>Andersen, M. J. *Portable Prairie: Confessions of an Unsettled Midwesterner.* New York: St. Martin's Press/Thomas Dunne Books, 2010.
>Austin, Greta. *Shaping Church Law around the Year 1000: The Decretum of Burchard of Worms.* Abingdon, Oxfordshire: Taylor & Francis, 2009.
>Balmain, Melissa. *Just Us: Adventures and Travels of a Mother and Daughter.* London: Faber & Faber, 1998.
>Belkin, Lisa. *First Do No Harm: The Dramatic Story of Real Doctors and Patients Making Impossible Choices at a Big-City Hospital.* New York: Fawcett Crest, 1994.
>Bennett, Brian. *Religion and Language in Post-Soviet Russia.* Milton Park, Abingdon, Oxfordshire: Routledge, 2011.

Boorstin, Julia. *When Women Lead: What They Achieve, Why They Succeed, and How We Can Learn from Them.* New York: Simon & Schuster, 2022.

Booth, Alison. *Greatness Engendered: George Eliot and Virginia Woolf.* Ithaca, NY: Cornell University Press, 1992.

Bosker, Bianca. *Original Copies: Architectural Mimicry in Contemporary China.* Honolulu: University of Hawaii Press, 2013.

Brooks, Oakley. *Tsunami Alert: Beating Asia's Next Big One.* Singapore: Marshall Cavendish International, 2011.

Brunetta, Leslie. *Spider Silk: Evolution and 400 Million Years of Spinning, Waiting, Snagging, and Mating.* New Haven, CT: Yale University Press, 2010 (with Catherine L. Craig).

Burris, Jennifer. *Foreclosed: Between Crisis and Possibility.* New Haven, CT: Yale University Press, 2011 (with Sofia Olascoaga, Sadia Shirazi, and Gaia Tedone).

Canine, Craig. *Dream Reaper: The Story of an Old-Fashioned Inventor in the High-Tech, High-Stakes World of Modern Agriculture.* New York: Knopf, 1995.

Challener, Daniel D. *Stories of Resilience in Childhood: Narratives of Maya Angelou, Maxine Hong Kingston, Richard Rodriguez, John Edgar Wideman and Tobias Wolff.* Boca Raton, FL: CRC Press Inc, 1997.

Chew, Alexa Z. *The Complete Legal Writer.* Chapel Hill, NC: Carolina Academic Press, 2016 (with Katie Rose Guest Pryal).

Choudhury, Kushanava. *The Epic City: The World on the Streets of Calcutta.* London: Bloomsbury, 2017.

Cohen, Elisabeth. *The Glitch.* New York: Anchor, 2018.

Coleman, Isobel. *Strategic Foreign Assistance: Civil Society in International Security.* Stanford, CA: Hoover Institution Press, 2006 (with A. Lawrence Chickering, P. Edward Haley, and Emily Vargas-Baron).

Crawford, Lacy. *Early Decision: Based on a True Frenzy.* New York: William Morrow, 2013.

Creange, Renee. *Classroom Routines That Really Work for PreK and Kindergarten.* New York: Scholastic Teaching Resources, 2001 (with Kathleen Hayes).

Crystal, Abe. *The Business of Courses.* Durham, NC: Ruzuku, Inc., 2021.

Deutschman, Alan. *Winning Money for College: The High School Student's Guide to Scholarship Contests.* Denver, CO: Peterson's, 1984.

Doshi, Sudeep, editor. *A Poem for Cry: Favourite Poems of Famous Indians.* New York: Penguin Global, 2007 (with Avanti Maluste).

Ferriss, Timothy. *The 4-Hour Workweek: Escape 9–5, Live Anywhere, and Join the New Rich.* New York: Crown Archetype, 2009.

Fisher, Marc. *After the Wall: Germany, the Germans, and the Burdens of History.* New York: Simon & Schuster, 1995.

Fleming, Michael, *Bags and Tools: Poems.* Brattleboro, VT: Green Writers Press, 2022.

Flippin, Royce. *Save an Alligator, Shoot a Preppie: A Terrorist Guide.* New York: A & W Visual Library, 1981 (with Douglas McGrath and Frank Williams).

Frazier, Mark. *The Making of the Chinese Industrial Workplace: State, Revolution, and Labor Management.* Cambridge: Cambridge University Press, 2002.

Gellman, Barton D. *Contending with Kennan: Toward a Philosophy of American Power.* Westport, CT: Praeger Publishers Inc, 1984.

George, Don, editor. *Wanderlust: Real-Life Tales of Adventure and Romance.* New York: Villard, 2001.

Gollin, Andrea, editor. *Lair: Radical Homes and Hideouts of Movie Villains.* Miami: Tra Publishing, 2019 (with Chad Oppenheim).

Gordinier, Jeff. *X Saves the World: How Generation X Got the Shaft But Can Still Keep Everything from Sucking.* New York: Penguin Books, 2008.

Graham, Lawrence Otis. *Ten Point Plan for College Acceptance.* New York: Putnam, 1981.

Gray, Margaret. *The Ugly Princess and the Wise Fool.* New York: Henry Holt Books for Young Readers, 2002.

Greider, Katherine. *From Home to Home: The Story of the International Rescue Committee.* New York: International Rescue Committee, 2008.

Ha, Thu-Huong. *Hail Caesar*. St. Louis: Turtleback, 2007.

Haase, Leif Wellington. *A New Deal for Health: How to Cover Everyone and Get Medical Costs Under Control*. New York: Century Foundation, 2005.

Hagedorn, Suzanne. *Abandoned Women: Rewriting the Classics in Dante, Boccaccio and Chaucer*. Ann Arbor: University of Michigan Press, 2004.

Hajari, Nisid. *Midnight's Furies: The Deadly Legacy of India's Partition*. Boston: Houghton Mifflin Harcourt, 2015.

Healey, Mark. *The Ruins of the New Argentina: Peronism and the Remaking of San Juan after the 1944 Earthquake*. Durham, NC: Duke University Press, 2011.

Henderson, Gretchen Ernster. *On Marvelous Things Heard*. Chicago: Green Lantern Press, 2011.

Hessler, Peter. *River Town: Two Years on the Yangtze*. New York: Harper, 2001.

Hoffmann, Stephen A. *Under the Ether Dome: A Physician's Apprenticeship at Massachusetts General Hospital*. New York: Scribner, 1986.

Itzkoff, Dave. *Lads: A Memoir of Manhood*. New York: Villard, 2004.

Jenkins, McKay. *The South in Black and White: Race, Sex, and Literature in the 1940s*. Chapel Hill: University of North Carolina Press, 1999.

Jerris, Randon. *Historical Dictionary of Golf*. Lanham, MD: Scarecrow Press, 2001 (with Bill Mallon).

Kalish, Nancy. *The Case Against Homework: How Homework Is Hurting Children and What Parents Can Do About It*. New York: Harmony, 2007 (with Sara Bennett).

Kalu, Uchechi. *Flowers Blooming Against a Bruised Gray Sky*. Jackson, WY: Whit Press, 2006.

Kavanagh, Preston. *Secrets of the Jewish Exile*. Eugene, OR: Wipf and Stock, 2005.

Kennedy, Elisabeth Robertson. *Seeking a Homeland*. Leiden: Brill, 2011.

Krist, Elizabeth Cheng. *Women of Vision: National Geographic Photographs on Assignment*. Washington, DC: National Geographic, 2014.

Landau, Susan. *Privacy on the Line: The Politics of Wiretapping and Encryption*. Cambridge, MA: MIT Press, 1999.

Lander, Eric. *Symmetric Designs: An Algebraic Approach*. Cambridge: Cambridge University Press, 1983.

Lander, Jessica. *Driving Backwards*. Cambridge, MA: TidePool Press, 2014.

Langfitt, Frank. *The Shanghai Free Taxi: Journeys with the Hustlers and Rebels of the New China*. London: PublicAffairs, 2019.

Larsen, Karen. *Breaking the Limit: One Woman's Motorcycle Journey Through North America*. New York: Hachette Books, 2004.

Lederman, Doug. *Taking Colleges Online: How Smart Institutions and Their Leaders Can Approach Online Education Now and in a Post Coronavirus World*. Washington, DC: Inside Higher Ed, 2020 (with Lindsay McKenzie).

Leff, Laurel. *Buried by the Times: The Holocaust and America's Most Important Newspaper*. Cambridge: Cambridge University Press, 2005.

Lemberg, Diana. *Barriers Down: How American Power and Free-Flow Policies Shaped Global Media*. New York: Columbia University Press, 2019.

Li, Lillian. *Number One Chinese Restaurant: A Novel*. New York: Henry Holt, 2018.

Lieberman, Evan. *Race and Regionalism in the Politics of Taxation in Brazil and South Africa*. Cambridge: Cambridge University Press, 2003.

Lipeles, Maxine. *An Environmental Law Anthology*. Durham, NC: Carolina Academic Press, 1996.

Loewenson, Carl. *Insider Trading: Law and Developments*. Washington, DC: American Bar Association, 2018 (with Ruti Smithline).

Massie, Robert. *His Image, My Image: Leaders Guide*. Nashville: Nelson Incorporated, Thomas, 1985.

Mathews, Francine. *Death in the Off-Season: A Merry Folger Mystery*. New York: William Morrow, 1994.

Mayeux, Sara. *Free Justice: A History of the Public Defender in Twentieth-Century America*. Chapel Hill: University of North Carolina Press, 2020.

Maynard, W. Barksdale. *Architecture in the United States, 1800–1850*. New Haven, CT: Yale University Press, 2002.

McAlpin, Heller. *Nostalgia*. New York: Scribner, 1982.

McGuinness, Aims. *Path of Empire: Panama and the California Gold Rush*. Ithaca, NY: Cornell University Press, 2008.

Mehnert, David. *Citizen Jane: A True Story of Money, Murder, and One Woman's Mission to Put a Killer Behind Bars*. New York: Onyx, 1999 (with James Dalessandro).

Miller, Samantha. *E-Mail Etiquette: Do's, Don'ts and Disaster Tales from People Magazine's Internet Manners Expert*. New York: Grand Central Publishing, 2001.

Morgan, Wesley. *Ten Years in Afghanistan's Pech Valley*. Washington, DC: United States Institute of Peace, 2015.

Morgenroth, Kate. *Kill Me First*. New York: Avon, 2000.

Moss, Peggy. *Say Something*. Thomaston, ME: Tilbury House Publishers, 2004.

Nielsen, Aileen. *Practical Time Series Analysis: Prediction with Statistics & Machine Learning*. Sebastopol, CA: O'Reilly Media, Inc., 2019.

Penney, Cynthia Tougas. *Going Back: An Oral History of Princeton*. Princeton, NJ: Princetoniana Committee of the Alumni Council, 1996.

Phillip, Leila. *The Road Through Miyama*. New York: Random House, 1989.

Preston, Richard. *First Light: The Search for the Edge of the Universe*. Boston: Atlantic Monthly Press, 1987.

Price, Jennifer. *Flight Maps: Adventures with Nature in Modern America*. New York: Basic Books, 1999.

Pruitt, Sarah. *Breaking History: Vanished! America's Most Mysterious Kidnappings, Castaways, and the Forever Lost*. Lanham, MD: Rowman & Littlefield, 2017.

Rainey, Kristen. *In Pursuit of the Triple Bottom Line: Economic, Social, and Environmental Commitment at Clif Bar, Stonyfield

Farm, and Starbucks. Chisinau, Moldova: Lambert Academic Publishing, 2011.

Rampton, Sheldon. *Friends in Deed: The Story of U.S.–Nicaragua Sister Cities*. Madison, WI: WCCN, 1988 (with Liz Chilsen).

Raphel, Adrienne. *What Was It For?* Milwaukee: Rescue Press, 2017.

Redd, Teresa. *A Teacher's Introduction to African American English: What a Writing Teacher Should Know*. Champaign, IL: National Council of Teachers of English, 2005 (with Karen Schuster Webb).

Reed, Bruce. *The Plan: Big Ideas for America*. New York: PublicAffairs, 2006 (with Rahm Emanuel).

Reiken, Frederick. *The Odd Sea*. New York: Delta, 1998.

Remnick, David. *Lenin's Tomb: The Last Days of the Soviet Empire*. New York: Random House, 1993.

Rigolot, Stephanie. *Combinatory Urbanism: The Complex Behavior of Collective Form*. Stray Dog Cafe, 2011 (with Thom Mayne).

Robertson, Aaron, translator. *Beyond Babylon*. San Francisco: Two Lines Press, 2019.

Rogers, Eugene F., Jr. *Thomas Aquinas and Karl Barth: Sacred Doctrine and the Natural Knowledge of God*. Notre Dame, IN: University of Notre Dame Press, 1995.

Ruxin, Robert. *An Athlete's Guide to Agents*. Burlington, MA: Jones & Bartlett Learning, 2009.

Salama, Jordan. *Every Day the River Changes: Four Weeks Down the Magdalena*. New York: Catapult, 2021.

Schlosser, Eric. *Fast Food Nation: The Dark Side of the All-American Meal*. Boston: Mariner Books, 2001.

Seay, Elizabeth. *Searching for the Lost City: On the Trail of America's Native Languages*. Lanham, MD: The Lyons Press, 2003.

Sharma, Akhil. *An Obedient Father*. New York: Farrar, Straus and Giroux, 2000.

Shtulman, Andrew. *Scienceblind: Why Our Intuitive Theories About the World Are So Often Wrong*. New York: Basic Books, 2017.

Sieck, Margaret. *Sports Illustrated for Kids: Super Bowl Heroes*. New York: Sports Illustrated, 1999 (with Richard Deitsch).

Smith, Lucia. *What Every High School Student Doesn't Know . . . Yet: A Guide for the College Bound*. Boulder, CO: Blue Mountain Arts, 2005.

Smith, Stacey Vanek. *Machiavelli for Women: Defend Your Worth, Grow Your Ambition, and Win the Workplace*. New York: Gallery Books, 2021.

Solomon, Amy. *Management Skills for the Occupational Therapy Assistant*. West Deptford, NJ: SLACK Incorporated, 2002 (with Karen Jacobs).

Spillenger, Clyde. *Principles of Conflict of Laws*. St. Paul, MN: West Academic Press, 2010.

Stengel, Richard. *January Sun: One Day, Three Lives, a South African Town*. New York: Simon & Schuster, 1999.

Swanson, Heather. *To See Once More the Stars: Living in a Post-Fukushima World*. Santa Cruz, CA: New Pacific Press, 2014 (with Daisuke Naito, Ryan Sayre, and Satsuki Takahashi).

Szanton, Andrew. *Have No Fear: The Charles Evers Story*. Hoboken, NJ: Wiley, 1998.

Tanner, Adam. *Frommer's Budget Travel Guide: Eastern Europe on $30 a Day: Albania, the Czech & Slovak Republics, Hungary, Poland, Slovenia & Romania*. New York: Hungry Minds Inc, 1995.

Tashi Slater, Ann. *Travels Within and Without*. Nashville, TN: Annandale Press, 2016.

Terrell, Whitney. *The Huntsman*. New York: Viking, 2001.

Tobin, David. *Securing China's Northwest Frontier: Identity and Insecurity in Xinjiang*. Cambridge: Cambridge University Press, 2020.

Tooke, C. W. *Ballpark Blues*. New York: Doubleday, 2003.

Trees, Andrew. *Decoding Love: Why It Takes Twelve Frogs to Find a Prince, and Other Revelations from the Science of Attraction*. New York: Avery, 2009.

Trimble, Cornelia Liu. *Cancer Obstetrics and Gynecology*. Philadelphia: Lippincott Williams & Wilkins, 1999 (with Edward L. Trimble).

Turpin, Andrea. *A New Moral Vision: Gender, Religion, and the Changing Purposes of American Higher Education, 1837–1917.* Ithaca, NY: Cornell University Press, 2016.

Vanderkam, Laura. *168 Hours: You Have More Time Than You Think.* New York: Portfolio Hardcover, 2010.

Vulchi, Priya. *Tell Me Who You Are: Sharing Our Stories of Race, Culture, & Identity.* New York: TarcherPerigee, 2019 (with Winona Guo).

Walsh, Bryan. *End Times: A Brief Guide to the End of the World.* London: Seven Dials, 2019.

Weiner, Jennifer. *Good in Bed.* New York: Atria Books, 2002.

Weiss, Gillian. *Captives and Corsairs: France and Slavery in the Early Modern Mediterranean.* Stanford, CA: Stanford University Press, 2011.

Whelan, Christine B. *Why Smart Men Marry Smart Women.* New York: Simon & Schuster, 2006.

Wolff, Katherine. *Culture Club: The Curious History of the Boston Athenaeum.* Amherst: University of Massachusetts Press, 2009.

Worth, Robert F. *A Rage for Order: The Middle East in Turmoil, from Tahrir Square to ISIS.* New York: Farrar, Straus and Giroux, 2016.

Wright, Robert. *Three Scientists and Their Gods: Looking for Meaning in an Age of Information.* Chicago: Times Books, 1988.

WuDunn, Sheryl. *Thunder in the East: Portrait of a Rising Asia.* New York: Knopf, 2000 (with Nicholas D. Kristof).

Yang, Dori Jones. *Pour Your Heart Into It: How Starbucks Built a Company One Cup at a Time.* New York: Hachette Books, 1999 (with Howard Schultz).

Yarbrough, Luke, translator. *The Sword of Ambition.* New York: New York University Press, 2016.

Zavaleta, Erika. *Ecosystems of California.* Berkeley: University of California Press, 2016 (with Harold Mooney).

14

Books by John McPhee's Children

"Ideas are where you find them."
—"WISHING I WERE JOHN MCPHEE:
HOW TO WRITE NARRATIVE NONFICTION
ABOUT A MASTER OF NARRATIVE NONFICTION,"
BY KERRI ARSENAULT, LITERARY HUB, NOVEMBER 15, 2017

THE FOUR daughters of John McPhee and his first wife, Pryde Brown (a photographer), all have published multiple books.

Jenny McPhee

Novels

The Center of Things. New York: Doubleday, 2001.
No Ordinary Matter: A Novel. New York: Free Press, 2004.
A Man of No Moon: A Novel. New York: Counterpoint, 2007.

Works of translation from the Italian

Crossing the Threshold of Hope by Pope John Paul II, translated by Jenny McPhee and Martha McPhee. New York: Knopf, 1994.
Canone Inverso by Paulo Maurensig. New York: Henry Holt, 1998.

Flaw of Form by Primo Levi, part of *The Complete Works of Primo Levi*. New York: Norton, 2015.

Natural Histories by Primo Levi, part of *The Complete Works of Primo Levi*. New York: Norton, 2015.

Family Lexicon by Natalia Ginzburg. New York: New York Review Books, 2017.

The Kremlin Ball by Curzio Malaparte. New York: New York Review Books, 2018.

Neapolitan Chronicles by Anna Maria Ortese, translated by Jenny McPhee and Ann Goldstein. New York: New Vessel Press, 2018.

Lies and Sorcery by Elsa Morante. New York: New York Review Books, 2023.

Laura McPhee

No Ordinary Land: Encounters in a Changing Environment, photographs by Laura McPhee and Virginia Beahan. New York: Aperture, 2005.

River of No Return: Photographs by Laura McPhee. New Haven, CT: Yale University Press, 2008.

Guardians of Solitude, photographs by Laura McPhee. London: Iris Editions, 2009.

Gateway: Visions of an Urban National Park, edited by Alexander Brash, Jamie Hand, Kate Orff, photography by Laura McPhee. Hudson, NY: Princeton Architectural Press, 2011.

The Home and the World: A View of Calcutta, photographs by Laura McPhee. New Haven, CT: Yale University Press, 2014.

Lost, Calcutta, photographs by Laura McPhee. New York: KGP Monolith, 2018.

Martha McPhee

Bright Angel Time. New York: Random House, 1997.
Gorgeous Lies. Boston: Houghton Mifflin Harcourt, 2002.
L'America. New York: Harcourt, 2006.
Dear Money. New York: Houghton Mifflin Harcourt, 2010.
An Elegant Woman. New York: New York: Scribner, 2020.
Omega Farm: A Memoir. New York: Scribner, 2023.

Sarah McPhee

Filippo Juvarra. Drawings from the Roman Period 1704–1714, vol. 2. Rome: Edizioni dell'Elefante, 1999.
Bernini and the Bell Towers: Architecture and Politics at the Vatican. New Haven, CT: Yale University Press, 2002.
Bernini's Beloved: A Portrait of Costanza Piccolomini. New Haven, CT: Yale University Press, 2012.

Laura, Martha, and Jenny McPhee

Girls: Ordinary Girls and Their Extraordinary Pursuits. New York: Random House, 2000.

ACKNOWLEDGMENTS

IN MANY ways, this book wouldn't exist without John McPhee. Because of all his writing, of course, and also much more.

He was gracious from the start, welcoming me on numerous occasions into his home and Princeton University academic office. I had the privilege of seeing his extraordinary mind and memory working at full speed, remembering and conceptualizing things I never would have expected. I was fortunate to get a sense of him in ways that his editors and former students have for decades. His suggestions and critiques were always keen. This book is far better for his cooperation and participation.

Besides all that McPhee told me, libraries and archives were the linchpin as I sought to find and examine his vast array of writings in a career spanning more than 70 years.

Daniel Linke, Princeton University's archivist, was a tremendous help at the start and throughout the project and I will always be thankful to him. The Princeton library staff, at the Seeley G. Mudd Manuscript Library and the Harvey S. Firestone Memorial Library, was professional and eager to assist.

Meredith Mann was my chief guide to the treasures of the Farrar, Straus and Giroux archive at the New York Public Library. It is an archive that includes thousands of folders and pages about Farrar, Straus and Giroux and its authors, McPhee included, from the publisher's decades of literary excellence. As someone who grew up in New York City and watched the trials and now the triumphs of the great New York Public Library, it was moving to work in the Brooke Russell Astor Reading Room for Rare Books and Manuscripts, whose staff was efficient and thoughtful.

A library where particular magic happened was The New York Historical, which holds the archives of *Time* magazine. I knew that McPhee had been a prodigious young writer for eight years at *Time*, but owner Henry Luce's group journalism idea held sway while McPhee was there and no bylines were given to credit writers. McPhee remembered his cover stories—which sadly had not gotten much attention over the years—yet there was no record of all the other articles he wrote.

At first stymied in my quest to document all McPhee's *Time* work, the librarians said there was someone else who could maybe help me: Bill Hooper, the longtime Time Inc. archivist. He had supervised the move of the archives to The New York Historical about a decade earlier, and he was still the archivist for *Time*. Hooper made a huge difference. I was thrilled when he told me about the set of bound volumes of *Time* magazines where each article had been marked by a copy editor with the initials of its writer. For weeks, I went through every page of each magazine while McPhee was on staff, eventually searching tens of thousands of pages for "JM" markings.

McPhee was indeed prolific at *Time*. After I found more than 500 stories attributed to him in the bound volumes, I checked with him to make sure the attributions were accurate. I've included in the book listings more than 70 highlights of his *Time* stories. Hooper credited Norman Pearlstine, who had been editor-in-chief and chief content officer of Time Inc., for the far-seeing act of saving the *Time* archives from destruction as the company downsized.

Another source of many significant McPhee items was the indefatigable Anne Lozier, the archivist at Deerfield Academy. McPhee attended Deerfield for an important year after Princeton High School and before Princeton University. Included in the archives is a trove of materials McPhee donated to Deerfield after he wrote his second book, *The Headmaster*, about Frank Boyden, who led the school for an astounding 66 years. The materials shed valuable light on McPhee's brilliant research and organizational methods.

I am lucky to be able to count the Library of Congress as a local library for me, and the librarians there gave me much good advice and service.

Much farther away, in Los Angeles, was the UCLA Film & Television Archive, which is one of the premier research centers for film and television. It was the place where I watched what is apparently the last existing video copy of a screenplay written by McPhee in the mid-1950s, "The Man Who Vanished," produced on the *Robert Montgomery Presents* television show. Later it was terrific to find paper copies of McPhee's script for "The Man Who Vanished" and another screenplay of his in the collection of Yale's Beinecke Rare Book & Manuscript Library. Moira Fitzgerald of the Beinecke did a skillful job of tracking down those two rare television scripts written by McPhee when he was in his mid-twenties.

At Colgate University, Sarah Keen and Cara Howe, the former and current university archivists, aided me greatly by digitizing and making publicly accessible recordings of McPhee in two settings that are representative of other public appearances during his career. He and his wife, Yolanda Whitman, did a reading at Colgate of McPhee's *Rising from the Plains*, and McPhee also visited an undergraduate English class to answer questions of student writers.

At Brown University, my alma mater, two superb archivists taught me much over the years about how to do research—the legendary Martha Mitchell in my student days and, more recently, Jennifer Betts.

A final library to acknowledge here is one where I have never set foot: the Cornell University library. Cornell was the college of E. B. White, another literary hero of mine and who, like McPhee, was an essential part of *The New Yorker*.

My late mother, Phyllis, was a librarian and book collector, and she helped me for years with my small collection, including of White. In 1979, Cornell produced the magnificent *Bibliographic Catalogue* of all White's published writings. My mother bought it for me, sadly not long before she died in 1985, and it sat on my bookshelf for decades. I looked at it a few times, and it must have marinated in my head. My idea to do this volume about McPhee is clearly related to my mother and her love of books and libraries.

This is my first book, a long-awaited milestone. I express great gratitude to three people who unwittingly signed up to be in my "kitchen cabinet" and generously shared their knowledge of the publishing world: Tom Maier, Bob Prior, and Larry Tye.

For teaching me so much about how to find and categorize books, I thank Ben Leubsdorf, a master reporter and librarian.

I was favored to have a number of energetic and intelligent research assistants throughout this project. Annie Knowles was the anchor and her cheerful can-do attitude made working with her a pleasure. Thanks also to a great crew of Brown University students who helped: Sunny Choi, Grace Holleb, Chiupong Huang, and Reem Ibrahim.

Princeton University Press has been a remarkable partner in this book. I have been extremely lucky to have Anne Savarese as my editor. She has made many wise suggestions, always in a calm and constructive way. Many others on the Princeton team have contributed, including James Collier, Karen Carter, and Anne Sanow.

I stand on the shoulders of many scholars whom I admire. Two who were particularly generous with me as I undertook this project are David Kertzer, professor emeritus of Brown University, and Alice Nakhimovsky, emerita from Colgate University.

Steve Russillo is himself a good McPhee story. In 2002, Russillo was an eighth-grade science teacher in North Carolina and needed more knowledge and motivation. He found his answer in McPhee's books and devoured them. Then he went on to create a webpage devoted to McPhee, listing much McPhee writing and including comments. I was delighted to stumble on the page in my searching and it further motivated me.

Early on, when my project was only a fledgling and I was trying to find my way, I was fortunate that Gregg Orr and Bernard F. Rodgers Jr.—scholars and bibliographers—patiently answered my questions and showed me their ways in successfully studying Jim Harrison and Philip Roth.

McPhee's publishing career is highly unusual. With the exception of one book (which the late publisher Roger Straus called an excused absence), his books have been brought out, beautifully, by Farrar, Straus and Giroux for 60 years. Current and past FSG people were generous with me and expressed pride in their association with McPhee. Devon Mazzone, head of subsidiary rights, gave me information about McPhee's legion of international editions, and Victoria Fox, permissions manager, aided on clearances. Alex Star, McPhee's editor at FSG since 2012, was helpful, as was Paul Elie, who edited McPhee from 1998 to 2011. Many other people at FSG past and present, especially the brilliant and colorful Straus, came alive in the pages of archives and McPhee's stories.

I appreciate and have been spurred on by many people connected with Deerfield Academy—leadership, faculty, and alumni—who fiercely claim McPhee as one of their own and nurture his memory, wanting to know more about his life.

Researching this book, I learned much about McPhee's impact on his Princeton students (544 of them, McPhee's meticulous records show) and about how those students have held so close their memories of his class and their friendship with him. Peter Hessler, who wrote the elegant, insightful foreword to this book, exemplifies this, and I have also valued comments from Nanci Heller McAlpin, Marc Fisher, and Joel Achenbach.

For graciously letting me into her house many times, including when COVID was still a significant threat, I am grateful to John McPhee's wife, Yolanda Whitman.

I thank Mike McNamee and Karla Taylor, longtime friends and fellow writers who patiently listened to McPhee stories for so long, and journalist Rich Cohen was another friend who offered good ideas.

I pay special tribute to my family, whose support has meant so much, especially my late father who encouraged me in many ways for such a long time, my daughter Bella, my sister Sarah, and brother-in-law Jim.

Last, and totally defying all categorization, is my wife, Amy Cohen. Not only did she listen to me with exquisite patience and give me boundless support, but she also offered careful and inspired advice whenever I showed her draft material or asked her endless far-flung questions. She was always game for a challenge, whether it was doing the copy photography for the book or offering her wise counsel on many subjects. Amy has meant a tremendous amount to this project and to me.

INDEX

Alaska: Images of the Country, 16
Annals of the Former World, 22, 142, 143, 172–174
Ashe, Arthur, 9–10, 39, 87
Assembling California, 20, 169–170, 192

Baez, Joan, 61–62
Basin and Range, 16, 161–163
Boyden, Frank, 8, 101, 148, 150, 191–192
Bradley, Bill, 4, 7, 8, 35, 43, 71–72, 150
Brigade de Cuisine, 15, 127–128, 160
Brower, David, 11, 102
Brown, Pryde, xxv, 11, 195, 196, 217
Burton, Richard, 49, 50, 63, 68

Casey's Shadow, 79, 202–203
Coates, Robert M., 117–118
Coming into the Country, 14–15, 100, 135, 141, 145, 148, 158–160
Control of Nature, The, 19, 141, 166–167
Crofter and the Laird, The, 10–11, 153–154
Curve of Binding Energy, The, 12, 155–156

Deerfield Academy, 5–7, 26, 28, 100–101, 107–109, 137–138, 148, 150–151, 191–192
Deffeyes, Kenneth, 16, 197
Deltoid Pumpkin Seed, The, 12, 155
Draft No. 4, 24, 145, 146, 147, 177–179

Encounters with the Archdruid, 11, 154

Founding Fish, The, 22, 174–175

Gibbons, Euell, 9, 99
Giving Good Weight, 15, 82, 160–161
Glaser, Milton, 12
Gleason, Jackie, 58–59

Harris, Anita, 16–17
Headmaster, The, 5–7, 8, 137–138, 148, 150–151, 191–92
Heirs of General Practice, 18, 165

In Suspect Terrain, 16–17, 163–164
In the Highlands and Islands, 18
Irons in the Fire, 22, 172

John McPhee Reader, The, 13–14, 157–158

Kauffmann, John, 15, 29
Kazmaier, Dick, 24, 30, 93, 109–110, 115
Keewaydin camp, 30, 31, 32, 103
Kelly, Jim, xx, 146, 181, 207

La Place de la Concorde Suisse, 17, 164
Levels of the Game, 9–10, 134, 137, 152
Love, David, 18–19, 27–28
Looking for a Ship, 20, 166–167

McAlpin, Heller, 1, 95, 145–146, 213
McGlynn, Robert, 26, 28, 100–101
McKee, Olive, xvii, 9, 11, 108, 142
McPhee, Harry R., 24, 70, 91, 103, 107, 197
McPhee, Jenny, 196, 217, 218, 219

McPhee, John
    connection to Princeton, xvi–xvii, 100, 103, 134–135, 136, 144–145
    fiction writing, xv, 12, 120–22
    foreign editions, 3, 14
    impact as teacher, ix–x, xx, 132, 134–135, 136, 146, 147, 194, 204–216
    poetry writing, xxviii, 104, 110–111
    Princeton Tiger and college humor, 95–96, 114–116
    Pulitzer prize, xxviii, 22
    reading aloud, 11, 142
    relationship with *The New Yorker*, xviii, 3, 70–72, 114–115, 144, 193
    strength of nonfiction writing, xiii–xiv, 40, 42, 127
    television screenplays, xix, 117–120
    Time magazine career, xvii–xviii, 44, 48–52
    Time magazine cover stories: Alan Jay Lerner and Frederick Lowe's *Camelot*, 56; Barbra Streisand, 67; Jackie Gleason, 58–59; Jean Kerr, 57; Joan Baez, 61; Mort Saul, 54; New York World's Fair of 1964, 67; Richard Burton, 63; Sophia Loren, 59
    writing about canoes, 13, 31–32, 103, 157
    writing about geology, 16–17, 18–19, 20, 22, 39, 44–45, 131, 134, 135, 142, 143, 147–148, 161–164, 165–166, 169–170, 171, 172–174, 192–193
    writing about tennis, 9–10, 98, 134, 137, 152
    use of language, xi–xii, 108, 134, 135
    use of structure, 5, 6, 7, 13, 79, 108, 129–130, 137, 145, 187
McPhee, Laura, 28–29, 102, 196, 197, 218, 219
McPhee, Martha, 134, 145, 148, 196, 219
McPhee, Mary Ziegler, 23–24, 101, 195
McPhee, Sarah, 196, 219

Montgomery, Robert, xix, 117–120
Moores, Eldridge, 20, 143, 192

Oranges, 8, 135, 151
Outcroppings, 19

Patch, The, 24–26, 147, 179–180
Pearson, Michael, 106, 130, 181, 183
Pine Barrens, The, 8–9, 15, 99, 102, 134, 144, 151

Ransom of Russian Art, The, 20, 170–171
Remnick, David, xx, 21, 41, 42, 44, 137, 144, 146, 171, 201, 207, 208, 214
Rising from the Plains, 18–19, 165–166, 192
Roomful of Hovings and Other Profiles, A, 9, 152
Rowell, Galen, 16

Second John McPhee Reader, The, 21, 171
Sense of Where You Are, A, 4, 35, 36, 43, 44, 45, 150
Shawn, William, 71–72, 97
Shenker, Israel, 80, 126
Silk Parachute, 23–24, 177, 193
Stengel, Richard, xx, 42, 44, 146, 207, 215
Straus, Roger, 15, 16, 100, 207
Streisand, Barbra, 49, 67
Survival of the Bark Canoe, The, 13, 157

Table of Contents, 17, 165
Tabula Rasa: Volume 1, 26, 148, 180–182
Taylor, Theodore B., 12, 17
Thoreau, Henry David, 13, 30
Twenty Questions tv show, xii, 116, 144

Uncommon Carriers, 22–23, 175–176, 193

Vursell, Harold, 13, 201

Waxham, Ethel, 18–19, 27, 28
Whitaker, Rogers E. M., 70
Wimbledon: A Celebration, 11–12, 154
Whitman, Yolanda, 142, 191, 192, 196, 197, 199

A NOTE ON THE TYPE

This book has been composed in Arno, an Old-style serif typeface in the classic Venetian tradition, designed by Robert Slimbach at Adobe.